THE TRUTH NEVER
STANDS IN THE WAY
OF A GOOD STORY

THE TRUTH NEVER STANDS IN THE WAY OF A GOOD STORY

Jan Harold Brunvand

With a Chapter on the Heroic Hacker
by Erik Brunvand

UNIVERSITY OF ILLINOIS PRESS

URBANA AND CHICAGO

Library of Congress Cataloging-in-Publication Data
Brunvand, Jan Harold.
The truth never stands in the way of a good story /
Jan Harold Brunvand ; with a chapter on the heroic
hacker by Erik Brunvand.
p.   cm.
Includes bibliographical references and index.
ISBN 0-252-02424-9 (cloth)
1. Urban folklore—United States.
2. Legends—United States.
3. United States—Social life and customs.
I. Brunvand, Erik.
II. Title.
GR105.B716   2000
398.2'0973'091732—dc21   99-6465
CIP
C 5 4 3 2 1

CONTENTS

THE TRUTH NEVER
STANDS IN THE WAY
OF A GOOD STORY

INTRODUCTION

My collecting and studying of urban legends for many years has benefited greatly from the voluminous correspondence with readers of my publications. On December 15, 1989, for example, Ron Thurston, a high school teacher in Fort Collins, Colorado, queried me about a story he had recently been told:

Have you heard this one? One of my wife's colleagues has a friend who knows someone who tells this story: When she was young and only recently married, she was having her first dinner party and had prepared a huge baked salmon. Just before the guests arrived, she discovered that the cat had gotten up on the counter and nibbled on the freshly baked fish. After considering her investment, as well as all of the alternative entrees at this late moment, she decided to simply clean it up as best she could, turn the salmon over to hide the tell-tale nibblings, and serve it.

It was a fine dinner, enjoyed by all. After the last guest left, she and her husband went to let the cat back in. To their horror they found the cat just outside the front door—dead. Fearing that the fish was tainted and had caused the cat's death, they anguished over what to do. Finally they called all their guests and told them the story. Everyone, including the hosts, went to the hospital and had their stomachs pumped. Returning home after their ordeal, they were met by their neighbor, who was anxious to explain about the cat.

It seems that the cat had been hit by a car and must have suffered internal injuries. The neighbor went on to say how he had brought the body of the cat to their house, but didn't want to interrupt the party he saw in progress, so he just left it by the front door.

I had, of course, heard Ron Thurston's story—*many* times. In fact, I had dubbed it "The Poisoned Pussycat at the Party" in my 1981 book *The*

Vanishing Hitchhiker and had reported a version from a 1963 San Francisco newspaper column in which the cat had been fed some wild mushrooms. I also heard a mushroom version in Romania in 1981, and that same year a German tabloid reported a similar incident that concluded with the cat, after eating some mushrooms, suffering from apparent convulsions, sending the family racing to the hospital. The Germans returned, weak and queasy, to find that their cat had delivered kittens.

The "poisoned" pet legend has been widely told both in the United States and abroad for decades, and it popped up again in the 1989 film *Her Alibi,* then yet again in the 1994 best-seller by John Berendt, *Midnight in the Garden of Good and Evil.* But the oral tradition of the story continued unabated, and many other readers have queried me about it, including, on September 24, 1990, Jean Wendland of North Royalton, Ohio:

> I heard a suspicious story recently, and would appreciate your opinion on its credibility.
>
> My sister's boyfriend knows a family who had this unfortunate incident happen to them. They were the hosts of a backyard barbecue, and were grilling fish. The hostess found their cat sampling the fish before it was served to the guests and chased it away. The guests, of course were never told of the cat's intrusion, and they all enjoyed what was left of the fish.
>
> Upon finishing the meal, and preparing to return home, they found the cat dead in the driveway. The hostess notified all that the fish must have been tainted, as the poor kitty had tasted some and met his maker. The host and hostess and all the guests made a beeline for the local emergency room where they had their stomachs pumped.
>
> Returning home, the host of the ill-fated barbecue found a note on his door from his neighbor: "Please accept our apologies for running over your cat. We will be happy to replace him."

The insistence on the truth of this bizarre story, the attribution to specific friends of friends, the age of the story, and (most of all) the variations in details among the different versions are all hallmarks of the modern urban legend, a lively category of contemporary folklore that has fascinated me since I began studying American folklore in the early 1950s. Presently I have on file thousands of letters, clippings, and photocopies—plus transcripts of oral versions and offprints of scholarly articles—all documenting several hundred urban legend plots in countless variant texts.

The same kind of narrative traditions exhibited in the poisoned pet stories are evident in another popular urban legend, as reported in a letter to the travel editor of the *Washington Post,* published on May 26, 1991:

Friends recently showed us the letter in the Feb. 24 Travel section about "grandmothernapping."

While living in Frankfurt, Germany, in the early '60s, our maid and her family went on vacation to Spain. They were a week late in returning and offered as their excuse the amazing tale of a grandmother dying there, and how—to avoid problems with Spanish police and to save money at border crossings—they wrapped their Oma (Granny) in a tent and covertly slipped her across borders back to Germany for a proper burial. However, when they stopped to eat, someone stole their van, with Granny aboard. The maid said she needed a few more days off to settle matters.

We were, of course, horrified and sympathetic. Later, we told the story to a young German lawyer and were flabbergasted when he cracked up laughing. This is a scenario, he said, that is commonly presented to first-year law students in Germany with instructions to determine and list all possible infractions of local and international law that could be involved.

We subsequently changed maids.

Harry V. Ryder Jr.
Arlington

"The Runaway Grandmother," as folklorists call this story, is another classic urban legend discussed in my first book. It has had extensive international circulation since at least the 1930s. The story has been echoed in novels by authors as diverse as John Steinbeck (in *The Grapes of Wrath,* 1939) and Anthony Burgess (in *The Piano Players,* 1986), as well as furnishing a gag for the 1983 film *National Lampoon's Vacation.* Variations include having the body stolen from where it was stashed in a canoe tied to the top of the car or in a boat being towed behind the car. Almost invariably, the family has stopped to eat when the vehicle and the corpse are stolen.

Not all the urban legends currently circulating are classics. In the late fall of 1990 a shocking story suddenly appeared concerning a dreadful mishap that befell a couple while they were on vacation in a tropical paradise. Here is a version sent to me on March 19, 1991, by the Denver journalist Alan Dumas:

This tale was told to me by an earnest young man who swears it happened recently to some friends of his parents.

An older couple took a long-anticipated trip to Costa Rica, and when they arrived they found to their dismay that their luggage had been stolen. The thieves had spared nothing except the couple's toilet articles and their camera case. It was assumed that the thieves didn't want the couple's personal toilet items, and authorities speculated that in their haste—loaded down with the other luggage—the miscreants simply were unable to manage the camera equipment.

Well, the couple were determined not to let the incident ruin their vacation. They bought some new clothes and, in fact, had quite an enjoyable two weeks. They took a lot of pictures.

Upon returning home they promptly had their film developed so they could share the experience with their friends. Having shot color slides, they quickly loaded them into a holder and began showing them to their kids. Halfway through the presentation they ran across a slide they hadn't taken. It must, in fact, have been taken by the thieves who stole their luggage.

It was a close-up picture of the couple's toothbrushes sticking out of two large hairy butts.

Absolutely true, I was told.

I have on file about sixty other reports—both oral and published—of this "true" incident as it supposedly happened in Jamaica, the Bahamas, Bermuda, or St. Maarten in the Caribbean and in other scattered locations from Australia to Europe. So far, however, nobody has stepped forward claiming to be the victims, nor has anyone produced the actual photograph.

Lately the Internet has become a prime medium for the rapid circulation and discussion of urban legends, although the people who forward the stories electronically are not always aware of their folkloric nature. One of the most repeated Internet legends is an updated version of the expensive recipe story discussed in chapter 4. Here's a typical example from my files:

> This is a true story that was forwarded to me. Read it and raise an eyebrow. Bake the cookies and enjoy them. Forward it to all you know!
>
> My daughter & I had just finished a salad at Neiman-Marcus Cafe in Dallas & decided to have a small dessert. Because both of us are such cookie lovers, we decided to try the "Neiman-Marcus Cookie." It was so excellent that I asked if they would give me the recipe and the waitress said with a small frown, "I'm afraid not." Well, I said, would you let me buy the recipe? With a cute smile, she said, "Yes." I asked how much, and she responded, "Only two fifty, it's a great deal!" I said with approval, just add it to my tab. Thirty days later, I received my VISA statement from Neiman-Marcus and it was $285.00. I looked again and I remembered I had only spent $9.95 for two salads and about $20.00 for a scarf. As I glanced at the bottom of the statement, it said, "Cookie Recipe—$250.00." That's outrageous!! I called Neiman's Accounting Dept. and told them the waitress said it was "two-fifty," which clearly does not mean "two hundred and fifty dollars" by any *POSSIBLE* interpretation of the phrase. Neiman-

Marcus refused to budge. They would not refund my money, because according to them, "What the waitress told you is not our problem. You have already seen the recipe—we absolutely will not refund your money at this point." I explained to her the criminal statues which govern fraud in Texas, I threatened to refer them to the Better Business Bureau and the State's Attorney General for engaging in fraud. I was basically told, "Do what you want, we don't give a crap, and we're not refunding your money." I waited, thinking of how I could get even, or even try and get any of my money back. I just said, "Okay, you folks got my $250, and now I'm going to have $250.00 worth of fun." I told her that I was going to see to it that every cookie lover in the United States with an e-mail account has a $250.00 cookie recipe from Neiman-Marcus . . . for free. She replied, "I wish you wouldn't do this." I said, "Well, you should have thought of that before you ripped me off," and slammed down the phone on her.

So, here it is!!! Please, please, please pass it on to everyone you can possibly think of. I paid $250 dollars for this . . . I don't want Neiman-Marcus to *ever* get another penny off of this recipe . . .

Neiman-Marcus Cookies

Ingredients:

2 cups butter	1 tsp. salt
4 cups flower	1 8 oz. Hershey Bar (grated)
2 tsp. soda	4 eggs
2 cups sugar	2 tsp. baking powder
5 cups blended oatmeal**	3 cups chopped nuts (your choice)
24 oz. chocolate chips	2 tsp. vanilla
2 cups brown sugar	

Procedures

**Measure oatmeal and blend in a blender to a fine powder.

Cream the butter and both sugars. Add eggs and vanilla; mix together with flour, oatmeal, salt, baking powder, and soda. Add chocolate chips, Hershey Bar, and nuts. Roll into balls and place two inches apart on a cookie sheet. Bake for 10 minutes at 375 degrees. Makes 112 cookies.

Yes, it does say "statues" and "flower" in about half of the Internet postings of this recipe, an indication that the item was probably forwarded without a close reading. The odd addition of "blended" oatmeal is another standard inclusion in this recipe. Just what effect a single eight-ounce Hershey Bar would have on a recipe for 112 cookies is not clear. What *is* perfectly clear, however, is that the story is purely fictional. (See the Neiman-Marcus Web site at http://www.neimanmarcus.com for the company's light-hearted response to the decades-old story in this latest version.)

These examples of just three recent urban legends suggest the variety and spread of such stories. And even this small sample demonstrates some of the common topics of modern legends—cars, death, crime, family emergencies, pets, commerce, and the like—as well as some of the typical themes—misunderstandings, poetic justice, business rip-offs, and revenge. Another clear lesson here is the important role of the mass media and electronic communications in spreading and confirming (or debunking) urban legends. And, of course, it all goes to show that the truth never stands in the way of a good story.

At this point the question of how we might define such a diverse and ever-changing genre of modern folk narratives must be raised. Here is my own attempt at definition, quoted from the latest edition of my textbook, *The Study of American Folklore:* "a story in a contemporary setting (not necessarily a big city), reported as a true individual experience, with traditional variants that indicate its legendary character. Urban legends (also called 'contemporary legends' and 'modern legends') typically have three good reasons for their popularity: a suspenseful or humorous story line, an element of actual belief, and a warning or moral that is either stated or implied."[1]

More concisely, I attempted another phrasing of the definition in the reference work I edited entitled *American Folklore: An Encyclopedia:* "an apocryphal contemporary story, told as true but incorporating traditional motifs, and usually attributed to a friend of a friend (FOAF)."[2]

But the International Society for Contemporary Legend Research (ISCLR, founded in 1988) bypasses the question of definition in its own mission statement, stating simply: "We study 'modern' and 'urban' legends, and also any legend circulating actively.[3]

During the 1980s the urban legend came into its own as a major topic for research in folklore, but there were some notable earlier studies. Alexander Woollcott included legends of the city in his 1934 book *While Rome Burns* as well as an extended discussion of "The Disappearing Lady" legend, which he called "a fair specimen of folklore in the making."[4] In 1941 Marie Bonaparte published a study of "The Corpse in the Car" legend in the psychiatric journal *American Imago*,[5] an essay she incorporated into her book *Myths of War*,[6] which also included the legends "The Doctored Wine" and "The Devil-Jew."

American folklorists began to collect "urban belief tales" (as they were then called) in the 1940s and 1950s. Notable early publications include Richard K. Beardsley and Rosalie Hankey's 1942–43 work on "The Vanishing Hitchhiker";[7] Ernest Baughman's 1945 article on "The Fatal Initiation";[8] J. Russell Reaver's 1952 article on "The Poison Dress";[9] and B. A. Botkin's 1954 book *Sidewalks of America*, which contained versions of several urban legends.[10]

Richard M. Dorson's 1959 textbook, *American Folklore*,[11] was a landmark in American urban legend studies; as I discuss in chapter 1, it included a number of "folktales and legends of the big city" in its chapter on modern folklore. Another ground-breaking publication was the first issue of the journal *Indiana Folklore* in 1968. For a number of years thereafter, in that forum and elsewhere, Linda Dégh and her students at Indiana University documented and analyzed many urban legends. Folklorists from then on, both American and foreign, became intrigued with analyzing the history, variety, persistence, and widespread acceptance as literal truth of such bizarre yet plausible modern narratives as "The Death Car," "The Hook," "The Kentucky Fried Rat," "The Snake in the Blanket," "The Spider in the Hairdo," and "The Roommate's Death."

My introduction to the genre came in the undergraduate class I took from Richard M. Dorson at Michigan State University in the early 1950s and in my graduate work with Dorson and others at Indiana University from 1957 to 1961. However, the stimulus to specialize in urban legend studies came from my teaching at the University of Idaho (1961–65), Southern Illinois University (1965–66), and the University of Utah (1966–96). I urged my students to explore the folklore of their own lives and times, and they responded often by producing wonderful collections and studies of urban legends. Eventually, I researched the subject and developed a lecture on urban legends that I delivered at Northern Arizona University in February 1980 and revised for publication in *Psychology Today* in the June 1980 issue.[12] I had no idea at the time that this was a turning point in my career, but before long I found myself much more deeply involved in urban legend studies than in anything else in folklore research.

Exploring this interest further, and drawing on earlier publications by my fellow folklorists, I published my first book on the subject in 1981— *The Vanishing Hitchhiker: American Urban Legends and Their Meanings.*[13] In this ambitiously titled book I dealt with thirty-six classic modern legends, but hardly exhausted the genre, as I had at first imagined. Three years later, using stories and clippings sent in by readers, and supplemented by my own wider study of the genre, I published a sequel, *The Choking Doberman and Other "New" Urban Legends,*[14] but even in this book I had only scratched the surface. Subsequently I published *The Mexican Pet: More "New" Urban Legends and Some Old Favorites, Curses! Broiled Again!: The Hottest Urban Legends Going,* and *The Baby Train and Other*

Lusty Urban Legends.[15] Also, from January 1987 through June 1992 I wrote "Urban Legends," a twice-weekly newspaper column distributed by United Feature Syndicate, and in 1999 W. W. Norton published my updated comprehensive urban legend anthology, this one entitled *Too Good to Be True.* (The title suggests that urban legends, although told as true, are too neat, ironic, and coincidental to be taken for absolute truth, especially since the same stories are attributed to so many different settings.)

Urban legend studies continue to thrive. International conferences on modern legends were held at the Centre for English Cultural Tradition and Language at the University of Sheffield, in July 1982 and 1983; at least two sessions on urban legends were held during the Eighth Congress of the International Society for Folk Narrative Research in Bergen, Norway, in June 1984. The ISCLR now holds annual meetings, either in the United States or abroad, and publishes a newsletter, *FOAFtale News,* and an annual journal, *Contemporary Legend.* Papers on urban legends are given at most national and regional folklore meetings nowadays, and a steady flow of books and articles on the subject continues. An indication of the popularity of these studies is that fully 1,116 items are listed in Gillian Bennett and Paul Smith's 1993 compilation *Contemporary Legend: A Folklore Bibliography.*[16]

I originally wrote the chapters of this book—each a case study of one legend or of a related group of legends—as either conference papers, academic journal articles, or both. Each essay has been revised and updated for this publication, and the original sources are indicated in the notes. In general, my approach is historical and comparative, since I am convinced that interpretations and analyses must be based on a large collection of data plus the clearest possible account of each story's history and development. To illustrate how the stories accumulate in my collection and how interpretations may emerge from documentation of the widespread variations, I often follow a first-person and chronological structure. Eventually, then, I am able to speculate about such matters as what social-cultural patterns constitute the "real" topics of the "Baby Roast" legend, why the cake baked from the expensive recipe is red, what a recent gang crime legend says about anxieties of our time, and how the supposed tension between science and religion is depicted in a quasi-scientific "evangelegend" (as another commentator has dubbed "The Missing Day in Time"). Readers will doubtless find other meanings to ponder in these stories, and I hope that my studies will suggest some approaches, techniques, and sources useful for further research.

Some of the legends studied here are classics of the genre (i.e., "The Baby Roast," "The Expensive Recipe," "The Exploding Toilet," and "The Ghost in Search of Help"). Others have only recently appeared as part of this ongoing narrative tradition (i.e., "The Brain Drain," "Lights Out!" "The Stunned Deer," and "The Story of Mel, a Real Programmer," which my son Erik Brunvand explores in chapter 13). In nearly every case, however, networks of modern media have transmitted the stories (via e-mail, fax, broadcasting, and print) beyond the workings, most familiar to folklorists, of face-to-face oral tradition. For much of this ephemeral material that races along the electronic superhighway I am indebted to the thousands of readers who have sent me letters, clippings, and photocopies. It is obvious that folklore nowadays travels by much faster and more modern methods than mere word-of-mouth transmission, even though the old oral channels are still flowing vigorously.

As a preliminary to our individual studies, we must consider briefly several problems in terminology for all urban legend studies. The term *urban* itself is the first difficulty, because many of the stories involved are modern without specifically concerning cities. In fact, the suburbs more often than the inner cities are the scenes depicted in urban legends. Second, *legend* may not always be the most accurate term, since a number of these items are often told as mere unverified reports (that is, rumors) rather than as plotted narratives, or as jokes; and not all of them are universally believed. (Belief is assumed to be a hallmark of the legend.) Most American folklorists, however, are content to refer to stories like "The Boyfriend's Death" and "Red Velvet Cake" or even to the less structured reports like "Alligators in the Sewers" and "The Procter & Gamble Trademark" as legends, recognizing that there is usually some narrative content to these traditions and that at least some people tell them as true. Substitutes for the term *urban* that have been suggested include *modern, contemporary, adolescent,* and *mercantile,* but *urban legend* is still the most common label for this kind of folk story.

Other difficulties arise with the "Americanness" and "newness" of urban legends collected and studied in the United States. In *The Vanishing Hitchhiker* I identified a few international variants of "American urban legends," but I gave the overwhelming impression that this was a largely native folkloric product. I was wrong about this, since most of the legends turned out to be international. As for the modernity of urban legends, the word *new* in the subtitles of my two sequels was put within quotation marks because the antiquity that was established for a few stories in the first book was much more impressive for several included in the second and third books. Also, as folklorists in other countries have collected and studied their own urban legends, the age and international character of the stories have become well established.

A last problem with terminology lies in the names assigned to individual legends by folklorists. Sometimes an arbitrary label like "The Solid Cement Cadillac" or "The Mouse in the Coke" suggests that these stories are static entities with consistent content, whereas they are really fluid oral narratives that change constantly as they are performed by oral storytellers in their dramatic reconstructions based on more-or-less clearly remembered traditional motifs. Further, the supernatural nature of "The Vanishing Hitchhiker" legend (in which a ghost haunts the roadside) is atypical for this narrative tradition, since few other urban legends have any consistent supernatural content. "The Choking Doberman"—a crime story—is, perhaps, a more appropriate piece to represent modern oral narratives, although not all urban legends are necessarily horror stories and certainly not all urban legends may be traced to such ancient roots as this one has.

The upshot of all this is that the field of urban legends—both the story types themselves and the scholarly study of them—still seems to be in its infancy. We should expect many more advances and discoveries as the research continues.

A Note on Type and Motif References

All mentions of folktale *types* and narrative *motifs* in this book refer to two major publications consulted by all folklorists for the classification and analysis of traditional stories. Rather than cite these references repeatedly, I will list them here:

Type refers to the stories indexed in the English version of Antti Aarne's 1928 catalog *Verzeichnis der Märchentypen* as translated and enlarged by the American folklorist Stith Thompson and published most recently as *Folklore Fellows Communications* no. 184 (1961) under the title *The Types of the Folktale.*

Motif refers to the myriad individual narrative units indexed in Stith Thompson's *Motif-Index of Folk-Literature* in the revised edition published in six volumes from 1955 to 1958 by Indiana University Press.

An important related work is Ernest W. Baughman's 1966 *Type and Motif-Index of the Folktales of England and North America* published by Indiana University Press as volume twenty in the Indiana University Folklore Series.

Notes

1. Jan Harold Brunvand, *The Study of American Folklore,* 4th ed. (New York: W. W. Norton, 1998), 205.

2. Jan Harold Brunvand, ed., *American Folklore: An Encyclopedia* (New York: Garland, 1996), 730.

3. This is stated in every issue of *FOAFtale News* and in the membership information for ISCLR.

4. Alexander Woollcott, *While Rome Burns* (New York: Viking Press, 1934), 93.

5. Marie Bonaparte, "The Myth of the Corpse in the Car," *American Imago* 2 (1941): 105–26.

6. Marie Bonaparte, *Myths of War,* trans. John Rodker (London: Imago, 1947), originally published as *Mythes de Guerre* (Paris: Presses Universitaires de France, 1946).

7. Richard K. Beardsley and Rosalie Hankey, "The Vanishing Hitchhiker," *California Folklore Quarterly* 1 (1942): 155–77, 303–55; 2 (1943): 13–25.

8. Ernest Baughman, "The Fatal Initiation," *Hoosier Folklore Bulletin* 4 (1945): 49–55.

9. J. Russell Reaver, "Embalmed Alive: A Developing Urban Ghost Tale," *New York Folklore Quarterly* 8 (1952): 217–20.

10. B. A. Botkin, *Sidewalks of America* (Indianapolis: Bobbs-Merrill, 1954), 520–29.

11. Richard M. Dorson, *American Folklore* (Chicago: University of Chicago Press, 1959).

12. Jan Harold Brunvand, "Urban Legends: Folklore for Today," *Psychology Today,* June 1980, 50–62.

13. Jan Harold Brunvand, *The Vanishing Hitchhiker: American Urban Legends and Their Meanings* (New York: W. W. Norton, 1981).

14. Jan Harold Brunvand, *The Choking Doberman and Other "New" Urban Legends* (New York: W. W. Norton, 1984).

15. Jan Harold Brunvand, *The Mexican Pet: More "New" Urban Legends and Some Old Favorites* (New York: W. W. Norton, 1986); *Curses! Broiled Again!: The Hottest Urban Legends Going* (New York: W. W. Norton, 1989); and *The Baby Train and Other Lusty Urban Legends* (New York: W. W. Norton, 1993).

16. Gillian Bennett and Paul Smith, *Contemporary Legend: A Folklore Bibliography* (New York: Garland, 1993).

1

Richard M. Dorson and the Urban Legend

In an issue of *The Unknown,* a small British magazine devoted to psychic mysteries, Michael Goss published an article on urban legends.[1] The author is described on the jacket of his book *The Evidence for Phantom Hitch-Hikers* as "a freelance writer specializing in the paranormal."[2] He offers in the aforementioned article the following capsule summary of early research on urban legends: "It was Rodney Dale who popularised 'foaf' in his [book] *The Tumour in the Whale* (1978). Until then few people, not even many professional folklorists, had been alert to the existence of the genre, although Richard Dobson [*sic*] had given fair warning in his *American Folklore* as early as 1959."

After we run that passage through our spell-checker to correct *Dobson* to *Dorson,* we may ask how accurately it presents the role of Richard M. Dorson in recognizing the genre of urban legends and in encouraging their study.

To begin with, we should note that Goss was not completely accurate about his countryman Rodney Dale. It's true that Dale did introduce, in his engaging book of stories, the useful term, much quoted by folklorists ever since, *FOAF,* an acronym for "friend of a friend."[3] But Dale was not the first among English writers on folklore to collect urban legends. And those who were first knew Dorson's earlier work. In 1965 Katherine Briggs and Ruth Tongue included four examples in their book *Folktales of England* (which had a preface by Dorson);[4] and in 1969 Stewart Sanderson published his important article "The Folklore of the Motor-Car,"[5] which included references to Dorson's American material.

As for Richard Dorson's larger contribution to urban legend studies, I would make a much stronger case than Michael Goss did. Dorson, I believe, launched the urban legend as a subject of serious study with the survey of the genre he included in his 1959 textbook, *American Folklore.*[6] While other American folklorists had published earlier notes on individual legends, Dorson was the first to perceive the stories as a separate category within the larger area of modern folklore. Although Dorson himself collected only a handful of urban legends,[7] he repeatedly reminded folklorists of the vitality of such stories in modern oral tradition, urging their further study.

The programmatic statement behind Dorson's textbook was his 1959 *Journal of American Folklore* article, "A Theory for American Folklore."[8] But neither there nor in his 1969 *Journal of American Folklore* article, "A Theory for American Folklore Reviewed," did Dorson say much about urban legends.[9] While he asserted in "A Theory for American Folklore" that "masses of oral materials floating in contemporary American culture merit the attention of folklorists," he cited no urban legends as examples. However, in his textbook he was specific.[10] There Dorson emphasized stories centering on the automobile, the "chief symbol of modern America." He wrote about "The Vanishing Hitchhiker," as recorded in folklorists' articles, about "The Death Car," which he had studied himself, and about "The Haunted Street," as reported in his students' papers. He also mentioned "The Economical Carburetor" and other traditions about remarkable inventions supposedly suppressed by big business. Turning from car stories to legends about department stores, he included "The Dead Cat in the Package" and an elevator accident story.

In the notes to this section of his textbook Dorson acknowledged the major journal articles from 1942 to 1959 on "The Vanishing Hitchhiker," and he cited two 1953 articles on other legends, including one found in the tiny newsletter *Arkansas Folklore.*[11] (However, he either missed or chose not to include four items from 1945–46 and 1952 on "The Poison Dress" legend in *Hoosier Folklore Bulletin, Hoosier Folklore,* and *New York Folklore Quarterly.*[12]) But, on the whole, Dorson provided in 1959 adequate if not definitive references to earlier studies of individual urban legends as part of an introductory textbook that became a standard teaching tool.[13] In 1977 Dorson revised the bibliographic notes in his textbook and added several urban legend references. (When I asked Dorson once why he did not update the entire modern folklore chapter, he replied, with characteristic modesty, "I don't believe in tampering with a classic.")

My recollections from Dorson's classrooms go back to the early 1950s, and I remember him frequently discussing urban legends with students, generally calling them "urban belief tales." In his textbook he used the unmodified term *legend* seven times, *modern legend* twice, *city* (or *big city*) *legend* twice, and *rumor* twice. He scattered terms like *story, tale,* and *motif* around for variety. In his preface to *Folktales of England* Dorson called them *modern legends,* and that term was used throughout the book. The earliest that I find Dorson calling them *urban legends* is in his chapter in the 1968 compilation *Our Living Traditions.*[14] Dorson may at that time have coined the now-common term *urban legend;* at least in his 1977 revised notes to *American Folklore* he had adopted the term, in the form *modern urban legend,* and in a 1980 introduction to a special double issue of the *Journal of the Folklore Institute* he used just plain *urban legends.*[15]

Whatever label Dorson used for such stories, he clearly had a distinct genre in mind, even though his list of favorite examples was small. In two 1968 papers, later reprinted, he mentioned only the same three: "The Death Car," "The Vanishing Hitchhiker," and "The Runaway Grandmother."[16] Most of Dorson's voluminous writings on legends as a separate narrative category focused on traditional frontier, supernatural, rural, and small-town stories; but in his essay "How Shall We Rewrite Charles M. Skinner Today?"—first presented at a 1971 symposium on the legend at UCLA— he made it clear that urban legends held a major place in his concept of the genre.[17] The three large divisions that he proposed for most American folk legends were stories associated with a place, stories about persons, and what he called "floating single-episode legends . . . usually told as second-hand memorats." The seven examples of the last group that he listed were these: "The Vanishing Hitchhiker," "The Stolen Grandmother," "The Death Car," "The Dead Cat in the Package," "The Hook," "The Killer in the Backseat," and "The Graveyard Wager." All, of course, are urban legends. The four additions to Dorson's usual list of three examples reflect material in the first issue of *Indiana Folklore,* which was devoted to studies of the modern legend in Indiana.[18]

Returning to Dorson's teaching, I want to illustrate a typical effect of his use of urban legends in the classroom on a student who did not become a professional folklorist but who did get turned on to folklore. Dean M. Wakefield (B.A., Journalism, MSU 1953), along with his girlfriend, who later became his wife, took a folklore class in the early 1950s from Dorson at Michigan State. Here is what Wakefield wrote me on October 29, 1986, about that class:

> [My girlfriend's] hand shot up when Dorson described ["The Death Car"] as folklore, and she insisted that her father, who was a casualty insurance lawyer in Detroit, had seen the car. He challenged her to track the story down.

We traced it back through five people besides her father before it petered out and we became convinced that Dorson was right. . . .

I subsequently heard the story many times—from the manager of the Elks Club in Lansing, from a fireman in Bowling Green, Ohio, from a basketball coach in Columbus, a grade school teacher in Midland, a landlord in Cleveland, and so on.

I smiled and told them the story was folklore and about my trying to trace it to its origins. None of them believed me.

I have, in general, stopped trying to enlighten people about folklore, but it's amazing how that incident has affected my life, causing me to reject surface explanations and shallow thinking of all sorts. It doesn't make one very popular, I think, to understand folklore. . . . But, leaving aside popularity, I can think of few things that impart a healthy skepticism quite so enjoyably [as folklore study].

There are two important discussions of urban legends in Dorson's mature work on modern folklore that I will not review here. These appear in the section "Druglore Legends" in *America in Legend,*[19] and the "Crimelore" chapter in *Land of the Millrats.*[20] Instead, I will focus on the first urban legend that Dorson collected and studied—one that he continued to mention in many of his subsequent writings on contemporary folklore—"The Death Car." Dorson notes in *American Folklore* that he heard the story from a colleague in 1944 (the first year Dorson taught at Michigan State University);[21] elsewhere he identifies that colleague as Russel B. Nye, one of the earliest American popular culture specialists.[22] Nye had heard from a Lansing, Michigan, Buick dealer about inquiries for a rumored inexpensive but highly desirable used car in which a man had died and the smell of death could not be removed. Subsequently, Dorson got many variations of the same story from students in his folklore classes at MSU.

In 1953 Dorson cited this example of the "widely believed modern city legend" in a talk on folklore that he gave in the community of Mecosta, Michigan, while he was collecting material for his *Negro Folktales in Michigan.* After the talk Dorson was approached by John Berry, "grandson of a fugitive slave," who told him what Dorson called "the first authenticated account of the phantom tale ever to come my way."[23] Berry told Dorson that in 1938 a white man in Mecosta named Dennings committed suicide in his 1929 Model A Ford after being rejected by a lover. The old car, with distinctive hunting and fishing designs painted on it, was parked off the road in the woods when it was found. Cracks in its floorboards and body had been chinked, and a hose from the tailpipe conveyed exhaust fumes inside. A used car dealer sold the car cheaply to a man named Clifford Cross, who attempted in several ways to get the bad smell out of the car, but nothing worked. One time a little white dog got inside when Cross wasn't looking and barked from the backseat, scaring Cross into thinking a ghost was in the car. The story concludes, "Finally he give up trying to get the smell out, and turned the car in for junk."

Dorson's note to this version summarized thirty-three texts of "The Death Car" from widespread states, all filed in the MSU Folklore Archive; he compared them briefly as to distribution, dates, and details.[24] In his summary of the case in *American Folklore,* Dorson wrote, in answer to his own rhetorical question whether this incident in Mecosta was the origin of the legend, "Unlikely as it seems, the evidence from many variants, compared through the historical-geographical method of tracing folktales, calls for an affirmative answer."[25]

I doubt that Dorson gathered any "Death Car" versions beyond the MSU collection and that he did the rigorous comparative study that this statement suggests. More likely, realizing that he had the earliest known American version of the story, he merely deduced in a casual way that later texts could have been derived from it. He did not attempt to trace how the story spread so far from Michigan so quickly with so many changed features, nor did he try to account for the loss of details from the Mecosta story, such as the specific model of car, its decorations, the motive for the suicide, or the little white dog.

In fact, there is one major leap forward from the local story to the widespread legend that would have to be explained in a theory of origin. The Mecosta local legend centers on an ineradicable remnant of death, in this instance a bad smell, and ends with the smelly old car being junked. The modern urban legend is primarily a story about the lure of buying a wonderful car for a bargain price. The widespread legend always focuses on a late model or classic sports car, not an old junker.

Such discrepancies led Stewart Sanderson to challenge Dorson's conclusions about the origin of "The Death Car." First, in "Folklore of the Motor-Car," published in 1969, Sanderson called attention to an English modern legend about a car with a similar remnant of death, "The Ineradicable Blood-Stain." Sanderson listed five oral versions of this legend from 1951 to 1962 and a literary version from 1957. He footnoted Dorson's "Death Car" text as an American variant.[26]

In 1981, in his Katharine Briggs Memorial Lecture, Sanderson devoted more attention to these two versions of similar themes. (Incidentally, in this lecture Sanderson also mentioned discussing modern legends with both Dorson and Briggs in 1963 during conferences in Portugal and Leeds.)

"The Deathcar" by Tristan Schane © 1994 Paradox Press. All rights reserved. Used with permission of DC Comics.

Sanderson expressed reservations about Dorson's theory since the 1938 Mecosta story describes a 1929 Model A with cracks in the body that had been "used in rough country" and was probably a candidate for the junkyard even before the suicide. He suggested that the folk idea of the smell of death in the car may well have infiltrated the retellings of the Mecosta incident, and this motif is itself a variant (perhaps polygenetically originated) of the ineradicable bloodstain theme.[27]

Although Sanderson cited no motif, the ineradicable bloodstain has the number E422.1.11.5.1 in Thompson's *Motif-Index,* wherein are cited English, Irish, American, and Danish versions. The citations of the motif are much expanded in Baughman's index, including several references to ineradicable bloodstains found in Dorson's works. So it is surprising that Dorson—as devoted to indexing folk narratives as he was—never made the same connection that Sanderson did between smells and bloodstains persisting after death in these legends.

Sanderson further proposed in his analysis that the formation of modern legends is not so much a matter of the reworking of facts about an individual event into a widespread fictionalized account. Rather, he suggested, it is a process by which "two or more historical incidents, all much alike . . . have passed into legend and gone on to generate sets of fictional variants."[28] In other words, the answer to the question, Where did that urban legend come from? is not nearly so simple as Dorson's case study had implied.

I made my own review of "The Death Car" variants in the Indiana University Folklore Archive (which includes Dorson's MSU student collections). I could not isolate exactly which thirty-three variants Dorson himself used, for there are fifty-nine texts on file collected by MSU students dated from 1939 to 1956, plus another fifty-two texts deposited subsequently from Indiana University students.[29]

Dating of the MSU texts is problematic, since informants would often mention only when they remembered a story told to them originally, and collectors did not always indicate when their texts were collected. So one text attributed to "about 1939," which would place it only one year after the Mecosta incident, was actually collected around 1946. In fact, there are no earlier "Death Car" stories in the MSU collection. Similarly, calling this the "Michigan" collection is misleading, since about one-quarter of the tales are actually attributed to other states by their tellers, including not only the nearby Midwestern states but places as far afield as Maine, Florida, and California.

A comparison of details in the Michigan versions (following the historic-geographic method in spirit if not in strict practice) does not point clearly to the Mecosta incident as the origin. In fact, if we judge by the numerical superiority and the widest distribution of traits, we would postulate an archetype in which a person dies of a heart attack in a recent model Buick or Cadillac, rather than an archetype about dying by suicide in a Model A Ford. Although a few variants mention suicide, none says that a broken romance was the motive; and while some allude to the dead person having gone hunting, just as many set the accidental death in a western desert as in a midwestern forest. And, as pointed out above, the invariable focus of the stories is on the bargain price for a desirable car, not on the death that took place in the car. In short, it is hard to see how the Mecosta story could have given rise to such a consistently different legend in wider circulation.

One contextual detail worth mentioning is that three of the storytellers from the late 1940s said they were shown the actual car standing on a dealer's lot, although none said they could actually smell anything, since they saw the car from a distance or at times when the lot was closed and the cars were locked. Two informants mentioned that a used car salesman spread the legend. Remembering the general shortage of cars just after World War II, this hoax-like feature of telling "The Death Car" legend about a specific car standing on a local lot may have been partly a matter of increasing the mystique of the already rare vehicles. Many texts of "The Death Car" that I have collected are remembered from the same period of time and make specific reference to the scarcity of cars and the allure of a great car at a bargain price.

The texts collected by Indiana University students give much the same impression: details are standardized, settings are sometimes localized, and the versions are never very much like the Mecosta incident, with one suspicious exception. A text dated 1977 is obviously a summary of Dorson's published text, complete with details like driving around in winter with the windows open. No wonder the student collector/plagiarist indicated on the archive release form that his material was "under no circumstances" to be published.

It may seem that I have reached a conclusion that Dorson overgeneralized what he knew about urban legends and then fudged the data on "The Death Car" legend in particular, but that is not my intent. Dorson did no worse trying to track a single modern legend to its source than any of us have done with other such texts. Probably such a source search can never be done in a definitive way, but we do learn from the endeavor.

I think Dorson's major contribution in this area was in early identifying that a group of such stories even existed and that they centered on significant topics of contemporary concern and ought to be collected and studied. By consolidating the few scholarly references to urban legends, and by introducing them into his influential textbook, and by encouraging students and professional colleagues to carry on their study, Dorson started the ball rolling. The bibliography of books and articles on urban legends—now more than forty years after the publication of *American Folklore*—is enormous. Following Richard Dorson's example, we take it for granted today that urban legends are a major form of modern oral narrative worthy of our attention.

Notes

This essay was originally presented in a session on Richard M. Dorson's views and work at the annual meeting of the American Folklore Society in Albuquerque, New Mexico, October 21–25, 1987. It was published in *Folklore Historian* 7 (1990): 16–22.

1. Michael Goss, "Legends for Our Time," *The Unknown*, July 1987, 10–16.

2. Michael Goss, *The Evidence for Phantom Hitch-Hikers* (Wellingborough, England: Aquarian Press, 1984).

3. Rodney Dale, *The Tumour in the Whale: A Collection of Modern Myths* (London: Duckworth, 1978). Dale's other suggestion—that urban legends be called "whale tumour stories" (or WTS's)—failed to catch on. There are discrepancies in Dale's terminology: his book is subtitled "A Collection of Modern Myths," although this is rendered on the dust jacket as "a hilarous [sic] collection of apocryphal anecdotes."

4. Katherine Briggs and Ruth Tongue, *Folktales of England* (Chicago: University of Chicago Press, 1965).

5. Stewart Sanderson, "The Folklore of the Motor-Car," *Folklore* 80 (1969): 241–52.

6. Richard M. Dorson, *American Folklore* (Chicago: University of Chicago Press, 1959).

7. For example, in the headnote to "The Runaway Grandmother" in Briggs and Tongue, *Folktales of England,* Dorson notes that he heard a version of that story on New Year's Eve, 1963.

8. Richard M. Dorson, "A Theory for American Folklore," *Journal of American Folklore* 72 (1959): 197–232.

9. Richard M. Dorson, "A Theory for American Folklore Reviewed," *Journal of American Folklore* 82 (1969): 226–44.

10. Dorson, "A Theory for American Folklore," 212; Dorson, *American Folklore,* 249–54.

11. Ibid., 306–9.

12. "The Poisoned Dress," *Hoosier Folklore Bulletin* 4 (1945): 19–20; Gloria Hochsinger, "More about the Poisoned Dress," *Hoosier Folklore Bulletin* 4 (1945):

32–34; Raymond Himelick, "Classical Versions of 'The Poisoned Garment,'" *Hoosier Folklore* 5 (1946): 83–84; J. Russell Reaver, "'Embalmed Alive': A Developing Urban Ghost Tale," *New York Folklore Quarterly* 8 (1952): 217–20.

13. He also called attention in a note to a literary treatment of five urban legends in a 1934 book by Alexander Woollcott.

14. Richard M. Dorson, "Legends and Tall Tales," in *Our Living Traditions,* ed. Tristram Potter Coffin (New York: Basic Books, 1968), 154–69, reprinted in Richard M. Dorson, *Folklore: Selected Essays* (Bloomington: Indiana University Press, 1972): 159–76.

15. Richard M. Dorson, "Introduction: The America Theme in American Folklore," *Journal of the Folklore Institute* 17 (1980): 93.

16. See Richard M. Dorson, *American Folklore and the Historian* (Chicago: University of Chicago Press, 1971), 157–72; and *Folklore: Selected Essays,* 159–74.

17. See the reprint in *Folklore: Selected Essays,* 177–98.

18. Linda Dégh, ed. "Folk Legends from Indiana," *Indiana Folklore* 1 (1968): 9–12.

19. Richard M. Dorson, *America in Legend* (New York: Pantheon, 1973).

20. Richard M. Dorson, *Land of the Millrats* (Cambridge, Mass., Harvard University Press, 1981).

21. Dorson, *American Folklore,* 250.

22. Richard M. Dorson, *Negro Folktales in Michigan* (Cambridge, Mass.: Harvard University Press, 1956), 218.

23. Ibid., 99; Richard M. Dorson, *American Negro Folktales* (Greenwich, Conn.: Fawcett Premier Books, 1967), 298–99.

24. Dorson, *Negro Folktales in Michigan,* 218.

25. Dorson, *American Folklore,* 252.

26. Sanderson, "The Folklore of the Motor-Car," 250.

27. Sanderson, "The Modern Urban Legend," *Katharine Briggs Lecture no.* 1 (1981): 3–15.

28. Ibid., 9.

29. I am indebted to Peggy Brooks, archivist of the Indiana University collection, for locating texts of "The Death Car" and providing me with copies.

2

"The Brain Drain" Legend of the Long Hot Summer of 1995 (and Beyond)

The summer of 1995 was a scorcher, helping to boost the average surface temperature of the whole earth enough to make 1995 "the warmest year since records first were kept in 1856," as reported in the *New York Times*.[1] While the average high temperature of 58.72 degrees, as the article put it, "may not sound like beach weather," it was hot enough to alarm climatologists and, enough, perhaps—combined with long periods of record-breaking summer temperatures in the Midwest, South, and East—to encourage the growth and spread of a new urban legend, the story of the woman trapped in her oven-hot car and suffering a frightening case of suspected "Brain Drain." (Then again, the heat may have had little to do with the story, since there are precedents for it in ancient folktales told in cooler eras.) At any rate, the modern story *popped* into my attention, so to speak, just as the heat wave got going in early summer, and it persisted even after the record cold, ice, and snow of the winter of 1995–96 began to arrive around Christmas. Since then, it has reappeared occasionally.

Six Months of "Brain Drain" Stories

I first encountered the story in a letter dated June 15, 1995, from a woman in Austin, Texas, who said it had been told to her husband, who works in a hotel, by a guest from Atlanta, a woman, who told it to him in the first person:

> [She said she was] in the parking lot of an Atlanta grocery store, on her way in, when she passed a car with the windows down and a woman sitting in the driver's seat with her hand on the back of her head, staring ahead. The guest did her shopping, and returned to the parking lot about half an

hour later. The woman was still sitting in the same position in her car, so the guest asked if she were all right.

The woman said in a feeble voice, "I've been shot!" The other woman ran back into the grocery store, shouting for 911. While someone called, she rushed back to the parking lot with the store manager. Both were afraid to try to move the poor lady, who wouldn't let go of her head. When the police and ambulance arrived, the paramedics gingerly peeled her hand away, revealing a whitish blobular substance on her hand and in her hair.

As the police looked around, they discovered that a can of biscuits had exploded and hit the woman. Apparently she heard the noise, felt the impact, and reached up, only to feel what she thought must be brain tissue.

The time on her receipt indicated that she'd been in the parking lot for one and one-half hours. The manager gave her another can of biscuits.

About a month later I got the same story in a letter from a woman in St. Louis, who mentioned that several weeks before that the temperature in that city had been in the nineties for a week straight. She also clarified that the "biscuits" were Pillsbury Poppin' Fresh brand refrigerated biscuit dough in a tube and that the woman was "hunched over to keep her brains from falling out." My correspondent heard the story in the St. Louis Art Museum, where she works, from her boss, who said it had happened to the mother of a man in a different department of the museum. Later another woman in the museum said that she had heard the same story told six months previously in Illinois.

"The Brain Drain" continued to show up, with minor variations. A man in Pineville, Kentucky, wrote in late July to say that he had heard it concerning three different local stores' parking lots. This time a man came to the aid of the stricken woman. One week later a woman in New York City wrote to say that she had overheard the story told in her office; it had supposedly happened to a FOAF vacationing in Florida, and it occurred not in a parking lot but along a highway. The victim heard the pop, felt the blow to her head, touched the biscuit dough, and immediately pulled over, thinking she had been the victim of a drive-by shooting. She was helped by a friendly man who stopped to investigate.

Next, a mother and daughter in Cincinnati wrote that the story was making the rounds there. They said a man had stopped to help a woman pulled over to the roadside and holding her head, "thinking her brains were hanging out." He moved her hand, saw the dough, and made the connection with the "popped" tube of biscuit dough on top of her grocery bag in the backseat. But my correspondents pointed out that "you have to peel the outer label off the package and rap it on the counter" to open these tubes of dough, plus pull the individual biscuits apart. Besides, the daughter had also heard a version that mentioned a grocery store parking lot and a bag boy from the store, who was collecting grocery carts and had helped the woman.

In mid-August I started getting versions via the Internet. In an e-mail message from Janesville, Wisconsin, a woman said that her friend Mary told her on a camping trip in Door County (up north) that *her* friend Susie had told her that it happened to a woman down (south) in Madison on a very hot day. The dough had come from a package of Pillsbury Crescent Rolls, and the victim had fainted when she felt the blow. "But there's something wrong with the story," my correspondent concluded. "If the dough exploded, wouldn't it just leak out rather than shoot a biscuit?"

In early September I heard from an Episcopal priest in Staunton, Virginia, who sent a printout of an e-mailed version of "The Brain Drain" received by the rector of his church. This came from Indianola, Mississippi, and stated that while shopping at Wal-Mart on a very hot day a dentist visiting her hometown saw an old woman hunched over the steering wheel. "I'm paralyzed, [*sic*] I can't move!" the woman said, fingering the gooey gray matter on the back of her head. The dentist figured it out when she saw "an open can of biscuits sticking out of the top of a grocery bag in the back seat."

In October I received three versions of "The Brain Drain" from Professor Susanne Ridlen of Indiana University in Kokomo, whose introductory folklore students had collected them. All three emphasized the intense heat of the past summer, and they specified the locales as either a Kroger store or along a road. The victims were women, but one of the helpers was a male sacker from the grocery store. The stories were collected in an electronics factory, in a grocery store, and from an office worker who had heard it by telephone from a relative in Ohio and whose friend had heard it from a relative in Texas as well. Although some of the Kokomo informants thought the story had been published in the *Indianapolis Star* or possibly reported by Paul Harvey, none of the students was able to verify these claims.

As autumn turned to winter in 1995 I heard from a man in Maryland who got the story from someone working in a hospital emergency department in Fresno, California, who said "The Brain Drain" incident had happened there. And I heard it from a friend in Salt Lake City who had heard the story told on a local radio talk show. And from the folklorist Joe Goodwin in Muncie, Indiana, who said that in some versions the dough was past its freshness date and had exploded from a build-up of gas (presumably CO_2). And from a woman on CompuServe who thought it sounded like a legend turned into a joke, or vice versa. And from another CompuServe user who thought she must have heard it in Florida before she moved to New Jersey to live with a man she had met on the Internet. And from another anonymous Internet contact who said she had witnessed tubes of biscuit dough oozing open—but never "popping"—when she had worked in grocery stores. And, finally, a few days before Christmas, from a man in Seymour, Indiana; at his workplace, someone reported to him that the incident had happened to a friend's aunt as she was exiting a shopping mall and spotted a woman clutching the back of her head.

In early 1996, a few versions of the story continued to drift in: an e-mailed version, heard back in August 1995, concerning a supposed incident in Texas City, Texas, in which the victim is found sobbing in her car; a version from Jackson, Mississippi, in which the sender traced it back, supposedly, four steps to the actual brother of the victim; a version from Marion, North Carolina, in which the teller's friend's son, an EMS worker, insisted it had really happened at a small country store nearby; a version from a woman in Tuscaloosa, Alabama, in which the teller claimed the incident had actually happened to her, and she had "rescued" herself without help. Early in 1997 "The Brain Drain" story was told on the National Public Radio program "Car Talk," and it also popped up as comic relief on an episode of the ABC-TV cop show "High Incident."

To summarize my several months of stockpiling this story: I got it from nineteen individuals residing in a dozen different states but who had heard the story reported in a total of fourteen different states, mostly midwestern, southern, or eastern, but literally from coast to coast. The distribution, variation, and multiple attribution of the story to FOAFs all confirmed it as an urban legend, call it "The Brain Drain" or maybe "The Biscuit Bullet." In common with other crime legends, the scene is often the parking lot of a store or mall. Themes evident in the legend, besides the summer's heat, include a misunderstanding leading to a comic result, a defect in a manufactured product, the danger of random criminal attacks, and the need to rely on the kindness of strangers. Also, like some other modern urban legends, "The Brain Drain" creates tension with the implication of grave danger or injury, then releases the tension in a humorous aftermath. In this respect, the story is similar to "The Elevator Incident" or "The Poisoned Pussycat at the Party."

In considering possible meanings of the legend, it is worth noting what the only two journalists who took the story seriously had to say. One of these went for a very broad theme, asking, "What has America come to

. . . when a woman's first thought upon hearing a loud noise is that she has been the victim of a random shooting?"[2] The second journalist was more limited in her interpretation: "things are not always what they seem; our imaginations can greatly distort the truth."[3] Speaking of distortions, I decline to consider here the possibility that the discharge of a viscous substance toward a woman and from a tube, not to mention in a car, may be a sexual metaphor, although similar elements in other stories have been given this interpretation in some studies.[4] Sometimes, I believe, a tube of biscuits is just a tube of biscuits.

So far, so good, but I was not the only person interested in the legend that year; in fact, discussion of it had been rampant on the Internet all spring and summer of 1995, and I was just a bit late in joining the conversation.

More Information from the Internet

As far as I can determine, "The Brain Drain" was first posted to the newsgroup alt.folklore.urban in mid-May 1995 by someone at Purdue University, who wrote, "I heard something last weekend that I'm sure *has* to be a UL." Joe Goodwin posted a similar query to the Folklore Discussion List in mid-July, writing that he had heard it in Muncie, Indiana, but that it may have been known in either North or South Carolina around July 1. Both these postings set off responses that continued well into the fall, and the story eventually found its way into several joke newsgroups as well as to groups discussing Fortean phenomena and "weird news."

The Internet chit-chatters added a few new details to the story (names of stores, dialogue among participants, other locations); they also pointed out similar scenes in popular culture and in real life. For example, several people mentioned accounts of "exploding" food (in pressure cookers, microwave ovens) told as newlywed bungling-bride stories, or they recalled scenes in old war or slapstick comedy movies or on recent TV sitcoms in which a food can was shot at or otherwise "exploded," spraying people with its contents and leading them to think they were more badly injured than they actually were. Other people added accounts of experiences of their own while opening packaged biscuit dough or experiences with "exploding" cans of other products. Still others dug into databases to uncover newspaper accounts of the story (about which more below), some of which they then posted to the Internet.[5]

The most interesting and useful information to emerge from the Internet chats was that the comedian Brett Butler, the star of the ABC sitcom

"Grace under Fire," had been telling a variation of the story—saying it had happened to her sister—as part of her stand-up act for some time. She had also told it on "Late Night with David Letterman" about a year before.[6]

Something about Brett Butler

My computer search for news reports mentioning both Brett Butler and biscuits yielded two hits, one of them really just an interesting miss. First, the miss: *USA Today Weekend* on June 18, 1995, in a feature on rising comics and their acts, referred to Butler as "the little biscuit eater from the South." (Why *biscuit* eater? There is no explanation in the article.) Second, the hit: almost exactly one year *earlier*, on June 19, 1994, the *Cleveland Plain Dealer,* in a review of a Brett Butler live performance in Cleveland, gave this valuable account: "Minutes later, she was recounting a hilarious tale about a sister who thought she'd become a victim of a highway shooting only to find out her Pillsbury biscuits in the back seat had exploded and whacked her in the head. Then, as if to truly plead with the audience to help her TV show become less sanitized, more real, she cried, 'I want (stuff) like that to be on "Grace Under Fire."'"

The word *stuff* was in parentheses in this review, evidently to indicate that it was a euphemism for another s-word. Note also that no "rescuer" appears in this version; indeed, one Internet commenter remembered from the Letterman appearance that Brett's sister supposedly had driven herself to an emergency room.

Something about Packaged Biscuit Dough

My computer search for articles combining biscuit dough with explosions yielded several good hits about "The Brain Drain," but also this nostalgic memory of packaged biscuit dough from the *Austin American-Statesman.* It was the lead-in to an October 6, 1994, review of good places in Austin to go out for brunch. The writer wrote of his childhood: "Mom would scramble at least a dozen eggs, adding our secret family ingredient: grated cheddar cheese. She put the fluffy eggs on a platter, always adorned with strips of bacon ready to crumble at your fingertips. We fought about who would get to take the cardboard cylinder containing the biscuit dough and whack it on the edge of the kitchen counter so it would explode open. . . . Not exactly *haute cuisine,* but a heckuva spread for 1970s suburbia."

What is revealing about this reminiscence is that the writer, a South-westerner, is referring *ironically* to refrigerated biscuit dough as part of "a heckuva spread," but also as an ingredient of the meal that is obviously not the best that regional cooking has to offer. A humorist from the Deep South, the late syndicated columnist Lewis Grizzard, quoted another Southern humorist, Jerry Clower, on this very topic: "'One of the saddest things,' Jerry once said, 'is the sound of them whomp biscuits being opened in more and more houses these days. Whomp! Another poor man is being denied homemade biscuits. No wonder the divorce rate is so high.'"[7]

Grizzard followed this passage with two pages of mouth-watering description of his mama's biscuits and all the good ways they were served: "Mama made her biscuits from scratch, the same as her mother had done. They were soft as angel hair," he began. The attitude that a southern cook who would resort to "whomp biscuits" is failing to uphold an important regional culinary tradition is clear here, and it adds another dimension to our understanding of the story's meaning. Indeed, when I mentioned "The Brain Drain" in a 1995 lecture in the public library of New Iberia, Louisiana, one woman commented afterwards, "Well, I'd heard that story, but I didn't really understand it, because we-all around here always make our biscuits from scratch."

Incidentally, despite various references to "whacking" or "whomping" the biscuit canister on the kitchen counter edge to open it, the directions on the package are both illustrated and quite clearly stated: "EASY OPEN CAN: Peel in direction of arrow until can pops." (Ah! But notice: "until can *pops*." And see below for more on "whacking" the canister.)

When people refer to packaged biscuit dough, they almost always mean a Pillsbury product, for, as a Pillsbury spokesman told a reporter in November 1995, "We are by far the biggest name in refrigerated dough products."[8] In a 1990 press release, Pillsbury—headquartered in Minneapolis, Minnesota—revealed that "in 1965, the Doughboy popped out of a tube of Pillsbury fresh, ready-to-bake dough for the first time." The release continued by naming the advertising agency executive who dreamed up the trademark character in 1965 while fantasizing about "what would pop out when a roll of Pillsbury refrigerated biscuits was tapped against the kitchen counter." So here we have the folk images, despite what's printed on the canisters themselves: the can is *tapped* and the contents *pop out*. Incidentally, probably to counter the negative associations of pre-fab biscuit dough, Pillsbury's original Poppin' Fresh slogan was this: "Nothin' says Lovin' like Something from the Oven and Pillsbury Says it Best."[9]

Some Help from Lexis-Nexis

The wonderfully helpful computer database Lexis-Nexis revealed that several journalists had picked up on "The Brain Drain" about the same time I did. Eight news stories or columns including or discussing the legend appeared from mid-June to mid-November 1995. Even better, a column published in the *Cleveland Plain Dealer* on January 19, 1994—just six months before information on the Brett Butler routine appeared in the same paper and some eighteen months before I started hearing the legend—gave this brief account of the story:

> True Story No. 1: A woman had been to the grocery store. Driving home, she heard a "pow!" and felt something hit the back of her head. With her hand, she felt a gooey substance on the back of her head. She immediately assumed she had been hit in a drive-by shooting and that her brains were leaking out through the wound.
>
> She drove to a hospital [like Brett Butler's sister], keeping her hand in place to stifle the flow of brain matter, stopped in front of the emergency room and started honking her car's horn. Emergency personnel rushed out and examined her head. It turned out that a can of biscuit dough had exploded in the back seat, hitting her head. What she felt was gooey biscuit makings.[10]

The author of the Cleveland column, whose name is Pat Truly, drew from this and another "true story" some lessons about trust, suspicion, and danger in modern life (some of which I quoted earlier). Truly ended by commenting, "How did we get to such a point? The only logical conclusion is that we've all been using biscuit dough for brains the last 40 years." To repeat, this was January 1994; so, evidently, "The Brain Drain" was already going around that early.

◤

A summary of the eight newspaper references located from 1995 about "The Brain Drain" story:

June 13—*Greensboro (N.C.) News and Record.* A friend of the columnist, a nurse, told him the incident happened inside a grocery store in Lucedale, Mississippi, to "Miss Lydia." Bystanders drive her to a hospital where the gray matter on her head is sampled for a lab analysis that reveals it to be you-know-what. The writer admitted, "I didn't check it out, because experience tells me that stories this good usually go flat when you check them out, and they won't sell newspapers."

July 11—Same paper, same columnist. Readers and friends have informed him that the biscuit incident really happened in Tennessee. Some had heard it told on the radio. The victim, trying to race to a hospital, is stopped by a highway patrolman. "Lady, your biscuits blew up and hit you in the head," he said.

August 13—*Lewiston (Idaho) Morning Tribune.* In a commentary on scary stories told among retirees appears this true story that happened to a woman in Springfield, Missouri. She is helped by an off-duty paramedic; when the police come, they recognize the biscuit dough.

October 1—*Charleston (S.C.) Post and Courier.* In a column of short takes entitled "Have You Heard the Latest Urban Myth?": It is said to have happened "right here in our fair city. . . . Seems the heat popped those Hungry Jacks right open."

November 6—Follow-up on the above. "Remember that urban myth? . . . A juvenile judge from Savannah called last week. . . . He originally heard it from a kid in his church youth group." The judge thought it must be a *new* myth because "he had just read a complete book of urban legends, and that one wasn't included."

October 4—*Baton Rouge Capital City Press.* In "Shot by the Doughboy?: Every So Often I Get One of Those 'Urban Legends'" a physician rushed to aid a woman sitting in the parking lot of the Wynn-Dixie store on Siegen Lane. *She* was "writhing in pain" and holding her head, and *he* spotted the biscuit canister.

October 6—Same paper, same columnist. A reader informs him that Brett Butler uses the story in her routine and adds, "All biscuit cans do is pop, split open and ooze out some contents under non-projectile capability pressure!"

November 15—*St. Louis Post-Dispatch.* The columnist had received two letters relating "The Brain Drain" story from readers in Wayne City, Illinois, and from the suburb of Kirkwood, the latter told by an "older adult" on an Old Age Transport System bus who claimed she was the one who aided the lady in distress. The columnist phoned me, then phoned Pillsbury. I updated her on the story, and a Pillsbury spokesman "gulped like he'd swallowed a raw biscuit" and "in a voice that chilled my buns" said this was the first he had heard of it.[11]

Yet another account of the story appeared in the *Denver Post* on April 6, 1996, in a column entitled "A Biscuit with Her Name on It," in which the story is identified as "another urban legend." And in the May 1996 issue of *U: The National College Magazine* the story was retold, tongue-in-cheek, as something that happened to a student at Northeastern University in Massachusetts.

These press references to "The Brain Drain" all pretty much play it for the laughs. Only two accounts—the earliest one, published in Cleveland, and the August 1995 one from Idaho—seem to take the story seriously, while all the others treat it lightly, and some even identify the story as an urban legend. We wonder, though, *where* did the Cleveland and the Lewiston, Idaho, journalists hear their "true" versions, and *why* did they believe them? I wrote to both of these journalists asking these questions. Pat Truly, who wrote the 1994 column for the *Cleveland Plain Dealer*, did not reply directly, but when I happened to get a call from another journalist with that same paper in March 1996 she researched the story for me, publishing her findings in a column of her own on March 27, 1996.[12] Pat Truly, a man, is a syndicated columnist in Fort Worth, Texas, whose column in this instance was picked up by the Cleveland paper and evidently by no other, at least none that I have discovered. Truly told the Cleveland journalist that he heard the story from his wife, and she got it from a co-worker, who got it from a friend. "Eventually," concludes the recent article, "Truly traced the tale to a woman in Hattiesburg, Mississippi."

As for the Idaho "true" account, it turned out that the son of the woman who wrote the story is a police officer in Springfield, Missouri; he called home one day and told his wife the story, and she phoned her mother-in-law in Idaho to repeat it. The newspaper ran the story without any further checking. It makes you proud of American journalism, does it not?

Some Folkloric Background

"The Brain Drain" legend of 1994–95 contains many contemporary elements, including a commercial product, a car, shopping, street crime, and the 911 emergency system. But there are also several traditional folkloric elements present in the stories.

Some general motifs come close to the central ideas of the urban legend, for example Motif J1820, *Inappropriate action from misunderstanding,* and Motif X1630, *Lies about hot weather.* The specific tall tales that combine motifs involving *both* heat and food, however, bear only the slightest similarity to "Brain Drain" stories; these traditional heat/food motifs include cooking bacon and eggs on a stone in the shade on a hot day, potatoes baking in the hot ground, and popcorn popping in the overheated fields. Such stories indicate only that the possible effects on food of extreme hot weather have been comically exaggerated for a long time.

More similar to our legend is Motif K473, *Sham blood and brains,* which is actually part of an animal tale (Aarne-Thompson Type 3) in which a fox (for one) covers his head with milk or other food, claims his brains have been knocked out, and thus frightens the bear (or another creature). This motif and type are often combined with Tale Type 4, *Carrying the Sham Sick Trickster,* and both of these tales are among the large cycle of animal tales studied by Kaarle Krohn in the 1880s. Types 3 and 4, plus incorporated motifs, have wide distribution, especially in Europe. The closest I've found to "The Brain Drain" scenario is a Russian version of Type 4 called "Little Sister Fox and the Wolf" collected by the folklorist Aleksandr Nickolaevich Afanas'ev and first published in the midnineteenth century. Here is the relevant section of the story in one translation: "[Fox has played another trick on the wolf; then the story continues] Little Sister Fox . . . got into a house where women were frying pancakes, stuck her head into a tub of dough, smeared herself, and ran away. The wolf met her. 'So that's the way you teach me?' he said. 'I was roundly beaten for my pains.' 'Eh, neighbor,' said little Sister Fox, 'all you have lost is some blood. But I have had my brains beaten out of me, and it was much more painful; I can hardly hobble along.'"[13]

Another curious instance of the dough-for-brains motif appears in an anecdote told by a Finnish-American man from Wisconsin in 1935. In "Old Paul's Story," Walter Jackola recorded the story of an old man who, after mixing some bread dough and hanging the bucketful on a hook to dry, got drunk and fell asleep. When his son arrived and woke him up, the man had a lump of dough stuck to his hair. The son was startled, and he blurted out, "Why father, your brains are sticking out of your head!"[14]

Stith Thompson, summarizing the historic-geographic scholarship on the group of European trickster animal tales, reported Krohn's conclusion that the cycle developed in northern Europe and may have existed there for about one thousand years.[15] Types 3 and 4 are seldom reported in American folklore, except, notably, in the Br'er Rabbit stories, where, however, no food on the head is mentioned. The rabbit merely claims he is too sick to walk, then tricks the fox into carrying him while wearing a saddle and bridle.

A similar folkloristic element not found in the *Motif-Index* but recorded in at least two early New England sources involves the entrails of a bear that has been shot that are mistaken by a hunter for his own insides. Ronald L. Baker reports this story from a work by Rowland E. Robinson published in the 1880s, and Richard Dorson discovered another version in the *Portland (Maine) Telegram* published in 1934. In both accounts the victim believes his guts are coming out and that he is dying, but those who come to his rescue identify the entrails as those of the bear, not the man, and they convince the hunter that he is not really wounded.[16] (A modern joke involving a person who swallows small-animal intestines to replace them, believing his own guts have come out, has been collected repeatedly. Often it is called "The Long-Handled Spoon," referring to the utensil employed for the swallowing.)[17]

The "leaky brain" motif took another twist in some versions of the old story classified by Baughman as K435(a), *Customer puts a quantity of butter under his hat*. In these stories the theft is detected when butter starts to melt and run down the thief's face and neck. Charles M. Skinner published an elaborate version of the butter-under-the-hat story in 1903 with this ironic introductory comment on the story's great popularity: "There is one narrative, formerly common in school-readers, in collections of moral tales for youth, and in the miscellany columns of newspapers, that is thought to have been a favorite with Aristophanes and to have beguiled the Pharaohs when they had the blues. . . . Every now and again it reappears in the periodicals and enjoys a new vogue for a couple of months."[18]

In *Jonathan Draws the Long Bow* Richard Dorson published another example of the butter story taken from the early New York "sporting weekly," as such papers were known, *The Spirit of the Times* in 1841.[19] Both Skinner's and Dorson's versions mention Vermont as the locale of the incident; yet the *Spirit of the Times* version was reprinted from the *New Orleans Picayune*. Dorson also mentions a version from Massachusetts published in 1892, a further indication of how popular the story had become in the United States. It came most likely from England, where both the old versions and some newer variations are still told. A writer to the *Sunday Express* in 1990, reading about a story involving an old lady who "had hidden a frozen chicken under her hat" in a supermarket was reminded "of a tale my father told more than 70 years ago." The older remembered tale is the butter-under-the-hat story and, in this version, the thief is scolded with this bit of dialect verse:

> Oh Buttery Dick, tha little did see,
> Tha farmer Gray were watching thee.
> He saw thi tak it and he did mutter
> He'd mak thi pay, and he'd bast thi wi butter.[20]

I have elsewhere discussed the international urban legend of the person stealing frozen food from a supermarket by putting it under his or her hat. I've compared it to a story told by Sherpa Tenzing Norgay concerning a lama who tries to steal some cooked sausages by hiding them under his hat. This thief is caught when the hot meat burns his head and the sausages slip out from under the hat.[21] None of these versions of food-under-hat stories connects the food to brains, however; it remained for Mark Twain to make that connection in his *Adventures of Huckleberry Finn* (1885). In chapter 40 of that book, after Huck is caught raiding the cellar cupboard for food and stuffs a "slab" of corn-pone and a "hunk" of butter under his hat to conceal them, Aunt Sally, suspecting nothing, detains him in the warm parlor until the butter begins to melt and run down Huck's neck. Noticing this, Aunt Sally exclaims, "For the land's sake what is the matter with the child!—he's got the brain fever as shore as you're born, and they're oozing out!"[22]

An Inconclusive Conclusion

What, if anything, may we conclude from viewing the contemporary "Brain Drain" legend against the background of similar traditional folkloric elements? As much as I enjoy citing parallels or analogues of modern folklore in older traditions, I must admit here that the matching details are very scattered and mostly pretty sketchy. In the two cycles of previous narratives discussed, the situations are considerably different, even if some details seem strangely similar.

In the animal tales, for example, a trickster puts food on his head, pretending it is his brains; this is a deliberate hoax on the part of the "victim," not a mistaken inference. In the thievery tale, a character hides butter or other food under his hat, but he is recognized as a thief when the butter melts or the other food somehow leaks out. In contrast, in the contemporary "Brain Drain" story there is no hoaxing or deliberate hiding of food; the food hits the head in the legend as part of the natural course of events in an ordinary situation, and the victim fools herself alone. (Only the story of the bear's entrails mistaken for a person's insides matches this thought process, but no food is involved, and entrails are not the same as brains.)

So—to be inconclusively conclusive—about all we can say at this time concerning the genesis of this new urban legend is that perhaps a cycle of traditional folkloric tales laid the groundwork for the emergence of the modern legend around 1994 by providing some of the essential motifs of the story. That same year a popular stand-up comic gave the story a further kick in the pants by incorporating it into her routine and repeating it on television talk shows. In the background of both her version and of the wider oral tradition of the same story lurks the Southern home-baked biscuits-from-scratch culinary tradition. Then, in 1995, possibly incubated by the long hot summer, and pressured by heavy news reporting of street crimes, "The Brain Drain" flourished, attracting into its orbit some familiar elements of other popular urban legends and elaborating the imagined possibilities of a canister of refrigerated biscuit dough popping open in the heat. (I believe I have mixed six metaphors in this final paragraph, which may be a record. Blame it on the heat of composition.)

Notes

An earlier version of this essay was presented at the Perspectives on Contemporary Legend conference, sponsored by the ISCLR, in Bath, England, July 27–August 1, 1996.

1. William K. Stevens, "'95 the Hottest Year on Record as the Global Trend Keeps Up," *New York Times,* Jan. 4, 1996.

2. Pat Truly, "The Unthinkable Is Becoming Less So Every Day," *Cleveland Plain Dealer,* Jan. 19, 1994.

3. Bonnie Wayne, "Things May Not Be as Bad as They Seem," *Lewiston (Idaho) Morning Tribune,* Aug. 13, 1995.

4. For a review of such interpretations of legends, see Gary Alan Fine, "Evaluating Psychoanalytic Folklore: Are Freudians Ever Right?" *Manufacturing Tales: Sex and Money in Contemporary Legends* (Knoxville: University of Tennessee Press, 1992), 45–58.

5. I am grateful to Joe Goodwin, Alan Mays, David Mikkelson, and Barbara Mikkelson for sending me materials gleaned from the Internet.

6. A sidelight on the Internet career of "The Brain Drain": A fictionalized version of the legend beginning "Beware the Dough-Boy. My friend Linda went to Arkansas last week to visit her in-laws . . ." soon became the standard version on the Forteana list and on several humor groups, one of which asked readers to rank the "joke" on a scale of 1 (not funny) to 10 (hilarious). Some versions of this joke begin, "Pillsbury Dough Boy wanted for attempted murder," juxtaposing the cute giggling little trademark guy with a killer's persona. Characteristic of these jokes, besides the opening line and the personal name, is the detail that rescuers had to break into the car to get at the woman.

The joke version soon took on a life of its own, apart from the circulation of the legend version; I received forwarded copies of it through June 1996. So it appears that the Internet has its own folklore subgroups that may develop their own variations of standard stories. One person posting a version of the "My friend Linda" story labeled it as "A found object, slightly edited." By March 1996 another "lady named Linda" variation was circulating on the Internet in a discussion on nutrition, and in 1997 the same version was posted on the "Darwin Award" list that was circulating on the Internet.

7. Lewis Grizzard, *Don't Forget to Call Your Mama . . . I Wish I Could Call Mine* (Marietta, Ga.: Longstreet Press, 1991), 69.

8. Elaine Viets, "Biscuit Bullets: Quite a Messy Tale," *St. Louis Post-Dispatch,* Nov. 15, 1995.

9. "Oh Boy! Pillsbury Doughboy Turns Twenty-Five!" PR newswire, Sept. 20, 1990, Pillsbury headquarters, Minneapolis.

10. Truly, "The Unthinkable."

11. Viets, "Biscuit Bullets."

12. Afi-Odelia E. Scruggs, "Legends Border on the Believable," *Cleveland Plain Dealer,* Mar. 27, 1996.

13. Aleksandr Nickolaevich Afanas'ev, *Russian Fairy Tales,* trans. Norbert Guterman (New York: Pantheon, 1945), 372.

14. Walter Jackola, "Finnish Folktales," in *Wisconsin Folklore,* ed. James P. Leary (Madison: University of Wisconsin Press, 1998), 181.

15. Stith Thompson, *The Folktale* (New York: Dryden, 1946), 220.

16. Ronald L. Baker, *Folklore in the Writings of Rowland E. Robinson* (Bowling Green, Ohio: Bowling Green University Popular Press, 1973), 180–81. Richard Dorson's report, "Just B'ars," published in *Appalachia,* n.s. 8 (Dec. 1942): 178–79, is cited by Baker on 193, n. 27.

17. John A. Burrison, "The Long-Handled Spoon," *Storytellers: Folktales and Legends from the South* (Athens: University of Georgia Press, 1989), 284–85; Ronald L. Baker, "The Mistaken Entrails," *Jokelore: Humorous Folktales from Indiana* (Bloomington: Indiana University Press, 1972), 99.

18. Charles M. Skinner, "A Travelled Narrative," *American Myths and Legends* (Philadelphia: J. B. Lippincott, 1903), 54–58.

19. See Richard Dorson, *Jonathan Draws the Long Bow* (Cambridge, Mass.: Harvard University Press, 1946), 19–20, and "A Melting Story," 89–91.

20. "Shoplift Tale Is Old Hat," *Sunday Express,* Jan. 14, 1990. The letter came from a reader in Haxley, York.

21. See Jan Harold Brunvand, *The Mexican Pet: More "New" Urban Legends and Some Old Favorites* (New York: Norton, 1986), 143–144; and *Curses! Broiled Again!: The Hottest Urban Legends Going* (New York: Norton, 1989), 178–79.

22. Mark Twain, *Huckleberry Finn* (New York: Norton, 1962), 211.

3

"The Baby Roast" as a "New American Urban Legend"

Although it is not possible from present evidence to trace a complete history of the baby roast legend, comparative and analytical study allows us to gain a better idea of its background, people's motives for telling it, and the meanings it has for storytellers and audiences. Material from the mass media and oral tradition as well as ideas from technology (how microwaves cook food) and psychology (the oven as a symbol) prove useful in understanding this piece of modern folklore.

The story in question is the widespread urban legend about the pet or baby that is put into a kitchen oven—most recently a microwave oven—and is killed by being cooked alive or exploded. It is probably a story that most readers have either heard or read about at some time. In reviewing past scholarship plus newly gathered data on this legend, we may understand better how research in verbal folklore proceeds, by what means modern oral narratives are disseminated, and what conclusions are possible about them as a result of research.

In *The Vanishing Hitchhiker* I described the legend that I am calling here "The Baby Roast" as a modernization of an earlier "pet in the oven" tradition that had possibly originated in people's realistic accounts of their pets accidentally getting into household clothes dryers or gas ovens.[1] I suggested that the older legends (going back to the 1950s) about cooked pets had simply been updated to become microwave oven stories and then had merged with other modern legends about baby-sitters to result in a new legend—"The Hippie Baby-Sitter"—known in American folklore since the early 1970s. This modern American legend, I surmised, had eventually spread to Europe and then, by some means, had even become known in Nigeria, as a tale quoted from an African student seemed to show. In the notes to the chapter I erroneously referred to a possible Brazilian analogue for the story published in 1951.[2] I concluded that "the distribution of the cooked baby story is doubtless more extensive in time and space than we can now demonstrate."[3]

Rather than repeat the material I covered in *The Vanishing Hitchhiker*, I will introduce the two main branches of this tradition with encapsulated versions. The source of the first two examples is Paul Dickson and Joseph C. Goulden's amusing anthology called *There Are Alligators in Our Sewers and Other American Credos: A Collection of Bunk, Nonsense, and Fables We Believe:*

The Poodle in the Microwave

A woman bathes her pet poodle and, in a hurry to dry it, decides to pop the animal in her new microwave oven for a few seconds. The poodle explodes.

The Baby and the Turkey

A baby-sitter waits until the parents have left and then takes LSD. Shortly thereafter she follows the instructions given to her: Put the turkey in the oven and put the baby to bed. She dutifully puts the baby in the oven and the turkey in bed.[4]

A longer version of the cooked baby legend is given in the English folklorist Paul Smith's collection *The Book of Nasty Legends:*

The Roast Dinner

An American couple, living outside New York, went out for dinner one evening leaving their baby son in the care of a teenage baby-sitter and her boyfriend. When they returned from the dinner the boyfriend was gone and the girl appeared to be acting rather strangely. They asked the girl if everything was all right to which she replied that everything was fine and that they had stuffed the turkey and put it in the oven.

The wife was rather puzzled by this remark as she did not remember having a turkey in the house and they began to realize that something was certainly wrong. Fearing the worst, they ran upstairs to check on their son but he could not be found anywhere. In desperation they started to search the house. In the kitchen the husband noticed a funny smell and that the oven was switched on. When he looked inside to see what was burning he found the baby in the roasting dish all set out like a turkey and surrounded by roast potatoes and all the trimmings. It transpired that the baby-sitter and her boyfriend has been using "Angel Dust", a powerful drug, and had roasted the baby while on a "trip".[5]

The language in this text—"to which she replied," "set out like a turkey," and "it transpired"—betray it as an authorial retelling, and a British one at that, of presumably an American oral legend. Smith cites no specific source for the story except to mention that "versions . . . have been reported in the United States since about 1970." He offers no analysis beyond that the story is "related to older folk narratives dealing with similar incidents."[6] Both of these published sources, which are popular rather than folkloric in nature, present the legends as being foolish whimsy and more like jokes than serious matters of concern—just "fables we believe." The professional comedian Robin Williams made a similar joke out of the story in 1978 in his parody of the children's television program "Mr. Rogers' Neighborhood": "Welcome to my neighborhood. Let's put Mr. Hamster in the microwave oven. O.K.? Pop goes the weasel!"[7]

A good example of how such legends are sometimes told and received as the truth in real life is the following excerpt from Marcus W. Muirhead's letter to me dated July 22, 1983—still a written version, but a much folksier one:

> I was told this story by my friend Jerry B . . . who worked as a recording secretary in the emergency room at Parkland Hospital in Dallas, Texas. As I understand it, his job involved writing down what materials were used during the hectic, hurried treatment of emergency victims, such as sponges, gauze, and tape, and to take statements from the patients as soon as they were in any condition to give them.
>
> According to Jerry, he was working the evening shift one day, in 1976 or '77, when they brought in a middle-aged woman in a state of extreme hysteria but otherwise apparently unharmed. Unable to calm her by other means, the doctor on duty put her under heavy sedation. When she started to come around several hours later, Jerry went in, and as gently as he could, asked her for a statement. This sent her into a frenzy only slightly less severe than the first. Again they sedated the woman. Another tactful attempt two or three hours later had the same effect, with less severity still. Predictably, the third attempt to elicit her story was successful.
>
> "I was washing Pepper," said the woman through her barely controlled sobbing and sharp intakes of breath, "and I was late for the dentist and I was afraid to leave him under the air conditioner wet like that so I toweled him off but he was still damp and everything so I thought . . . well I didn't want him to catch cold or anything . . . and . . . well" (She is fast losing control.) ". . . so I put him in the microwave, and I just put it on warm, but Pepper 'sploded!!" Here she breaks down completely and must be sedated again. Pepper, of course, turns out to be her pet poodle.
>
> You may imagine my chagrin when I read your versions of that same

story, and realized that I had been duped by my friend. He even went so far to say that Newsweek had carried a filler on the story. I am usually skeptical of such stories, but this one sucked me in completely, being told by someone I trusted, as a firsthand account.

Evidently, this storyteller performed "The Pet in the Oven" as a hoax story, although the emergency room is a frequent setting for telling "true" stories about either horrible or hilarious accidents involving exploding toilets, Super Glue, skiing mishaps, and the like.

Even more likely a story than "The Pet in the Oven" to be narrated in a completely serious manner and to give rise to worried discussion by listeners concerning its pros and cons is "The Baby Roast" legend, often known as "The Hippie Baby-Sitter." Here, for example, is a version with commentary collected in 1971 by William J. Kreidler, a student of the folklorist Lydia Fish at the State University College in Buffalo, New York. (Fish "took the first official scholarly notice [of this story] in the United States . . . in 1971."[8]) Kreidler's informant was training as a nurse in Boston when she heard the story:

> It seems these people hired a really freaky college girl to baby-sit. They had a little baby; it must have been less than seven months old.
> The mother called in the middle of the evening—they were at a play and it was intermission. The girl told her everything was fine, she had just stuffed the turkey and was going to put it in the oven. The lady knew she didn't have a turkey, and I guess she thought the girl sounded strange, so she told her to wait, they would come home right away.
> They called the police who went to the apartment and they found that the girl had stuffed the baby and was going to bake it. I don't know if they saved the baby, but I do know the girl was on some kind of drug.
> I'm sure this is a true story. One of the nurses told it to me when I was working in the hospital one night. She heard it from a friend of hers who worked in Bellevue where I think it happened.

Another student of Fish, Janet Hilinski, wrote out her own version with comments as she remembered it from her hometown tradition in Orchard Park, New York:

> Some parents left their baby with a neighborhood teenage girl while they attended a party. The girl had previously taken LSD and she began hallucinating. Thinking the baby was a turkey, she prepared it for roasting and put it in the oven.
> The mother called from the party to check and see how things were going

at home. The girl sounded normal and she mentioned that she had just put the turkey in the oven.

Later that evening the mother realized that they did not have a turkey at home. Her husband agreed that they should go home and find out was was going on. When they returned, they were horrified to find their baby in the oven, and the babysitter gone.

I first heard this tale over the phone from a girlfriend who said she heard it from a neighbor whose cousin (or sister) had read it in the paper. I think we both believed it at the time. This was in 1967 or '68, when the weird effects of LSD were being widely circulated; thus it did not seem too outrageous.

Later, in 1970, when I was a senior at Orchard Park High School, a girl in my home economics class brought it up again. Most of the class had already heard of it. The teacher was so interested in it, that the entire period was spent exchanging weird tales. I think most of us believed them.[9]

These folk versions more than the pop versions I have quoted underscore themes that are fairly consistent in this modern legend tradition. The reliability of the stories, for instance, is frequently buttressed by some reference to a knowledgeable FOAF or to an alleged published version. The settings in which the stories are told or with which they are associated are often more or less "official" places, such as a hospital or a school; the precise locale may directly suggest the theme of the story, such as an emergency room (with its accident victims) or a home economics classroom (with its ovens) did here. In "The Pet in the Oven," the implied reason for the mistake is the foolishness of the pet owner, while in "The Hippie Baby-Sitter" the warning is directed against either an eccentric personality type, a young person, a drug user, or, most often, all three. The baby-sitter legend often seems to imply that the parents, by going off to a party, to a restaurant, or to the theater, are neglecting their child; then the surrogate parent harms the child. The tellings of both legends often lead directly to discussions of their possible authenticity or of the lessons they contain.

Betty J. Belanus, a folklorist trained at Indiana University, pursued this latter point in a 1979 graduate research paper on microwaved-pet stories.[10] Confirming that the folk do perceive "messages" in their lore, Belanus collected discussions of the "drug" and "hippie" themes in the legend, people's speculations about the actual dangers of microwaves, and even conversations inspired by the stories concerning what kind of person would have a poodle for a pet and would shampoo and dry it regularly. (Poodles were described by some of her informants as "lap dogs" wearing "diamond choke collars" and with "painted toenails" and "yappy barks"; only a "silly society woman," it was stated, would own one and refer to it as "the dear little thing.") Belanus also reported that people recalled personal experiences (though sometimes secondhand ones or something remembered from published sources) that involved pets getting into household appliances.

Indeed, mail I have received provides good evidence that the cooked-animal theme is as much a part of personal narratives as it is of urban legends, though there is often a possibility that people think they are relating a true story when they are only repeating a tradition. A possible case in point is this story sent to me by a reader in Minnesota:

> When my mother was about six or seven years old (she was born in 1930), she was playing with a pet cat in the pasture behind her house. At the time my mother lived in Deatsville, Alabama, a small town about thirty miles north of Montgomery. While playing with the cat, the animal fell in the "branch" or stream running through the pasture. My mother retrieved the cat from the water, and took it inside the house. Once inside, my mother decided to dry the cat in the oven. As you might guess, the cat was forgotten and was "dried" to death.

My correspondent supplied her mother's address so that I could write to her for verification of the event. (I wanted to know how it was that the cat failed to utter any sound loud enough to call attention to its fate. Was it perhaps dead from drowning already?) Unfortunately, my letter was never answered.

Other personal narratives about pets getting into scrapes involving home appliances are told by people who stand close enough to the incidents to establish their truth. This one came from a reader in Portage des Sioux, Missouri: "A friend of mine was doing her laundry. Like most housewives, she put a load in the washer and went upstairs to make the beds. Down again to put in another load and upstairs to do the dishes. Somewhere along the line her daughter's cat got in the dryer to sleep because it was warm. Imagine her surprise when she opened the dryer. All the clothes had to be pitched, but the hardest part was telling her daughter what happened to her cat when she came home from school."

My acceptance of this story is based on the fact that the source this time is a friend, not merely a FOAF, and also that at the very time I was writing this essay one of our family cats did truly climb into the warm clothes dryer between loads. Our cat did not get shut in the dryer, however, and so our family did not make a personal narrative out of the incident. The point for folk legend research about such experiences is that they may easily become traditionalized as they are repeated from person to person and from generation to generation, and such a process possibly underlies the whole cooked-pet cycle of stories.[11]

Another direction that the folk tradition may go is toward developing "one liners" that treat the basic story motif as a joke. For instance, a letter to the editor of *Newsweek* began: "I was amazed by your article 'Is SAT a Dirty Word?' . . . Intelligence is more important than memory. I've known people who knew every general involved in World War II but didn't have enough common sense not to dry their dog in the microwave."[12] Or, even more succinctly, a successful writer of romance novels who is the mother of five boys was quoted as saying, "My seven-year-old's antics, such as drying the cat in the microwave, can be distracting!"[13]

Joking aside, microwave radiation is nothing to fool with, and certainly some uneasiness about the potential dangers of microwaves to living creatures underlies the popularity of these legends in the United States. What we commonly term "microwaves" are concentrated into a single frequency in a microwave oven and cause foods to heat by exciting the molecules of water present in them. A similar heating effect is induced under certain conditions by the microwaves used for radio and television transmissions or in radar. Microwaves—whether in small appliances or large installations—have been connected to such diverse health problems as simple burns, cataracts, sterility and other sex-related problems, cancer, and potential genetic disorders. The whole subject was carefully and chillingly studied by Paul Brodeur in a series of articles in the *New Yorker* that grew into *The Zapping of America: Microwaves, Their Deadly Risk, and the Coverup*. Brodeur had concerns of much greater magnitude than exploding poodles to deal with, though he did hint at a body of "folklore, based on a mixture of intuition, observation, and apprehension" that he found had developed during World War II, taking such forms then as what he termed "black humor, scuttlebutt, and quasi-medical practice."[14]

Another writer on microwave ovens also alluded to "numerous adverse effects from exposure to radiation from microwave ovens" but discounted the reports (specifying them only as the "tingling of skin," burns, and interference with pacemakers) because they were unverified. The closest that this source came to a microwaved-pet reference was the mention of "silkworm-cocoon cooking" as a possible commercial use for microwave ovens, but nothing is said about the possibility of the creatures exploding when zapped.[15] However, as cooks are often warned, potatoes, whole eggs, and other completely encased foods will explode when they are microwaved unless holes are punched through their outer membranes to allow steam to escape during cooking.

Although many references in oral tradition to supposed published accounts of cooked- and microwaved-pet stories cannot be verified, this does not mean that none has *ever* appeared in newsprint. In some cases, however, inattentive readers may recall reports of folklore studies (such as this one) as genuine news items. For instance, the *Des Moines Tribune* for April 26, 1978, in a story about Thelma C. Johnson of Sioux City, Iowa, and her personal collection of urban legends, printed this: "Told to Johnson four or five times in the span of one week [was the story] about a cat that had been drenched in a rain storm. The children who owned the animal tried to dry it out—by placing it in a microwave oven. The cat is said to have exploded all over the kitchen."[16] A similar piece of hearsay that got into print in 1983 was a San Francisco law student's description to an inquiring reporter of "the cat in the microwave case" in which, he understood, "the person sued the microwave company for a defective latch on the door and won."[17]

An actual lawsuit involving a microwaved cat in Warwick, Rhode Island, was reported by United Press International in September 1980. I have clippings from the *Muncie (Ind.) Star* and the *Chicago Tribune* that name the convicted man as well as the judge and the defense lawyer and state the amount of the fine ($200).[18] Although this incident is undoubtedly authentic (and was widely reported in the press that week), part of the UPI wording for the story also echoes the style of legend telling: "The singed cat," it reads, "had its claws imbedded in the oven's grill when they opened the door." The unsuccessful appeal of this case was reported in some detail in Murray Loring's "Cats in Court" column, which described how "from the smallest state in these United States" came "one of the most flagrant and outrageous cruelty cases, involving a feline."[19] The appeal was denied and dismissed by the Supreme Court of Rhode Island (*State v. Tweedie*, April 27, 1982) and the judgment was confirmed. In his discussion, however, Loring omits the description from the published appeal record of exactly how the cat died, a passage that is interesting in terms of the folklore involved, though it might have been too gruesome for the pages of *Cats Magazine*. Two things are evident here: first, the cat did not explode; second, the official account of its death differs from what the newspapers said. In crisp, unemotional legal style, it reads: "The record reflects that a scratching noise was heard coming from the oven. As the door was opened the rear legs of the cat fell out. The cat was alive but died shortly after."[20] (A clinical report of a small dog burned in a microwave oven—with no apparent connection to the legends—appeared in a veterinarians' journal.[21])

Probably there are many other suffering-pet news stories that have not come to my attention, though I happen to have two more from the spring of 1983. On April 14 the *Ogden (Utah) Standard-Examiner* carried an Associated Press story about a Montana State University fraternity member putting a kitten that was frozen inside a block of ice into a punch bowl; on June 3 the *Skagit Valley (Ore.) Herald* carried an AP story about a teenager in Lillooet, British Columbia, sentenced to six months in jail and two years' attendance at Alcoholics Anonymous meetings for killing a cat in a microwave oven. Modern life, we can see, may sometimes be as horrifying as legend.

Returning to the baby roast legends, we find that they consistently include three themes that are never part of the pet tragedies: parental neglect, treating the child as food, and drug-induced behavior. Even a short text written out by a fourteen-year-old Midwestern girl has these three typical elements (and little else): "A girl went to some people's house to babysit their baby. The mother asked her to put a roast in the oven around an hour before they came home. The parents came to find the baby buttered and prepared like you'd do a roast and in the oven cooked. The babysitter was tripping on LSD."[22]

The two further American variations on the cooked-baby stories that I have collected are about the mother who returns home because of a strong sense of danger—arriving just in time to save her baby—and about a "group of hippies," high on drugs, who roast a baby in a grotesque ceremony. Versions in which the baby is *microwaved* rather than roasted are not numerous, though they are known since the mid-1970s. One reference to this tradition appeared in "The Straight Dope" column of the Chicago weekly paper *Reader* (February 3, 1984). The columnist Cecil Adams responded to a reader's query about microwaved-baby legends by summing up my discussion of them in *The Vanishing Hitchhiker* and admitting that he could find no evidence that such an actual event had ever occurred.[23]

Most unfortunately, something resembling the microwaved-baby legend *did* occur in Michigan in 1982.[24] On December 18 the *Detroit Free Press* carried a small item datelined Hastings, Michigan, stating that "a baby who police say might have been burned in a microwave oven was placed under court protection." The victim was identified as a ten-week-old girl who had been in a Grand Rapids hospital since October 31 and had suffered burns that required amputation of part of her right foot and several fingers from her left hand. The *Lansing State Journal*, on January 21, 1983, carried a longer story (headlined "Baby Burned, Mom Charged") concerning the incident. Doctors had concluded that the child's burns were caused by radiation, but the mother claimed that she had only heated a bottle of formula in her microwave oven while the child was lying nearby on an ironing board. Various experts testified that the oven was not faulty, and while the court was considering the case further the baby was put into a foster home. On July 21, 1983, the *Lansing State Journal* reported ("'Microwave' Baby Returns to Mother") that the baby had been returned home from foster care as a ward of the court. Later the mother was sentenced to five years' probation and ordered to perform one hundred hours of community service. No news story that I have seen has clarified how just *part* of a body could be burned by microwaves even if the oven-door safety lock was operating properly.

There have been other news stories about cruelty to children, sometimes involving burns and ovens, and the Michigan case is cited only as a representative example. What should be noted here are the ways that the reported case is different from the baby roast urban legend. There is no baby-sitter, the child is neither prepared as food nor killed, no drugs or other mind-influencing substances are mentioned, and—most striking of all—the specific names, places, and dates (some of which I have omitted) are included. The news story, then, is not an urban legend, although it may remind readers of a legend; and possibly the events described may even have been influenced by an urban legend. Some readers of such stories in the mass media may later believe that they once read about a case "just like" the baby roast story that someone tells them. A quotation like a policeman's comment in one of these Michigan news items that the baby's toes had been cooked "through and through" comes rather close to the style of a modern horror legend, and it is just the kind of dramatic detail that a reader might well remember.

Following the appearance of *The Vanishing Hitchhiker* in an English paperback edition in spring 1983,[25] I soon began to hear from readers throughout Great Britain and in Australia and New Zealand about urban legends they had heard. It became clear then that the cooked-pet story was well known in these countries in forms very similar to the American versions. I received letters about cats trapped in "spin dryers," old women's poodles being washed and then microwaved, and in several instances I encountered the notion, not well known in the United States, that the pet's owner had successfully sued the microwave oven manufacturer for selling a hazardous product. But although an English book on urban legends had mentioned "current microwave oven myths" as a general topic as long ago as 1978,[26] the only cooked-baby story sent to me from an English-speaking country was an Australian report of a supposed news item about it being an American incident. The following is from a letter from Dianne Smerdon dated July 17, 1983:

> This was a newspaper report anything up to six years ago. As I recall, it was in "The News" and datelined somewhere in the U.S.A. . . .
>
> Hospital staff are watching a ?-month-old baby in their care. His fourteen-year-old babysitter put him into the microwave oven and turned it on "to see what would happen." The doctors are unsure of what damage has been done, as a microwave cooks from the inside out.

That the American "Hippie Baby-Sitter" legend had quite early migrated to Europe, however, is shown by a letter from Carl Freeman of Switzerland dated December 27, 1983: "I first heard a version of 'The Hippie Babysitter' in Geneva about ten years ago. Not having heard of 'urban legends' I took it at face value. In the local tale the baby-sitters were Geneva University students who had freaked-out on dope. When the mother phoned home to check, she was told that the baby had been 'smeared with mustard' and was all ready for the oven. Luckily the parents got back in time to save the child." We recognize here the familiar pattern known in the United States since the early 1970s: mother absent, child cooked as food, and baby-sitter taking drugs.

The Nigerian version that I collected from a student in 1979 (as she remembered it from 1976) seemed at the time nothing more than a transplanted American legend. As the text appears in *The Vanishing Hitchhiker* (to summarize), the mother telephoned home from work to check on her baby-sitter, who appeared to be doing her job well. But when the mother returned home in the evening, she found that the sitter had roasted the baby. Also reminding us of urban legend tradition in the United States is the association of this story with particular sections of the city (Calabar, Nigeria) and with particular friends of friends who presumably knew the facts of the case. What is *different* in the story, however, is that the baby-sitter's misbehavior is caused not by drugs or malice but by simple misunderstanding of the mother's orders. The baby's mother had used an expression (given in the Efik language) for "sit him up" (that is, "get him out of bed"), which the sitter, a novice at her job, interpreted as a homophonous expression meaning "cook the baby." Her error, then, lay in conscientiously following the mother's instructions exactly as understood. The warnings given in this story, then, are against careless word choice and thoughtless interpretation of orders rather than against eccentric or drug-induced behavior.

The version of the legend from Buenos Aires mentioned in *The Vanish-*

ing Hitchhiker has features reminiscent of the American stories, but surprisingly it was circulated in 1949, some twenty years before the legend had been collected by folklorists in the United States. Paulo de Carvalho-Neto reports it in this fashion, in his book *Folklore and Psychoanalysis,* referring to it as if it were an actual event or, as he puts it, a "pathological case which occurred under the influence of the Evil Mother":

> A young married couple hires a servant since the wife is pregnant and almost due. The baby is born. A few weeks later the husband and wife go to the movies one evening, leaving the baby in the servant's care. Until that time she has always been reliable. *According to one version,* on their return she receives them ceremoniously dressed in the wife's bridal gown and tells them she has prepared quite a surprise for them. She bids them come into the dining room to serve them a special meal. They enter and find a horrifying spectacle. In the middle of the table, placed there with great care, they see their son on a large platter, roasted and garnished with potatoes. The poor mother goes insane at once. She loses her speech and no one has heard her utter a single word since then. The father, *according to several versions,* is a military man. He pulls out a revolver and shoots the servant. Then he runs away and is never heard from again.[27]

In her 1951 book *Maternidad y sexo* Marie Langer had originally published this story. Langer described this particular baby roast story in her psychiatric study *not* as an actual clinical case but rather as a "modern myth" or rumor that, as she wrote, had been rampant in Buenos Aires during June 1949, especially among servants, taxi drivers, and barbers. In the space of a single week in Buenos Aires she collected nine versions of the story that differed only in details. The one that she quoted (and that Carvalho-Neto repeated) was merely "the most complete version of this strange story that was making the rounds."[28] Langer also commented that the story "was accepted as truth by people generally capable of critical judgment."[29] In other words, it was in every respect typical of an urban legend.

"The Evil Mother" mentioned by Carvalho-Neto is a Freudian concept explained by him as "the son's image of the mother resulting from the castration complex."[30] Langer introduced the baby roast story as she had heard it in 1949 into a chapter on the unconscious image of the evil mother (*madre mala*)—the opposite of the ideal of a wholly *good* mother that is cherished by both children and adults. In Langer's opinion, a "suppressed unconscious situation" based on "infantile anxieties" concerning the actual "goodness" of mothers could generate stories depicting grossly evil mothers; these stories, then, might circulate in oral tradition and even lead to neuroses. She compared instances of evil parents (both mothers and fathers) in myths and fairy tales (including "Hansel and Gretel") to the similar theme in the modern "rumor" without mentioning that the recent story really depicts a *neglectful* rather than an evil parent. The servant, however, in wearing the mother's bridal gown assumes the role of the real mother, and both women in the story lose their minds.

Interpreting the baby roast legend in psychological terms is tempting, especially with regard to the core idea of putting a child into an oven. As a doctor in the Columbia University College of Physicians and Surgeons wrote in a letter to *Psychology Today* in 1980, "One discovers the same theme in fairy tales. For example, the wicked witch attempted to cook Hansel and Gretel in the oven."[31] According to orthodox Freudianism, the stove or oven, as well as many other images of rooms and containers encountered in dreams or folklore, all symbolically represent female genitalia; this means that, as one analyst put it, "the womb is the 'stove' inside which the child is 'baked.'"[32] This symbolic meaning recurs in other examples of folklore, such as the familiar "Pattycake" rhyme or the euphemistic phrases "to put a bun in her oven" and "to have one in the oven" (i.e., to be pregnant).[33] The Jungian psychologist Erich Neuman cited further oven-as-womb proverbial sayings as part of his argument for "the thoroughgoing identification of the oven with the Feminine."[34]

Before accepting an absolute oven/womb equivalency in the folk stories, however, it is well to remember that the two abandoned children in the fairy tale did not finally perish in the oven (only the witch did). We would also have to explain how or why the act of roasting or microwaving a baby might reasonably be equated with returning it to the womb. Possible symbolism aside for the moment, the tale of Hansel and Gretel has a completely different plot and certainly cannot be taken as the historical prototype for our modern legend.

Although at least the *threat* of cooking Hansel in the oven is a standard part of the international tradition of "Hansel and Gretel,"[35] commentators on the story have generally refrained from calling this detail a sexual symbol. Max Lüthi, for example, in *Once upon a Time: On the Nature of Fairy Tales,* sees the witch only as "a personification of evil . . . [who] perishes by her own devices." This illustrates, Lüthi says, how "evil consumes itself."[36] Jack Zipes in *Breaking the Magic Spell: Radical Theories of Folk and Fairy Tales* is more specific. He interprets the witch as a symbol of "the entire feudal system or the greed and brutality of the aristocracy"; her destruction by the clever children, he says, illustrates how the European peasants might have learned "to act to improve their lot."[37] Even the psychiatrist Bruno Bettelheim, in his well-known work *The Uses of Enchantment: The Meaning and Importance of Fairy Tales*, emphasizes the "starvation anxiety" and "oral regression" (poor family, abandoned children, eating the witch's house, threat of the oven, and so forth) rather than a sexual theme.[38] Despite Zipes's contention that Bettelheim usually follows Freudianism as a "strait-jacket theory" Bettelheim here eschews a strictly Freudian symbolic reading.[39] In fact, he nearly ignores the oven. Although an oven does undeniably symbolize a womb in other folkloric manifestations, I am no readier than Bettelheim was to say that it positively does so either in "Hansel and Gretel" or "The Baby Roast." Certainly, however, some symbolic meanings and neurotic behavior are involved in the baby roast legend.

The theme of mental illness, as suffered by the servant and the mother in the Argentinian version of the story, is mentioned specifically in a report of a Middle Eastern version sent to me by Dr. Seyfi Karabais of Ankara, Turkey. He wrote on September 15, 1980 (quoting a friend of his): "These babysitters may do terrible things. For example, one of them, a woman discharged prematurely from the mental hospital, almost roasted the poor baby in the oven. She thought it was a turkey." When I asked Dr. Karabais to inquire further into the story, he replied (November 4, 1980), "If and when I can catch my friend I will try to find the owner of the oven in which a baby almost got roasted. I discussed it with her on the phone and she is positive that this negative event took place." There is also an allusion to a Swedish instance of a mentally ill woman roasting her baby. According to this source, in about the early 1950s a story was current in Sweden "about a young mother who, psychotic after childbirth, serves the baby roasted to her husband."[40]

Yet another similar legend has circulated far away from the other known texts. This version of "The Baby Roast" was collected in the South Pacific area of Micronesia on the island of Yap by the folklorist Roger E. Mitchell in 1971 and published two years later. The story, told by a forty-five-year-old man in Yapese through a translator, begins with the observation that the older children in Micronesia are often left to care for their younger siblings while their mothers work in the gardens. But the story soon begins to sound very much like the Nigerian version, when the mother instructs her daughter, "While I'm in the garden, you be sure to make your brother hot." After some deliberation, the girl concludes that in order to comply with her mother's orders she must indeed cook her little brother, so she puts the child into a pot with some food and builds up the fire. When the mother returns, the daughter tells her mother, "I did what you told me. You told me to heat my brother and so I cooked him because that's how we can get hot." The mother beats her daughter, breaking her arms and legs, and throws her into a stream. The daughter drifts along in the stream singing a mad song about her deeds (somewhat like Ophelia in Hamlet) until she drowns. Mitchell's note mentions that "this little tale is considered a true happening on Yap, and some informants dislike to tell it, since it is offensive to the girl's living relatives."[41]

Other versions of this Micronesian tale, however, establish it as being a traditional plot—one resembling the African and Argentinian stories—rather than an account of a bizarre local happening. (Even so, Mitchell's field notes mention another Yap informant's version of the same story with the notation, "The family is still alive, the story well known, and it would be embarrassing if it was published in a book.")

Two unpublished Micronesian versions in Mitchell's collection are filed in the Indiana University Folklore Archive; both were recorded in 1970, and both resemble the Yap versions in having the person who cooks the baby being severely punished and cast out to wander away and die. The first of these, from Satawan Atoll in the Truk District, is the more detailed. Here an older son, named Lipok, is told by his parents to cook an octopus and tend to the baby while they go out to gather taros to complete the meal. The tale continues: "He didn't know whether they were referring to the baby or the octopus because he didn't find the octopus. He thought that maybe they were referring to the baby. . . . So he killed the baby and he went out and gathered some breadfruit leaves, very big ones, came back and wrapped the baby in them. Then he put it on the fire. When it was cooked, he took it down and put it where they stored their food." After telling this story the informant commented that the expression "to have the ear of Lipok" had become proverbial among his people for getting something wrong or mixed up. The second archived text in Mitchell's collection is from Ulithi Atoll in the Yap District. Here an older son cooks his brother simply because "he was tired of doing the same thing, so he put his brother in their pot and cooked him."

Confirming that the Micronesian "Baby Roast" legends of 1970–71 are not just recent importations from abroad revised into local traditions, Mitchell cites several analogues published in the older anthropological literature. The two closest versions were those published by Wilhelm Müller from Yap in 1918 and a Papuan (New Guinea) version published by Annie Ker in 1910.[42] Here are summaries, slightly edited, as provided by Mitchell:

Müller: Fathali was a lame girl to whom mother said she should remain with her younger sister. Fathali said, "Then I will cook her." "Certainly not," said mother. Fathali repeated she'd cook her. "Therefore good then," answered the mother, annoyed. She inspected the child and went to the field to work. When she came home, she asked where the child was. "I have cooked her," answered Fathali; and when mother took cover from pot, child lay within. [Her mother strikes her, breaking her leg; Fathali tells the neighbors what has happened, jumps into the sea, and is covered with black mud which hardens into a stone that is still seen today.]

Ker: The parents went to the gardens and left two daughters to bathe their brother and cook some food so he could eat. Older daughter: "Mother said to stay and cook brother. Let us obey her." Younger disagreed, but older prevailed. They cooked the brother. Parents returned, and drove them out.

These five versions of the baby roast legend available from the South Pacific range in time from 1910 to 1971 and fall into two main subtypes. The first type has the distinctive features of the parents' orders being misunderstood; such is true of the Papuan version of 1910, the Trukese variation of 1970, and the Yap text of 1971. The second subtype contains the alternate theme of the baby-sitter cooking the infant in anger; this occurs in the Yap text of 1918 and the Ulithian version of 1970. It is clear as well that the Nigerian version of 1976 matches the first subtype while the Argentinian one of 1949 seems to stand apart (along with the Swedish and Turkish versions) in that the child cooking there is the result of the servant's mental illness.

In pursuing what is evidently an international story cycle about cooked babies, Stith Thompson's *Motif-Index of Folk-Literature* provides a little help, but only a little. Mitchell classified his texts under the general heading of Motif S10, *Cruel parents,* but this is too general to be useful, especially when we consider that the story is mainly not about a cruel parent but about the foolish (or insane) behavior of a surrogate parent. Motif K1461, *Caring for the child: child killed,* has some relevance, but the only two instances that Thompson cites for it are far from our legends. (The first, Rune No. 31 of the Finnish epic *The Kalevala,* concerns a man who becomes crazed from being rocked too much as a baby and who later tortures and kills [but not by cooking] a baby that is left in his charge. The second, a story collected in the 1930s from Indians of the Chaco region of Argentina, concerns a trickster in the shape of a fox that deceives a mother into leaving and then kills her baby left in its care by sucking out its insides.)[43]

Another promising motif reference is S112.6, *Murder by roasting alive in oven or furnace,* for which Thompson supplies two examples: a motif-index of Jewish legends that lists various fiery furnace scenes (no babies, no sitters) and a Tongan tale in which a man's concubines (but no babies) are pushed into an oven and burned to death.[44] Still another unrelated, though faintly similar, item to our modern legend is the Greek myth about how the goddess Demeter nursed the human baby Demophoön for its parents, trying to grant it immortality by anointing it with ambrosia and putting it into a fire; but its mother, failing to understand, intervened. While this story does have a baby and a caregiver, there is no oven and no murder.[45]

As for the particular cause of the baby roasting—that is, the psychology involved—Motif J2460, *Literal obedience,* contains the key idea and proves to be a widely known concept. The submotif J2460.1, *Disastrous following of misunderstood instructions,* in fact, is precisely what occurs in several versions discussed above. Thompson's sole example of the theme is a Chinese tale in which a person is told to burn the land (in order to clear it for planting) and then to sow the seed; but he does just the opposite: he sows the seed first, then burns the land.[46] While there is no baby, no oven, and no cooking in this story, it does contain the idea of reversed instructions found in such baby roast legends as the Papuan (bathe the baby and cook the food), the Trukese (cook the octopus and tend the baby), and some American ones (put the turkey in the oven and the baby in bed). In the Chinese story the *order* of instructions is reversed, while in the baby roast stories the *actions* to be performed on the two creatures or objects are reversed.

What the *Motif-Index* provides in this instance is clear exposure of the common international concern with basic themes of our legend—cruelty, deception, choosing carefully those who will tend babies, mental illness, and tragically foolish misunderstanding of orders. Viewed as a complete tale rather than a mere collection of motifs, versions of the baby roast plot are strikingly similar over a wide extent of time and space, although not nearly so universal as the Jungian theory of "archetypal" origins drawing from common patterns in a "collective unconscious" would predict. In fact, the situation for this tale is somewhat like that for the worldwide stories about witches and ogres who threaten children. As Thompson wrote in connection with "Hansel and Gretel," the versions are such that "one is frequently puzzled to know whether we are dealing with a borrowing or with an independent invention."[47]

The argument for the borrowing of the baby roast legend from one culture to another—especially for many modern versions—lies in the repetition of specific details within similarly patterned texts. Time and again the parents have gone to a party, a play, or a film. They leave some ambiguous instructions for the baby-sitter and later telephone home to check on her. The child is served to them as food (often a turkey) and is appropriately garnished (frequently stuffed or with potatoes on the side) by someone who is either literally insane or temporarily "crazed" (i.e., by youthful naïveté, language problems, jealousy, or drugs). The Jungian writer Marie-Louise von Franz, however, offers a possible psychological model, similar to Marie Langer's, for the independent formation of such stories: "When something strange happens it gets gossiped about and handed on, just as rumours are handed on, then under favourable conditions the account gets enriched with already-existing archetypal representations and slowly becomes a story."[48] But whether such stories were independently invented or just widely borrowed from a common original, the modern person's trust in the urban legends about cooked pets and babies seems to hinge on faith that such "strange" things can and have happened, this belief being "enriched" by the lurking fears the supposed happenings symbolically project.

The historical origin and the dissemination routes of the baby roast legend remain something of a puzzle, but the adaptations of the plot to fit different cultures are clear. These range from references to the child-care and food-gathering customs of Micronesia to problems of modern working mothers in Nigeria to anxieties about drugs, "hippies," and microwave ovens in Europe and America. Underlying all versions of the legend are both a concern about the parents' appropriate role in child rearing and a sense of guilt for leaving the job to others.[49] While the folks are away the infant's caregiver foolishly, childishly, insanely, or jealously destroys his or her charge. Shoving the baby into the oven may well be taken as an equivalent for returning it to the womb or "putting it back where it belongs," just as serving it up as food for the parents is a way of trying to return it to its place of origin.

As Alan Dundes has suggested, the psychological device of projection allows people (via their folklore, in this instance) "to attribute to another person or to the environment what is actually within themselves."[50] Thus, the sins of the baby-sitters in the baby roast legends may represent suppressed fears or desires in the minds of the parents and storytellers. Surely, these urban legends convey some of the same guilt feelings that Dundes identified in the dead baby joke cycle—in particular, as he put it, "a protest against babies in general."[51] But while Dundes postulated such trends as legalized abortion efforts and easier access to reliable methods of contraception in our time as underlying reasons for guilt, the baby roast legends focus on changing child-care practices of modern parents. The descriptions in this cycle of popular American legends of drug-crazed hippies (who were earlier failures of child-rearing) thrusting babies left in their charge into gas or microwave ovens may really symbolize unconscious anxieties, shared widely with people in other cultures, about the manner in which parents tend to their children. More specifically, these legends are about the manner in which American parents believe that they fail to tend to them personally nowadays, in contrast to the practices of the past. Earlier in the legend cycle such disastrous neglect or ignorance resulted merely in deaths of substitute children—pet cats or dogs—but eventually the legends explicitly described the deaths of children themselves.

Epilogue: Further Versions of "The Baby Roast"

After most of the above study was written, I received a letter containing yet another version of the story, which allowed me to review my interpretation in the light of new data. The letter, dated May 15, 1985, contained the following version of "The Baby Roast" from Beatrice Faust of North Carlton, Australia. She referred to her experience with various horror stories about abortions performed late in pregnancy and to the supposed results—both physical and psychological. One such story, Faust recalled, involved cooking a baby, and it was similar to other baby roast legends in being an unverified account that assumes the mother's insanity and describes the baby being prepared as food. Faust had believed the story to be true at the time she heard it; but, becoming aware of the urban legends about cooked babies, she wondered now if this might have been a traditional legend or perhaps a fabrication. What the story seems to be, in fact, is yet another example of a specific local adaptation of "The Baby Roast" made consistent with attitudes and social problems of the time and place in which it was told:

> I do not have the leisure to write down all the abortion legends that I have heard but I shall offer you a variant of the roasted baby story that I heard from a female social worker attached to one of Melbourne's two major maternity hospitals:
> "The woman had a history of mental illness when she became pregnant for the fourth or fifth time. Her social worker referred her to a consultant gynecologist with a view to having her aborted. At the time, abortion was legal under precedent law in Victoria, but illegal under statute law. The gynecologist did what many doctors do still: he procrastinated. The Christmas vacation intervened and after that the pregnancy was too advanced to be terminated by then practiced techniques. In due course, the baby was

born and the unwilling and unbalanced mother took it home where she roasted it for the family's midday Sunday meal."

The story was told to me in about 1964 by a social worker who claimed that it happened to a patient at her hospital but not directly under her care. She attributed the experience to "someone else in this department," i.e., an immediate colleague. I never heard any corroboration. The implication was that the woman had been quietly institutionalized because it was too dreadful a case to be brought to court and because the (masculine) medical mafia did not want to see one of their members embarrassed by bad publicity.

In March 1987 Stephen Jacquot of Charlottesville, Virginia, called my attention to a version of "The Baby Roast," or more correctly, "The Baby Chill," published in William F. Buckley's column in the *National Review*.[52] Buckley dubbed the story "untranslatable, imperishable" and quoted it verbatim "from a French paper." This time a Spanish maid, Carmen, is working for a French family. Her employers instruct her to put the cake (in French, *gateau*) into the refrigerator. Carmen misunderstands this as a reference to the cat (in Spanish, *gato*). So she puts the cat—a magnificent angora named Fonfon—into the fridge. On June 6, 1989, Frank Naylor of England wrote to tell me a more standard cooked cat version of the story as he had heard it in France. The instructions given were "*Mettez le gateau dans le four a onze heurs*" (Put the cake into the oven at eleven o'clock). The Spanish maid, of course, cooks *el gato*, the cat. Yet another variation on the theme is a version of the story in which an English couple uses French to communicate with their new Spanish maid.[53] Proving that forms of the traditional story continue to circulate is the following "news" item published with only a vague indication of source in the English paper *The Independent* on July 30, 1991:

Maid service

A maid accidentally killed a one-year-old baby in China after trying to bathe him in a washing machine, reports the *People's Public Security News*. The tragedy occurred in the far-west region of Xinjiang at the home of Aierguma and his wife Paheerguli, both school teachers. While at home in their lunch break the couple decided to teach their 16–year-old maid how to do the laundry in the washing machine. "After finishing the washing," the father said before they left for work "don't forget to bathe the baby." The maid finished washing the clothes, put the child in the machine and switched on the power. The baby drowned. The report said "the couple regretted hiring an uncultured nanny."

If nothing else, these examples illustrate how important it is always to accept new versions of old stories into our studies. Apparently the last word on "The Baby Roast" has not yet been written.

Notes

An earlier version of this essay was published in the third edition of my textbook, *The Study of American Folklore* (New York: W. W. Norton, 1986), 476–501.

1. Jan Harold Brunvand, *The Vanishing Hitchhiker* (New York: W. W. Norton, 1981), 62–69.
2. I should have have identified the source as Argentinian, not Brazilian. See below.
3. Brunvand, *The Vanishing Hitchhiker,* 73.
4. Paul Dickson and Joseph C. Goulden, *There Are Alligators in Our Sewers and Other American Credos: A Collection of Bunk, Nonsense, and Fables We Believe* (New York: Delacorte Press, 1983), 137, 145.
5. Paul Smith, *The Book of Nasty Legends* (London: Routledge and Kegan Paul, 1983), 104. Smith also gives stories about a chef's microwaved innards and an old woman's microwaved Persian cat. See 64–65 and n. 48.
6. Smith, *The Book of Nasty Legends,* 104.
7. "The Robin Williams Show," *Time,* Oct. 2, 1978, 86.
8. Brunvand, *Vanishing Hitchhiker,* 65.
9. Fish sent me the papers by William J. Kreidler and Janet Hilinski in 1979 with permission to quote from them.
10. Belanus's paper is discussed in *The Vanishing Hitchhiker,* 64–65, 72; it was published as "The Poodle in the Microwave Oven: Free Association and a Modern Legend" in *Kentucky Folklore Record* 27 (1981): 66–75.
11. Another example of a "folklorized" personal experience story is given in Jan Harold Brunvand, *The Choking Doberman and Other "New" Urban Legends* (New York: W. W. Norton, 1984), 71–73.
12. *Newsweek,* Aug. 9, 1982, quoted in Brunvand, *The Choking Doberman,* 216.
13. Parris Afton Bonds quoted in Kathryn Falk, *Love's Leading Ladies* (New York: Pinnacle Books, 1982), 23.
14. Paul Brodeur, *The Zapping of America: Microwaves, Their Deadly Risk, and the Coverup* (New York: W. W. Norton, 1977), 14.
15. Helen J. Van Zante, *The Microwave Oven* (Boston: Houghton Mifflin, 1973), 153.
16. A copy of this news story, plus many other interesting reports of urban legends in her area, was sent to me by Johnson.
17. Conti, "Question Man," *San Francisco Chronicle,* Jan. 30, 1983, quoted in Brunvand, *The Choking Doberman,* 215.
18. Thom Tammaro of Ball State University sent me the Muncie clipping of September 28, 1980, and Elaine Viets of the *St. Louis Post-Dispatch* sent me the September 26, 1980, *Chicago Tribune* clipping.

19. Murray Loring, "Cats in Court," *Cats Magazine,* Nov. 1982, 19.

20. *State v. Tweedie,* R.I., 444 A.2d 855; the quoted passage is on 857.

21. Lloyd M. Reedy, D.V.M., and Fred J. Clubb Jr. D.V.M., Ph.D., "Microwave Burn in a Toy Poodle: A Case Report," *Journal of the American Animal Hospital Association* 27 (Sept.–Oct. 1991): 497–500.

22. Carolyn Eastwood, "Folklore among Adolescents," *Indiana English Journal* 11, no. 2 (Winter 1976–77): 43. Other sources of published oral texts are given in Brunvand, *The Vanishing Hitchhiker,* 72–73.

23. This clipping was sent to me by Catherine Collins of the *Chicago Tribune.*

24. I am grateful to John R. Halsey, state archaeologist in the Michigan History Division in Lansing, and to Todd Marsh of Center Line, Michigan, for sending me clippings about this case.

25. Jan Harold Brunvand, *The Vanishing Hitchhiker* (London: Picador, 1983).

26. Rodney Dale, *The Tumour in the Whale: A Collection of Modern Myths* (London: Duckworth, 1978), 72–73.

27. Paulo de Carvalho-Neto, *Folklore and Psychoanalysis,* trans. Jacques M. P. Wilson (Coral Gables, Fla.: University of Miami Press, 1972), 43–44, emphasis added. This is a translation of the second (1968) edition of his book published in Spanish.

28. Marie Langer, *Maternidad y sexo: Estudio psicoanalitico y psicosomatico* (Buenos Aires: Editorial Nova, 1951), 98 (my translation). No English edition has appeared. Chapter 4 of this book also appeared as "Le 'Mythe de l'enfant rôti,'" trans. Madelaine Baranger, *Revue Française de Psychoanalyse* 16 (1952): 509–17.

29. Langer, *Maternidad y sexo,* 98–99 (my translation).

30. Carvalho-Neto, *Folklore and Psychoanalysis,* 43n.

31. *Psychology Today,* Sept. 1980, 6.

32. Gerhard Adler, *The Living Symbol: A Case Study in the Process of Individuation* (New York: Pantheon, 1961), 157. See also Sigmund Freud, *A General Introduction to Psycho-Analysis* (New York: Liveright, 1935), 139.

33. See Beryl Rowland, "The Oven in Popular Metaphor," *American Speech* 45 (1970): 215–22.

34. Erich Neuman, *The Great Mother, an Analysis of the Archetype* (New York: Pantheon, 1955), 286.

35. "Hansel and Gretel" is folktale Type 327A, discussed by Stith Thompson in *The Folktale* (New York: Dryden, 1946), 36–37.

36. Max Lüthi, *Once upon a Time: On the Nature of Fairy Tales* (Bloomington: Indiana University Press, 1976), 64.

37. Jack Zipes, *Breaking the Magic Spell: Radical Theories of Folk and Fairy Tales* (Austin: University of Texas Press, 1979), 32.

38. Bruno Bettelheim, *The Uses of Enchantment: The Meaning and Importance of Fairy Tales* (New York: Knopf, 1976), 159–66.

39. Zipes, *Breaking the Magic Spell,* 162.

40. Mentioned by Bengt af Klintberg in a review of *The Vanishing Hitchhiker* published in *Arv: Scandinavian Yearbook of Folklore* 37 (1981): 188–89.

41. Roger E. Mitchell, "Micronesian Folktales," *Asian Folklore Studies* 32 (1973), Tale 54, 156–58, n. 257. I am grateful to Mitchell not only for providing me with a copy of this publication but also for sending me summaries of other texts

discussed in relation to his published one.

42. The two original sources, unavailable to me, are Wilhelm Müller, Yap, vol. 2, *Ergebnisse der Südsee-Expedition 1908–1910* (Hamburg: Friederichsen, 1918), and Annie Ker, *Papuan Fairy Tales* (London: Macmillan, 1910).

43. There are, of course, plenty of world folk narratives concerning cruel parents, as Elizabeth Tucker, for one, shows in her article "The Cruel Mother in Stories Told by Pre-Adolescent Girls," *International Folklore Review* (1981): 66–70; few if any of these bear any relationship to the baby roast legend. For the ancient Finnish example, see Francis Peabody Magoun Jr., trans., *The Kalevala* (Cambridge, Mass.: Harvard University Press, 1963), Rune no. 31, esp. 225–26. For the Argentinian example, see Alfred Métraux, *Myths of the Toba and Pilaga Indians of the Gran Chaco,* Memoir Series vol. 40 (Philadelphia: American Folklore Society, 1946), 133.

44. Dov Noy, "Motif-Index of Talmudic-Midrashic Literature" (Ph.D. diss., Indiana University, 1954); Edward Winslow Gifford, *Tongan Myths and Tales,* Bernice P. Bishop Museum Bulletin no. 8 (Honolulu: Bishop Museum, 1924), 189–90.

45. See Robert Graves, *The Greek Myths* (London: Penguin, 1955), 90.

46. David Crockett Graham, *Songs and Stories of the Ch'uan Miao,* Smithsonian Miscellaneous Publications, vol. 123, no. 1 (Washington, D.C.: Smithsonian Institution, 1954). This includes material collected from 1921 until the early 1930s.

47. Thompson, *The Folktale,* 36–37.

48. Marie-Louise von Franz, *An Introduction to the Psychology of Fairy Tales,* 2d. ed. (Zurich: Spring Publications, 1973), 14.

49. A Russian story mentioned without a citation by Paul Smith has the baby cooked in a different way but preserves the theme of parental neglect: "The Tale is related of a mother bathing her baby in a tub of warm water. Placing the tub on top of the apparently unlit stove, the mother goes out and stands gossiping with a neighbor for some time. On returning indoors she is horrified to discover the draught of the open door has rekindled the fire and cooked the baby in the tub." See *Nasty Legends,* 65n.

50. Alan Dundes, "Projection in Folklore: A Plea for Psychoanalytic Semiotics," *Interpreting Folklore* (Bloomington: Indiana University Press, 1980), 37.

51. Alan Dundes, "The Dead Baby Joke Cycle," *Western Folklore* 38 (1979): 154.

52. William F. Buckley, "Notes and Asides," *National Review,* Mar. 26, 1968, 281.

53. Paul Smith, *The Book of Nastier Legends* (London: Routledge and Kegan Paul, 1986), 97.

4

What's Red and White and Baked All Over?

The answer to the title riddle is Red Velvet Cake—the famous bright red cake with white frosting that, according to legend, was served to a woman once at the Waldorf-Astoria Hotel in New York City. When she requested the recipe, the woman was charged an outrageous amount for it, which she found that she was obliged to pay since she had asked for the chef's secret. (Sometimes her lawyer advises her to pay, and then *he* charges her another outrageous amount for professional advice.) Even more annoying, the "secret" was merely a fairly standard cake recipe with a large dollop of red food coloring added. In revenge, the woman duplicated the recipe and sold it cheaply or distributed it among her friends, sometimes including it with her Christmas cards.

That woman must have had lots of friends. The same essential story attached to a copy of the recipe has circulated in the United States for at least forty years, despite the efforts of the Waldorf, yours truly, and others to debunk it. Eventually—in the manner of so many urban legends—the expensive recipe story developed other variations. Ultimately it became a legend about a chocolate chip cookie recipe sold for a rip-off price; this version, usually attached either to Mrs. Fields Cookies or to a Neiman-Marcus department store restaurant, continues to circulate, especially on the Internet. In fact, the expensive recipe story is one of the most durable and widely known American urban legends of all time.

I have a nostalgic attraction to this particular legend. The first note that I published on *any* urban legend was a brief item in the 1963 mimeographed newsletter *Oregon Folklore Bulletin* reporting the "Red Velvet Cake" story from Idaho and its surroundings.[1] The first publication in a scholarly context of a Red Velvet Cake recipe and story that I am aware of came in 1977 in Suzi Jones's collection *Oregon Folklore*.[2] (Jones's version, collected in 1973, had a woman pay $350 to the Waldorf for a recipe requiring two ounces of red food coloring. The woman gave out free copies of the recipe written on three-by-five cards.) In 1981 I discussed this legend in *The Vanishing Hitchhiker*,[3] and in 1989 I reviewed the material, including the cookie versions, in *Curses! Broiled Again!*[4]

The Classic Legend

The earliest known complete version of the classic form of the "Red Velvet Cake" legend is still the one I reported in 1963. It contains all four elements that we associate with the full story: a red cake, served at the Waldorf-Astoria, sold for a rip-off price, and leading to the victim's revenge. In this version, given to me by a University of Idaho student and originally distributed in a home economics class there in 1961, a woman from Seattle visits the Waldorf, pays $300 for the recipe, then circulates it among her friends. The amount of red food coloring added is two ounces. In January 1962 a similar story was published in the Canadian Pacific Railroad magazine *Spanner:* A British Columbia woman paid $200 for a recipe containing one-quarter cup of red food coloring. Although not identified specifically, the source was said to be "a hotel chef"; and although revenge is not mentioned, the recipe was said to have been "much publicized lately." Another Northwest source of 1962, a recipe sheet distributed by the Spokane, Washington, *Spokesman-Review,* included a recipe for red velvet cake containing two ounces of food coloring.

With varying amounts of detail, the story flourished from then on, seldom mentioning any other kinds of cake than red or any other place of origin than a hotel. My files bulge with letters, clippings, and notes documenting the popularity of the story in dozens of states—from Massachusetts to Hawaii, from Canada to Mississippi, and from Idaho to Arizona. The prices paid for the recipe range from $100 to $1,000, but most are $200 to $300. In revenge, the woman may give the recipe away, sell copies for $1.00 each, or in one instance supposedly publish it in the *New York Times.* Occasionally the recipe is for a cake *frosting,* or the cake is called something like "Red Carpet Cake" or "Waldorf-Astoria Christmas Cake," but the majority of the versions vary only slightly in details.

Besides newspaper articles and food columns, the most common published sources of Red Velvet Cake legends and recipes are locally compiled cookbooks produced by church groups, Junior League chapters, arts groups, and the like. For example, the recipes in the 1964 *Saint Louis Cookbook*[5] were gathered by "friends of the St. Louis Symphony," while recipes in the 1972 *Mississippi Cookbook*[6] were compiled by the state's agricultural extension service. Often the Red Velvet Cake recipe appears in such compilations alongside other novelty recipes for desserts like Crazy Cake, Coca-Cola Cake, and Scripture Cake.

The ingredients in the recipe are highly standardized, containing, besides the usual white cake ingredients, nearly always some buttermilk and some cocoa. Many recipes include a small amount of vinegar as well, although some of the directions caution, "Do not make your buttermilk." (Other directions, however, explain how to sour milk using vinegar to produce a buttermilk substitute.) In most recipes the cook is directed to make a paste of the cocoa and the red food coloring before adding that mixture to the rest of the batter. The amount of cocoa called for is usually small—a couple of tablespoons or so—with the notable exception of the recipe in the 1982 *Hershey's Chocolate and Cocoa Cookbook*,[7] which calls for one-quarter cup of Hershey's Cocoa. (Another recipe featuring Hershey's Cocoa is published in Ceil Dyer's book *Best Recipes from the Backs of Boxes, Bottles, Cans and Jars*.[8] It calls for only three tablespoons of cocoa. In the recipe's headnote Dyer suggests that Red Velvet Cake was a favorite in the 1930s, but, as discussed below, solid evidence is lacking for such an early date.)

There is some variation in the *statement* of how much red food coloring to add, but the actual *amount* to be added is consistent. Most recipes state "two ounces," but others say two small bottles, or one-quarter cup. Since food coloring usually comes in one-ounce bottles, and one-quarter cup is two ounces, all of these measurements are identical. If a frosting recipe is given, the color is always white, and the consistency is said to be soft, fluffy, or "like whipped cream." Several published recipes beginning in the 1970s emphasize that the dramatic red and white coloring of the cake makes it especially popular at Christmas, Valentine's Day, or Independence Day.

How well known the legend is in a community may be judged by the experience of my own local newspaper. In April 1975, the *Salt Lake Tribune,* in its food section, published a query for the Red Velvet Cake recipe and later published names of fourteen readers who had submitted their own copies. Again in July 1979, the *Tribune* requested Red Velvet Cake recipes, and in August published the names of eighteen different readers who had submitted them.

Allusions to red velvet cake also appear in popular culture. For example, the 1988 catalog of Swiss Colony, Inc., of Monroe, Wisconsin, offered "Red Velvet Petits Fours" and "Red Velvet Cake . . . a legend recreated for you. This regal dessert originated at New York's landmark Waldorf-Astoria hotel." The 1990 Swiss Colony catalog offered "Red Velvet Christmas Torte . . . made memorable by New York's Waldorf-Astoria hotel. . . . As beautiful as poinsettias on white linen." In the comic strip "Arlo and Janis" for March 11, 1989, a woman who has gained weight comments, "I knew I shouldn't have made that red velvet cake for Christmas." The most interesting popular culture artifact reflecting this legend, however, is a decorated cake platter copyrighted in 1983 by Royal China Co. The platter, measuring eleven and one-half inches in diameter (just right for a normal nine-inch layer cake), was found at a New York garage sale. The plate's design includes a woman in a red-and-white Victorian outfit gazing through her lorgnette at the familiar cake recipe, which is captioned "Miss Mary's Red Velvet Cake." The recipe calls for two one-ounce bottles of red food coloring. There is no mention of or allusion to any legend concerning the cake.

By the late 1980s, most references in print to the "Red Velvet Cake"

story linked it to an urban legend, perhaps reflecting readership of my 1981 book. The author of an article headlined "Red-Faced over Cake Recipe" in the *Tulsa Tribune* of May 13, 1992, described a local woman's Waldorf-Astoria Cake as "delicious" but "a fraud." The writer summarized the story from several local sources who said prices for the recipe ranged from $250 to $1,000. Even more an *analysis* of the tradition was Karola Saekel's article "Waldorf Astoria's Chocolate Layer Cake Enjoys a Rousing Revival" in the *San Francisco Chronicle* of July 8, 1992. In this piece Saekel reviewed local readers' versions of the story, one going back "nearly fifty years" and another from a 1970s fund-raising cookbook. A follow-up column in December 1992 quoted my debunking of the recipe's origin legend.

The last year for which I have any "Red Velvet Cake" references, apart from simple mentions of it in comparison to the later-emerging cookie variation of the legend, is 1992. Notable in 1992 was an Ann Landers column of September 25. After earlier publishing the Neiman-Marcus cookie story, Landers printed a letter from a North Carolina reader recalling the old "Red Velvet Cake" story. The quoted reader said the story went back forty years, and Ann Landers commented that she had received the same essential story from "at least fifty people."

Looking back over two dozen plus references to "Red Velvet Cake" published or reliably dated from about 1961 to 1992, I am struck by how few of the versions actually contain all four "classic" elements (red cake, Waldorf hotel, rip-off price, and revenge). Often the sources considered it sufficient merely to mention the Waldorf or to hint that the recipe is known widely, without describing details of either a rip-off or a revenge. Perhaps the whole story would have been better preserved if the original "folk" sources had been quoted in full; instead, local cookbooks, newspaper articles, and the like were usually content to mention the large numbers of people who knew and had copies of the recipe. In later articles, it was often my own books that were cited for the details, making one wonder to what degree the folklorist has influenced the tradition. At any rate, the legend seems to have been well established by the early 1960s, and then by the 1980s the story seems to have begun to fade in memory, although sometimes it was recalled to mind (as in Ann Landers's experience) by the "new" urban legend of the expensive cookie recipe.

The Waldorf-Astoria's Position(s) on the Legend

In 1965 I wrote to the Waldorf-Astoria in New York City asking what the management knew about the story. The reply I got, dated August 10, 1965, from Lola Preiss, director of public relations, asserted firmly that the story was false, that "there is no bright red cake on our menus, and our Executive Chef does not recall any such recipe." The letter stated that although the hotel had "letters and clippings . . . going back more than ten years which give numerous versions of this story" (with recipes priced from $5 to $1,000, and sometimes chocolate, sometimes red), after "a thorough check," the story was judged to be "completely false."

The firm and positive tone of this letter, however, is contradicted by a second reply I got from the same hotel (different spokesperson) after I read a syndicated article published in the *Denver Post* on December 20, 1978, stating that chef Arno Schmidt of the Waldorf-Astoria "had refused to share his recipe for red velvet cake requested by many readers because he said it was loaded with red food coloring. . . . 'We're not into dyes,' he said." Frances Borden, in replying to my second inquiry, on July 24, 1979, amazed me by forwarding a copy of what was entitled "The Authentic Waldorf Red Velvet Cake Recipe," along with the comment, "Our Chef says that the recipe goes back many years, and it has never been a particularly delicious cake, or a favorite." The recipe contains one-quarter cup of food coloring, but no cocoa or chocolate; the frosting recipe, rather oddly, includes "red color to suit."

Reflecting an apparent weariness on the part of the Waldorf management with the legend, the 1979 letter from the hotel comments, "The legend of the Red Velvet Cake and the varying costs of the 'secret recipe' go on and on. We do not keep a clipping file because the clippings are too numerous to store, and because the story is untrue." My guess is that the "Red Velvet Cake" legend does not trouble the Waldorf nearly as much as it once did, now that the tradition has moved on to another dessert food and to other companies. (My latest query to the Waldorf-Astoria in the summer of 1997 did not even receive a reply.)

But if the story did not start with the Waldorf-Astoria's kitchen and restaurant, then where did it originate?

The Prehistory of Red Velvet Cake

Although some writers and some of my correspondents have suggested that the Red Velvet Cake recipe and legend go back as far as the 1930s and 1940s, there are no reliably dated versions of the complete story before the early 1960s. The director of public relations for the Waldorf-Astoria in her 1965 letter dated the problems with the legend going back "more than ten years," but that is only to around 1955. But there *are* prototypes for the "Red Velvet Cake" legend, and these usually follow one of two themes: various traditions of *rip-off recipes* for other dessert foods and various recipes for *red cakes*, without reference to a secret recipe or to a rip-off price.

One reader claimed to remember a rip-off price charged for the Chicago Blackstone Hotel's chocolate ice cream recipe going back to the 1930s, but other early rip-off recipe stories concern candy, and these date only to the 1940s. The candy stories include one reader's memory of a 1949 recipe for "Mrs. Stevens $100 Fudge" and another person's memory of a $200 price charged for the recipe for See's Candies special fudge, sometimes referred to as "Million Dollar Fudge." (Mrs. Stevens and Sees are confectionery store chains.) Closer to the "Red Velvet Cake" legend is an Indiana woman's memory of a story from the 1940s concerning a woman who had to pay $25 for a chocolate cake recipe "in a restaurant down south somewhere." Similarly, a California woman provided a recipe for "One Hundred Dollar Cake," a chocolate cake containing the odd ingredient "One cup Miracle Whip Salad Dressing." This woman said that in about 1955 her father, a physician, received the recipe from a patient who said it came from a New York City restaurant that had charged someone a cool $100 for it.

The earliest published rip-off-priced cake recipe I have found appears in *Massachusetts Cooking Rules, Old and New* (1948), compiled by the Women's Republican Club of Boston.[9] This recipe for "$25 Fudge Cake" is credited to a woman in Whitman, a town southeast of Boston, who said she got it from a friend who "had to pay $25 upon the receipt of the recipe from a chef of one of the railroads." A similar recipe for "The Hundred-Dollar Chocolate Cake" appears in Marion Flexner's 1949 book *Out of Kentucky Kitchens*.[10] The capsule story attached to this recipe is this: "It is rumored that a certain Louisville matron, having tasted it in a New York restaurant, wrote back and asked for the recipe." She was charged $100 for it, advised by her lawyer that she must pay, and in revenge gave it to her church circle, who made a profit by selling the recipe to others. Neither of these cookbooks from the late 1940s describes a *red cake*, although the Kentucky book does include a pink peppermint frosting to use on the $100 chocolate cake.

I have *one* version of the rip-off story—with a chocolate cake recipe and mentioning the Waldorf-Astoria—that allegedly goes back to the 1940s. This recipe came to me from the Missouri folklorist Rebecca Schroeder, who got it in 1992 from an acquaintance in Columbia, Missouri, who had read an account of the Neiman-Marcus cookie story. "The

Waldorf-Astoria Story," as the typescript sheet is entitled, relates that "many years ago a friend of Aunt Mary stayed at the Waldorf-Astoria." This FOAF was charged $150 for the chocolate cake recipe that completes the sheet; she consulted a lawyer, had to pay, then gave it away to any desiring it for free. As for the dating of the story, the woman who supplied the sheet handwrote on it in 1992 that the "Aunt Mary" mentioned lived in Milwaukee and that the story "dates from ca. 1940." If we can trust this date, then we have all the ingredients of our story here, with the exception of the red coloring, some twenty years before my earliest dated version of the complete legend. That the color of the Waldorf cake did not shift from chocolate to red for another decade or so is suggested by the recipe for "$100 Waldorf Astoria Cake" published in Beth Tartan's compilation *North Carolina and Old Salem Cookery,* originally published in 1955.[11] This recipe, too, is for a rich chocolate cake without a hint of red.

As for *red* cakes, then, according to *James Beard's American Cookery,* a red devil's food cake had been a popular favorite in this country for a long time. Beard described it as "a cake that had great popularity at the beginning of this century and was made very red by the use of a good deal of soda, which achieved its purpose but had an objectionable flavor." Beard's own version of the recipe contains cocoa and a moderate amount of baking soda; he advises coating the cake with "boiled white frosting to intensify the red color."[12] (Similarly, in an older edition of *The Joy of Cooking* the editor remarks, concerning Red Devil's Food Cake, "Generally popular—but not with me, which is not to be taken as a criterion, 'likes' being what they are."[13]) James Beard follows his version of red devil's food cake with a recipe for Red Velvet Cake, which he says is "often called the hundred-dollar cake," but there is no explanation in his book for the nickname or any reference to the Waldorf-Astoria.[14] Beard's version of the classic recipe reduces the amount of red food coloring to one teaspoon but adds a teaspoon of cinnamon; the recipe also contains both cocoa and buttermilk.

A reference to a red cake actually dubbed "Red Velvet," but without the rip-off or revenge motifs, comes from a Texas reader born in 1943. She wrote that she had never heard any legend associated with the cake, but that Red Velvet Cake itself "has been a staple here in my part of the South since I can remember. My mother made it often." The Texas reader included with her letter a photocopy of a printed recipe calling for three products made by the Adams Extract Company of Austin, Texas. The products called for are "Adams Best" vanilla, Adams red food coloring, and Adams butter flavoring. The recipe also includes both cocoa and buttermilk, and a three-layer red cake is pictured.

The Adams Extract Company is legendary itself, and it seems to have been a major influence in popularizing Red Velvet Cake in this part of the Southwest. Its founder, John A. Adams, was selling extracts in Michigan in 1889, but moved his family and business to Beeville, Texas, in 1909, then to Austin in 1922 (where it has flourished under the direction of four generations of Adamses). According to its World Wide Web page, supplemented by information sent to me by Katherine Murphy, the associate advertising manager, Adams's products are sold in grocery stores in Texas, Louisiana, New Mexico, Arizona, and Mexico. Adams Extract has long promoted sales of its red food coloring by giving away copies of the Red Velvet Cake recipe, sometimes at in-store displays of the product topped by a large color photo of the cake. The oldest of the recipe sheets, judging by typography and layout, could well be from the 1940s or earlier, and one of the most modern-looking examples mentions that the cake is "also known as '$500 cake' or the 'Waldorf-Astoria' cake." So here we have the cake, given the traditional name, linked to a rip-off price and to the Waldorf Astoria in texts possibly as old as the late 1940s.

The Ingredients Combine, Forming the Classic Legend

Exactly how and when the rip-off recipe legend began is unclear, but possibly by the 1930s and certainly by the 1940s such stories were circulating widely by word of mouth and in print. The product was always a sweet of some kind—ice cream, fudge, chocolate cake, fudge cake, or a cake frosting—and the source of the recipe was variously described as a railroad chef, a large hotel in the South, or a hotel or restaurant in a big city, often New York City. The lowest price mentioned (in the earliest accounts) was $25, but $100 (mentioned in 1949) or more became standard. A 1955 reference to "$100 Waldorf Astoria Cake" establishes the early association of the legend with that particular hotel, and by the early 1960s the Waldorf story had focused definitively on a *red* cake, albeit one that includes chocolate (in the form of cocoa) among its ingredients.[15]

Red devil's food cake, according to James Beard, was a popular American kitchen creation even as early as the first part of the twentieth century, and references to non-rip-off red cakes, eventually to Christmasy red cakes, continued right up to the 1960s, when all such references become fixed as the Waldorf-Astoria hotel Red Velvet Cake rip-off recipe tradition, a legend form that lasted until the recent shift in the early 1980s to the version about an expensive cookie recipe.

The Waldorf-Astoria (now a Hilton hotel) surely must have attracted the legend to itself partly because of what Gary Alan Fine has dubbed "the Goliath Effect." Here he refers to the typical attachment of mercantile legends to the largest companies and manufacturers, especially to those holding the largest share of their market.[16] The very name of this hotel, Fine writes, "is still synonymous with luxury hotels, fine service, class, and wealth," although Fine also asserts that "the Waldorf has slipped from its position as the preeminent New York hotel."[17] The Waldorf itself, which as we have seen eventually adopted the legend even while debunking it, continues to bill itself, quoting from their 1996 World Wide Web page, as "the 50–story Grand Dame of luxury hotels . . . a New York landmark for over 100 years." True, that description is a bit exaggerated since the present hotel building, according to the same Web page, was built only in 1931. But with its location in the heart of midtown Manhattan, its over 1,400 rooms starting at $212 per night and running up to $875 for a deluxe suite, and its famous name intact, it is the Waldorf-Astoria and not, say, the Plaza Hotel, that was always associated with the legend. And thus it was also the Waldorf, in Fine's words again, that was characterized in the legend as "uncaring, manipulative, hostile, greedy, and/or incompetent."[18] The "red velvet" alluded to in the cake's name projects this sense of tradition and luxury, as does also the occasional reference to it as a "red carpet" cake. Another factor that probably contributed to the attachment of the recipe to this hotel is that the Waldorf was already the source of another well-known popular food tradition, Waldorf salad.

The redness of the cake provides another clue why the story appealed for so long to Americans, and this has not escaped the attention of at least one folklorist. In a parody of Freudian analysis of legends Keith Cunningham found "significant evidence" that this was indeed a "sexy cake . . . to wit, the words 'red' and 'velvet' are certainly verbal sexual symbols, or at least sexy adjectives; and the cake, at least in one variation, is covered all over with a thick, white, gooey icing."[19] Cunningham went on about the slicing of the cake with "a sharp, pointed object [that is] held erect," about the offering of "a piece" of the sexy cake to someone, and so forth, but by then he had wandered away from the legend itself to the context in which it is told, a subject about which we have little hard evidence.

The redness of the cake, however, does seem significant; in fact, it's really the only reason, other than revenge against the hotel, for preserving the story, circulating the recipe, and baking the cake. Surprise your guests by serving them a white-frosted cake that turns out to be bright red inside! Very few accounts of the "Red Velvet Cake" legend make much of the supposed superior taste or texture of the cake; it's the redness that counts. None of the ingredients, apart from the food coloring, is unusual. True, buttermilk is an ingredient for which the typical cook would have little other immediate use, but many recipes allow for artificially souring a cup of sweet milk with vinegar as a substitute. All the other ingredients—flour, sugar, butter or shortening, eggs, cocoa, salt, vanilla—will be found in the kitchen of any good cook, except that most cooks would probably have to make a special trip to the store for the red food coloring. As one cook who sent her Red Velvet Cake recipe (written on red paper) to a newspaper wrote, "This is a very special cake and is especially fun to serve on holidays." Another commented, "Fussy to make, but good and pretty."

What a red cake *is,* I believe, is primarily a *fun* cake—jolly, surprising, frivolous, festive, and most often a dessert served at a celebration or at a holiday meal. Red cake is part of the American tradition of "playing with food," comparable to all those other "wacky cake" recipes that may include unusual *ingredients*—like salad dressing, tomato soup, or even sauerkraut—or may include combining the ingredients in unusual ways— like making little piles of dry ingredients and adding some of the liquid ingredients to each pile. (Does it really matter, by the way, that you mix the red food coloring with the cocoa to form a paste before adding the mixture to the batter?) Other aspects of playing with cakes emerge as bizarre decorating themes (I once saw a pink naked female torso cake at a Louisiana dance party) or with the tradition of baking an object (like a coin or a ring) inside the cake; and we should not forget the cakes that are turned upside-down between the baking and the serving. Of course people do play with foods other than desserts; witness how some people eat their mashed potatoes and gravy or their "sunnyside up" fried eggs. But sweets served at the end of a meal constitute the most appropriate area of "guilty pleasures" in which to exercise our imagination and have some special fun with the food. We eat cakes, cookies, candies, fudge not for their nutritious value but to satisfy our sweet tooth. Pies at least may have fruit in them, although we play with pies too, making a mock apple pie, for example, out of Ritz Crackers. With cakes, the shape, texture, color, and decoration are just as important as the taste or the food value; otherwise, why would anyone eat Twinkies or those pink Snowballs sold mostly in convenience stores and from snack machines?

The fun value of a red cake is enhanced by the irony that it is baked from an ordinary recipe whose only "secret" is a simple trick—loading it up with food coloring. Compounding the irony is the notion that this dirty trick was peddled for a high price by the archetypal luxury hotel of New York. The Waldorf-Astoria, in my opinion, reacted in the spirit of the legend by eventually distributing free copies of their own version of the "authentic" recipe. (Of course, their simultaneous disavowal of the cake as not up to modern nutritional standards also emphasizes its fun-food status.) Perhaps the strongest statement of the fun-with-food nature of Red Velvet Cake is a Wrigleys Spearmint Chewing Gum advertisement of 1962. Here a company whose product is the epitome of a nonfood that nevertheless is put into the mouth and masticated strictly for its sweetness ("Double your pleasure, double your fun!") suggests making a bright red holiday cake by simply treating a white cake *mix* with a heavy dose of red food coloring.

As shown above, the "Red Velvet Cake" legend held up strongly through the 1980s and was mentioned by food writers as recently as 1992, but the seeds of the story's demise—or rather its significant variation—were sown as early as 1977, the year that Debbi Fields began to sell her chocolate chip cookies in a Palo Alto, California, shopping mall. By 1982 when Fields

Mrs. Fields **RECIPE**

HAS NEVER BEEN SOLD

There is a rumor circulating that the Mrs. Fields Cookie recipe was sold to a woman at a cost of $250.00. A chocolate chip cookie recipe was attached to the story. I would like to tell all my customers that the story is **not true**, this is not my recipe and I have never sold the recipe to anyone. Mrs. Fields recipe is a delicious trade secret.

Sincerely,

Debbi Fields
Debbi Fields

P.S. Mrs. Fields ingredients are exclusively blended to our specifications and can not be purchased anywhere.

THE RUMOR IS NOT TRUE!

moved the company headquarters to Park City, Utah, a new form of the expensive recipe legend was already sprouting, and by 1983 the story had attached itself firmly to the by then phenomenally successful Mrs. Fields Cookies Company. As Debbi Fields herself wrote in her 1987 bio-business history *One Smart Cookie,* "Of all the problems . . . that are going to be dropped on your doorstep if you run a large company, the worst, absolutely the worst, are the rumors."[20] The rip-off cookie recipe legend bedeviled Mrs. Fields for several years, and her response to it was different from the Waldorf-Astoria's, though perhaps more successful, since the legend moved on more quickly this time. The Mrs. Fields company simply denied the legend firmly on posters and other advertising and then refused to acknowledge the story any further.

By 1989 the expensive recipe legend had shifted to the Neiman Marcus company and was being circulated mostly through the Internet. Responding in kind, Neiman Marcus now debunks the story on its World Wide Web page, identifying it correctly as a long-standing American urban legend. Thus, the Internet is the latest context for the old but still vigorous legend of the rip-off recipe foisted upon an innocent customer by a big company.

Notes

An earlier version of this chapter was presented at the annual meeting of the American Folklore Society in Austin, Texas, October 29–November 2, 1997.

1. Jan Harold Brunvand, "Two Items of Recent Food Folklore," *Oregon Folklore Bulletin* 2.1 (1963): 5–7.

2. Suzi Jones, *Oregon Folklore* (Eugene: University of Oregon and the Oregon Arts Commission, 1977), 108.

3. Jan Harold Brunvand, *The Vanishing Hitchhiker* (New York: W. W. Norton, 1981).

4. Jan Harold Brunvand, *Curses! Broiled Again!: The Hottest Urban Legends Going* (New York: W. W. Norton, 1989).

5. Women's Association of the St. Louis Symphony Society, *Saint Louis Cookbook* (Louisville, Ken.: Cookbook Collectors Library, 1964), 49.

6. *Mississippi Cookbook* (Hattiesburg: University and College Press of Mississippi, 1972), 378.

7. *Hershey's Chocolate and Cocoa Cookbook* (Nashville, Tenn.: Ideals, 1982), 27.

8. Ceil Dyer, *Best Recipes from the Backs of Boxes, Bottles, Cans and Jars* (New York: Galahad Books, 1993), 435. This book is based on three volumes originally published in 1979, 1981, and 1982.

9. Women's Republican Club, *Massachusetts Cooking Rules, Old and New* (Boston: Women's Republican Club, 1948), 176–77.

10. Marion Flexner, *Out of Kentucky Kitchens* (New York: Bramhall House, 1949), 232–33.

11. Beth Tartan, *North Carolina and Old Salem Cookery*, rev. ed. (Chapel Hill: University of North Carolina Press, 1992), 274, originally published by the University of North Carolina Press in 1955.

12. James Beard, *James Beard's American Cookery* (Boston: Little, Brown, 1972), 678.

13. Irma S. Rombauer and Marion Rombauer Becker, *The Joy of Cooking* (Indianapolis: Bobbs-Merrill, 1953), 612.

14. Beard, *James Beard's American Cookery*, 678.

15. Two further sources of Waldorf cake recipes are Junior League of Lafayette, Louisiana, *Talk about Good* (Junior League of Lafayette, Louisiana, 1969), 388, and *Rowe Kitchens, 1785–1985* (Rowe, Mass. 1985), 127.

16. Gary Alan Fine, *Manufacturing Tales: Sex and Money in Contemporary Legends* (Knoxville: University of Tennessee Press, 1992), 141–63.

17. Ibid., 155–56.

18. Ibid., 4.

19. Keith Cunningham, "Reflections and Regurgitations upon the Well-Known Urban-Belief Tale 'The Red Velvet Cake,'" *Folklore Forum* 5 (1972): 147–48.

20. Debbi Fields and Alan Furst, *One Smart Cookie: How a Housewife's Chocolate Chip Recipe Turned into a Multimillion-Dollar Business—the Story of Mrs. Fields Cookies* (New York: Simon and Schuster, 1987), 152.

5

Was It a Stunned Deer or Just a Deer Stunt?: The Story behind a Missouri Legend

This chapter resulted from doing folklore research by long distance, via U.S. mail and the telephone. I remained home in Salt Lake City while tracing a legend that was spreading and changing in the state of Missouri and elsewhere. This absentee research method derived from my five years of writing a syndicated newspaper column. While the column was running I developed a network of correspondents, including journalists as well as ordinary readers of my books. These contacts were the "informants" who contributed to my study of "The Stunned Deer" or "The Hunter's Nightmare."

Specifically, it was Elaine Viets, a daily columnist for the *St. Louis Post-Dispatch,* who first called me about the story she had heard. Viets later sent me copies of her correspondence with a principal character involved in the legend as well as a tape recording purporting to be a copy of the original tape that's part of the legend.

First, here's the basic story—paraphrased—as Elaine Viets reported it in January 1989 as she had heard it from a St. Louis teacher who had heard it from another teacher who had heard it from her husband who had heard it at the brewery where he works.[1]

A Missouri man returning from an unsuccessful hunting trip hit a deer, a rather small one, with his car, and he believed that he had killed it. It seemed like the first good luck of a frustrating weekend, so he decided to keep the deer—illegal though the practice was.

The man put the animal, which was merely stunned, into his backseat, and shortly afterward the deer revived and began thrashing around. Grabbing a tire iron from under the front seat, the man swung at the terrified deer while struggling to steer the car. Unfortunately, he beaned his faithful hunting dog with one wild swing of the tire iron, and the dog bit him.

The man stopped his car and jumped out, pursued by his angry dog. He ran to a telephone booth, slammed the door, and dialed 911. When the call was answered, the man screamed to the operator that he was trapped there by his dog, while the deer was kicking out the windows of his car. He begged the police to come and shoot the two animals for him. The officer on duty, highly amused by the man's predicament, patched the call onto the office intercom, where it entertained everyone on duty that day, and the officer as a matter of routine made a tape of the emergency call. Later, he duplicated the tape for some of his co-workers and friends.

Funny story, but is it true? Elaine Viets—one of my frequent callers and correspondents, whom I have met just one time in person—thought that it *sounded* like an urban legend. She began to make some inquiries.

Local law enforcement authorities whom Viets called told her that "The Hunter's Nightmare" had not happened in the St. Louis area, but in Poughkeepsie, New York. A St. Louis executive of the 911 system said that he had heard the story about three or four years before told at a conference for 911 coordinators by a policeman from Poughkeepsie.

But when Viets called the Poughkeepsie Police Department, she learned that, at that time at least, they didn't even operate a 911 service there. Then Viets called me, and I admitted that I had not heard this exact story, although it certainly reminded me of urban legends in which stunned animals revive and mistreated animals gain revenge.

For example, in a legend I call "The Deer Departed," a deer or elk stunned by a hunter's shot gets up and walks away with the hunter's rifle caught in its antlers.[2] (The hunter had placed his rifle in the antlers intending to pose for a self-timed photograph with his trophy animal.) But I hadn't heard the story about the man in the car, the deer, the dog, and the frantic call to 911.

So Viets gave up the search for the origin of the incident and wrote her first column about it, published in the *St. Louis Post-Dispatch* on January 3, 1989. In the column she asked, "Is this an urban legend? Or did it really happen?"

Within a week Viets heard from twenty-five readers in the St. Louis area who had copies of the tape, some of whom sent her copies to "prove" that it was no legend. Most respondents had some connection with law enforcement, but they disagreed whether the incident had happened in Missouri, Arkansas, or Colorado.

"They were all wrong," Viets wrote in her follow-up column published one week later, on January 10, 1989.[3] She had called Poughkeepsie again and spoken to another police officer who explained that although there was no 911 service, the emergency call about the deer and the dog had actually been received, not just three or four years ago, but back in 1974 as a regular police report. He said the call was taken by "the legendary Al Clouser, now retired," who was working on the midnight shift when the call came in during February 1974. Note that this was fully fifteen years before the story was reported in Missouri.

The Poughkeepsie officer gave this description of what happened when the police arrived on the scene: "By the time we got there," he said, "the guy was gone. All we found was some auto glass, some seat stuffing, a little fur and a little blood." This officer also claimed that as many as fifty thousand copies of the tape were circulating, and that Scotland Yard, the White House, and the FBI academy all had copies.

Impressive explanation, but is it all true?

"The Hunter's Nightmare" seemed, at best, to be an emergent urban legend, based on an actual incident. Something *like* the stunned deer story had evidently happened fifteen years previously in New York State, and the story had spread to Missouri and perhaps elsewhere. The tape recordings definitely do exist.

Viets sent me one of her copies of the tape recording; it has extremely poor sound and may have been doctored by someone somewhere along the line during the intervening years. The caller's language, however, sounds very realistic; and, in fact, it's largely unprintable, as you might expect from a man involved in such a situation.

Viets published a sanitized transcript of the tape, and I quote a small portion of it from her second column:

> Man: I need a man with a gun up here.
> Police: You do?
> Man: I do. This @#$% . . . Let me tell you what happened. This dog chased this deer, understand? And this @#$% chased the deer into my car. Now I picked the deer up and put him in the back seat. I was gonna take him to get him fixed, understand? This @#$% is tearing my car apart. . . . This deer is tearing the @#$% out of the back seat. That @#$% bit me in the neck and that was it. I thought I was dead.
> Police: Where you at?
> Man: I'm in a damn telephone booth. The dog chased me into a telephone booth. . . .
> Police: Hang in there and I'll send a car over.
> Man: @#$% bit me, too. Send somebody with a gun to shoot him, too. I stabbed him with my knife and hit him with a tire iron and he bit me good.

Although it's a hilarious tape, I doubt that fifty thousand copies are floating around, as has been suggested, and I don't see what the White House or the FBI would want with it. But it does tell approximately the same story as summarized above, with the addition of the man also trying to defend himself with a knife and a tire iron.

On January 7, 1992, three years after the columns were written, Allen Clouser, a retired officer of the Poughkeepsie Police Department, wrote to Elaine Viets thanking her for writing the columns and explaining the truth behind "The Hunter's Nightmare" story. Clouser, of course, was the "legendary" officer who actually took the call in February 1974 from the man claiming to have been attacked by a wounded deer and an angry dog. ("Legendary" in this context means that Clouser had achieved local fame because of his involvement with the stunned deer story.) Clouser had evidently mislaid Viets's column sent to him three years before.

The man who made the call asking for help, Al Clouser believed, was intoxicated, but Clouser said there was definitely a "very angry dog" (in his words) barking excitedly in the background. He said that several policemen were dispatched to search for and assist the caller, but they were unable to locate him. In a second letter to Elaine Viets, on January 31, granting permission for me to quote his earlier letter, Clouser wrote, "This 'deer' event was merely a routine call for me. It amazes me how it has spread and become a 'legend.'"

Clouser's recollection of the incident closely follows the scenario outlined at the beginning of this chapter. He says that everything Viets heard from the Poughkeepsie police officer about the incident was true, except the ending statement. Rather than actually locating the site of the incident and finding it strewn with broken glass, car seat stuffing, and blood, Clouser reveals what the police actually found—nothing: "We checked every location we could think of fitting the description given. That location was never found. We have no idea of the location, or of the person involved that night." This clarification raises the possibility of a hoax or a crank call made to the police, although Clouser himself did not suggest this. It also suggests that the police in Poughkeepsie were improving on the story as they told it among themselves.

The "deer tape" that Elaine Viets sent me establishes that her transcription, quoted above, was reasonably accurate, although my ears cannot detect any sound of a dog barking. I *can* hear the increasing level of humor in the voice of the policeman taking the call. The caller does not sound especially drunk to me; his speech patterns and vocabulary, however, do seem to display some traits of Black English.

The evidence examined so far proves that the stunned deer emergency call did really come in to the Poughkeepsie Police Department in February 1974, and that tapes of the call have circulated quite widely, in part through distribution at a conference of 911 coordinators. Although the testimony of the officer who took the call is that the site of the alleged incident was never located, a current officer on the force gave Elaine Viets a detailed description of what was supposedly found at the site. He also made doubtful claims for the notoriety of the tapes, and he referred to Al Clouser as "legendary," indicating his awareness of the spreading fame of the incident. Thus we can detect some signs of a legend beginning to take shape. That process continued as the story spread.

In the St. Louis area, the story became localized and was retold as the supposed experiences of a FOAF. In other words, the stunned deer story had become an urban legend, albeit one that, despite having roots some fifteen years deep, was still rather narrow in its distribution.

That "The Hunter's Nightmare" legend had become a bit more popular later was shown by a letter sent to me in March 1991 by a reader in Cape Girardeau, Missouri. This reader, two years after Viets's columns were published (and without mentioning them), summarized the story, calling it "the latest tale to come my way," as follows:

> I overheard this in a coffee shop and did not get the entire yarn. It seems that some buddies in a big city decided to get some fresh venison and went out for a deer hunt. Well, it was a good day (none of them got shot), and a bad day (no deer got shot), and with evening at hand they decided to head home.
>
> One guy had his family van, and after leaving the others he headed down the interstate. Not too far along he found a deer by the side of the road. It had been struck by a car.
>
> The hunter decided to take the carcass with him, and he loaded it into his van. But it seems the deer had only been knocked unconscious, and it revived in the warm interior. Frightened, the deer began kicking; the man was startled and ran off the road. The animal escaped, and the police who pulled the van out of the ditch had a good laugh.

Now we can see that in the oral tradition—separately from the actual police tape or in the summary of the incident in the newspaper feature story—"The Hunter's Nightmare" legend has developed some distinctive features. Now there are several hunters ("some buddies from a big city"), as well as a van and an interstate, but there is no dog, no tire iron or knife, and no telephone booth. The police still find the incident amusing, and they also assist in pulling the van out of the ditch. The story, obviously, had acquired a life of its own by 1991.

Further evidence of this fact appears in another letter I received in January 1991—seventeen years after the Poughkeepsie incident and two years after Viets's columns—from a reader in Marble Falls, Texas. This reader made the revealing comment that many of those who have told it to him claimed to have seen a news story confirming it, although none could produce a clipping. (I suspect that perhaps Elaine Viets's 1989 columns were reprinted by some out-of-state newspapers.) At any rate, this reader judged that the incident "may or may not have happened."

In the Texas report a specific nearby small town is named where the incident is said to have happened. There are two hunters in the car that strikes the deer, and they tag the trophy-size buck with a tag that they had no other use for during their unsuccessful day of hunting (a new detail). While the men are stopped in a cafe for coffee, the stunned deer revives and begins to trash the inside of their station wagon. They release the deer from the car and it runs away, although in a variation reported by my Texas correspondent, one of the hunters is injured by the deer during its frantic attempts to escape the car. According to another variation a game warden was in the same cafe and cited the hunters for tagging a deer they had not shot. According to yet another variation the deer was in the car of a good samaritan who had rescued the stunned creature from a Houston area freeway and was trying to transport it to a veterinarian or to the humane society for treatment.

"The Hunter's Nightmare" story continued to circulate. On October 2, 1992, I received a telephone call from someone at a San Francisco radio station who had received a supposed 911 tape concerning a hunter/deer/dog/car encounter. On December 6, 1992, John Landis in his "Outdoors" column of the *Quincy (Ill.) Herald-Whig* published a tape transcript different from Viets's, prefacing it by writing, "With the assistance of one of Quincy's finest, I have acquired a copy of the actual recording of an emergency call for help, as it was received by an ambulance service near Kansas City." In 1993 I received two more queries about the story from Michigan and New York. The former reported that the tape "will be found in the 'chuckles file' of many police stations in Lower Michigan," and the latter reported that the story was circulating on the Internet, identified as an incident that had occurred in Georgia.

Within the broader related tradition, there are various other unverified stories about a deer stunned by a collision with a car or truck or about a deer (or a cow) that is struck by a vehicle and then flies up and lands in or on a second vehicle. There is also the very popular (at least in Utah) "California hunter" genre of stories in which an out-of-state hunter shoots a mule, cow, horse, or other large domestic animal, mistaking it for a game animal.

"The Stunned Deer," or "The Hunter's Nightmare," legend has joined this larger tradition because of an actual incident, and the story developed by a combination of personal embellishment, word-of-mouth changes, a poor-quality tape recording that exists in different versions and in multiple copies, and at least two newspaper articles. None of this is unusual in modern folk narratives, I might add.

Just a hint of a somewhat more elaborate, but definitely related, story came in a letter I received in December 1989 from a woman in Chico, California:

> In the early 1970s friends of mine in St. Louis related the following supposedly-true incident:
>
> While deer hunting in the Missouri woods, a man shot and wounded another hunter. When the judge asked the man how he could have been so stupid as to fire at a human being, the man replied that when he got a glimpse of the bright orange safety vest the other hunter was wearing, he thought he was seeing a wild turkey.
>
> The judge then said that since there was a ban on hunting wild turkeys, and the fine for same was $100 for each pound of the turkey's weight, he was going to fine the defendant $100 for each pound that the wounded man weighed.

This story was supposedly "heard in the news," the woman from California concluded, "but it sure sounds like an urban legend to me."

Speaking of turkeys, dead or alive, here is a story that "walks, gobbles, and explodes like a UL," as someone phrased it when quoting the story to me via e-mail as he read it in the August 1992 issue of the magazine *Car and Driver*. This is reported as having been heard on a car radio while driving: "A hunter, having shotgunned an unsuspecting wild turkey, placed the unfortunate fowl in the trunk and headed home. In a burst of monumental stupidity, he stored his loaded fowling piece in the baggage compartment as well. Unaccountably, the turkey revived, scratched but in a panic, and set off the shotgun. The explosion destroyed the rear seat and sprayed the driver with buckshot."

A variation of the turkey story showed up in an ad for Sauza "Conmemorativo" tequila published (among other places) in *Men's Journal* for November 1995. The full-page color ad featured this item, made to look exactly like a newspaper clipping:

Wounded turkey shoots man

Missouri, Oct. 6—A man showing off a turkey he thought he killed was shot in the leg when the wounded bird thrashed around in his car trunk and triggered his shotgun.

"The turkeys are fighting back," the County Sheriff said.

To make matters worse, it turns out that the man, in his early 40's, and his son, Junior, 16, were hunting a week before the start of turkey season and will probably be fined, the Sheriff said.

The caption on the ad reads, "Life is Harsh. Your tequila shouldn't be."

But, in conclusion, back to the deer stories.

Elaine Viets asserted in one note during the course of our exchange of correspondence that "the deer and dog story turned out to be true!" My findings on the matter are more along the lines of "not quite 100 percent rock-solid pure-gold unequivocally true." There's *some* truth behind the story, but there is also a good deal of communal re-creation going on as well. But then, as we all know, the truth never stands in the way of a good story. This is simply another prime example of how urban legends grow and spread.[4]

Notes

The first version of this essay was presented at the annual meeting of the Missouri Folklore Society in Hermann, September 25–27, 1992, then revised and published in *Missouri Folklore Society Journal* 15–16 (1993–94): 111–18. A condensed report on this legend appeared as "The Hunter's Nightmare" in *The Baby Train and Other Lusty Urban Legends* (New York: Norton, 1993), 270–72.

1. Elaine Viets, "A Man, a Deer, a Dog, and 911," *St. Louis Post-Dispatch,* Jan. 3, 1989.

2. Jan Harold Brunvand, *The Mexican Pet: More "New" Urban Legends and Some Old Favorites* (New York: W. W. Norton, 1986), 24–25.

3. Elaine Viets, "Year's Wildest Tale: Man, Deer, Dog," *St. Louis Post-Dispatch,* Jan. 10, 1989.

4. An audience member at the Missouri Folklore Society conference in September 1992 pointed out that the stunned deer story appears in essentially the folk form in Louise Erdrich's 1984 novel *Love Medicine*.

6

Bedtime for Bozo: The Legend of the Clown Who Cussed the Kids

In my 1984 book *The Mexican Pet* I devoted a few paragraphs to debunking two versions of a story (whether rumor, anecdote, or legend) that I called "Bozo the Clown's Blooper." According to one of these accounts a children's television show host in the character of Bozo was cussed once by a kid while broadcasting live on the air; the second version of the story was that Bozo himself had once cussed the kids on the air. I mentioned as background to the two Bozo stories similar tales that are told about various hosts on children's radio shows, most often about the broadcaster who was known as Uncle Don. I concluded my discussion thus: "these are traditional versions of broadcasting history as people think it *should be,* not as it really was."[1]

Few things that I've written about individual contemporary legends have brought me more dissenting mail than these remarks about Bozo the Clown's and Uncle Don's alleged bloopers.[2] Many, *many* readers wrote to tell me that they believed one or both of these blooper stories to be true, not because they had heard or seen the incident themselves, but because they had heard the stories on the supposedly good authority of FOAFs.

In defense of my position—and just out of curiosity—I diligently compiled all the information I could find concerning the two stories, and I was not persuaded to change my original conclusion. Eventually I presented my findings in two newspaper columns that were published in 1991. Since then I've been sending copies of these columns to readers who continue to write me asserting that they know someone who knows someone who, they believe, actually heard or saw the radio or TV children's show host being cussed by or himself cussing the kids.

This chapter is an expansion of those two columns—heavier artillery, as it were, to use in my campaign to put this particular blooper story to bed at last.

My first column on the subject[3] was written as a reply to an imagined letter from Bozo himself that neatly summed up the essence of both legends:

"DEAR PROFESSOR: Please, can you help clear the good name of Bozo the Clown? For years people have been spreading the false story that either Bozo cussed a kid or a kid cussed Bozo on live TV. The result was that Bozo was supposedly yanked off the air. Didn't that really happen to Uncle Don, a long-ago children's show host?—[signed] BOZO"

My reply began:

"DEAR BOZO: I'm not really sure which Bozo you are, because since 1950, at least 180 different people have portrayed Bozo the Clown on children's television shows across the nation, and at its peak there were more than 80 Bozo shows on local TV. But I do know that at one time or another, some form of the story I call 'Bozo the Clown's Blooper' has been told about most of them."

"Bozo the Clown's Blooper" is not one story, really, but two. However, the similarity of the two tales, and their link to Bozo the Clown, demands that they be regarded as different variations of a single legend.

The first version of the story focuses on a child who is a contestant on a local Bozo the Clown TV program. The child misses a shot in a game of dexterity and utters a curse. When Bozo attempts to comfort him, the child snaps, in the most common version, "Cram it, clown!" The outburst goes out over the airwaves, shocking the clown's young audience—and no doubt the parents too.

In the second version of the story, the offensive words are uttered by Bozo himself. The clown, exasperated by his young contestants, calls one of them an unprintable name. The comment goes out over the air, and irate parents call the TV station in protest. Before long, the local Bozo the Clown show is canceled.

Former Bozo actors and agents deny that the story of the child's naughty remark is true, and the many variations I've heard support them. I've heard the story told about the Bozos of Baltimore, New Orleans, Chicago, and Los Angeles; I've heard that Bozo called the child's remark a "Bozo No-no"; and I've heard that the kid said "ram it" or "shove it" or "climb it" instead of "cram it." I've been told that the child made an obscene gesture and said much naughtier words—the f-word, even—as well as "Screw you, Bozo!" and "Eat shit, Bozo!" I've heard that the child was playing a ball-in-bucket game, a block-building contest, an egg-in-a-spoon game, or was taking part in a quiz game. I've heard that the child asked Bozo a variant of this riddle: "Why is a woman like a frying pan? Answer: Because you have to get both hot before you put the meat in."

I've been told that the story is so well known that the expression "Cram it, clown!" became a generic comeback to any kind of frustration among the generation that grew up watching Bozo. I've been told that the actual incident occurred anytime from the late 1950s up to 1974.

But I've never ever heard the story told by anyone who was in the TV studio when the alleged event occurred, although it's true that games of skill or luck, riddles, and jokes were a regular part of every Bozo show, and such a mishap could easily have happened. Nor has anyone telling the story, at least to me, claimed to have witnessed the event firsthand on TV. The storytellers, as happens so often with urban legends, invariably heard the anecdote from friends and it supposedly happened to a FOAF.

An article that appeared in the *Chicago Tribune* in 1986 reported: "[Former clown] Bob Bell says that the great story about a kid missing Bucket No. 6 and telling Bozo to perform an impossible act is a myth."[4] Bozo's home station is WGN-TV in Chicago; Larry Harmon originated the character of Bozo there in 1949, and Bob Bell followed him, playing the clown character there for twenty-three years before retiring in 1984. If *anyone* knows, Bob Bell would be the one.

The second version of the legend (the clown cussing the kids), too, has been told to me by sources from coast to coast. People attribute the story to periods from the 1950s through the 1970s. Each of them, again, says that he or she knows someone who knows someone else who actually heard Bozo—or "Uncle Gus," "Uncle Bucky," "Captain Bob," "Uncle Bob," or even Art Linkletter—say something naughty on the air.

There seems to be some confusion of names here with Buffalo Bob of the Howdy Doody television series, on which a clown named Clarabell did appear (but never spoke, and certainly did not swear). There's also probably some confusion with the name of the aforementioned Uncle Don, about whom more is explained below.

A similar story is recounted by Hal Morgan and Kerry Tucker in their book *Rumor!* The pair attributes the story to the 1960s and phrases it like this: "A children's television show host was taken off the air after he said, 'That ought to shut the little bastards up!' on live television during what he thought was a commercial break." The authors of *Rumor!* insist that the event never occurred, and they comment, "The statement was attrib-

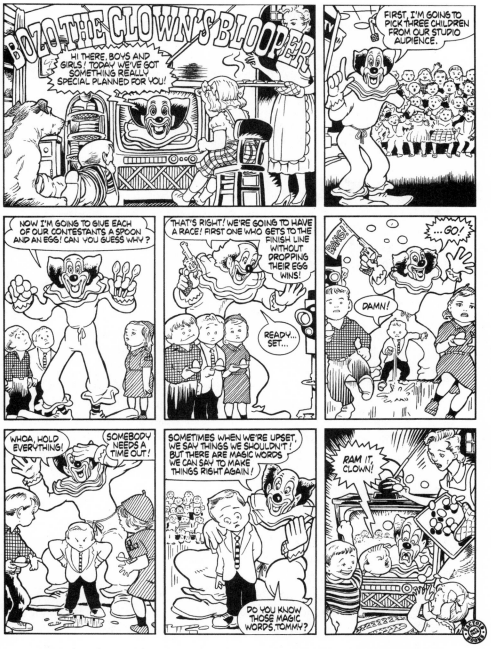

"Bozo the Clown's Blooper" by Ned Sonntag © 1994 Paradox Press. All rights reserved. Used with permission of DC Comics.

uted, in different versions of the tale, to virtually every local children's-show host around the country."[5]

But Bozo was right, in a way, in the letter that I invented, in suggesting that the second version of "Bozo the Clown's Blooper" (the clown cussing the kids by referring to them as "little bastards") was probably transferred to the television clown from an event attributed years earlier to the exceedingly popular children's show radio host who called himself Uncle Don.

But I don't think Uncle Don said it either, and that belief was the subject of my second column[6] on the blooper tale; that column too began with a letter from a reader:

"DEAR PROFESSOR: I read your reply to Bozo the Clown supporting his claim that he was never bumped from the air for cussing the kids or being cussed by kids. But how can you say this never happened to Uncle Don when I've heard it with my own ears on a blooper record?—[signed] UNCONVINCED"

My reply began:

"DEAR UN: I get a dozen or more letters like yours every year, many of them accompanied by taped copies of portions of various blooper records that do, indeed, seem to contain dubs of the infamous Uncle Don on-air goof. I've analyzed these recordings, and I've sought other evidence for their reliability, and here's what I've found."

First, let me say once again that I believe it is very likely that the version of the "Bozo the Clown's Blooper" legend, in which the children's television show host makes an unprintable remark on the air, was transferred to Bozo the Clown from an event attributed to the early children's show radio host who called himself Uncle Don. This alleged radio incident, however, is debunked in every available reference work on broadcasting history.

For example, John Dunning in *Tune in Yesterday,* a history of old-time radio, reported that the story of the host's signing off saying, "There! I guess that'll hold the little bastards for another night" was merely "a delightfully unsubstantiated story" that became attached to a former vaudeville musician named Howard Rice who changed his name to Don Carney and then adopted the name "Uncle Don" for his broadcasts. The "little bastards" story, John Dunning admitted, "has become one of radio's classics, despite being totally unverified." "Carney swore in every interview that it never happened," Dunning wrote, "and once [he] suggested that the story had been started by one of his rivals."[7]

If such sabotage by a radio rival had been attempted, it was to no avail.

Although Uncle Don's popularity peaked in 1928 and 1929, the show stayed on the air until 1947. It was never dropped, as the legend claims, because the host broadcast an off-color remark.

Other books on radio agree that Uncle Don did not utter the alleged blooper. For example, Frank Buxton and Bill Owen reported in *The Big Broadcast, 1920–1950*: "The one story about Uncle Don that has been told the most never even happened." This book quoted the alleged remark as, "I guess that'll hold the little bastards."[8]

If nobody ever heard the remark on the air, and if radio historians say it never happened, why do so many people seem to believe the story? The simple reason is that they *have* heard Uncle Don cuss the kids. They, or someone they know, actually heard it on a blooper record or on a spin-off blooper film or book or television show. Even those who have heard it, however, differ somewhat on the words they believe were used: "little bastards," "little brats," hold them "for another week," "for tonight," and so forth. These ear-witnesses also differ on whether Uncle Don's show was canceled or was just temporarily suspended as a result of the cuss words.

What about these blooper recordings? Beginning in 1952, Kermit Schafer, a radio and television producer, founded an empire on publishing blooper records and books. For a time he also presented gold Bloopy awards, appeared in night clubs and on the lecture circuit, wrote blooper columns for newspapers and magazines, and had a Blooper Snooper Club, among other activities. His company, Blooper Enterprises, Inc., of South Miami, Florida, seems to have gone out of business; mail to that address is returned. The modern blooper television specials hosted by Ed McMahon and/or Dick Clark are his heirs, though I'm not aware that they have touched on the Bozo or Uncle Don story.

Some of Schafer's publications, or the blurbs about them, even imply that he coined the term *blooper,* but dictionaries disagree. In the *Dictionary of American Slang,* Harold Wentworth and Stuart Berg Flexner document the term *bloop* in the sense of unsuitable or unwanted sounds as a word used in the film, recording, and broadcasting industries since the mid-1920s. *Blooper* was also used to describe a long slow punch thrown in a boxing match since 1939 and to refer to a slow, high-arching pitch or a similarly ineffective slow-moving hit in baseball usage since 1945. Another term for a blunder, *bloomer,* was applied to President Truman in a 1949 citation, while the term a *political blooper* was credited to President Eisenhower in 1951. Probably at the root of all these variants, Wentworth and Flexner suggest, is the imitative sound of a recorded "bloop" being committed.[9] At any rate, Kermit Schafer's popularization of broadcast "bloopers," beginning in 1952, did give increased currency to the word, but Schafer clearly did not coin the term or even seriously modify its usual meanings.

In his heyday, about forty-five years ago, Schafer issued his blooper recordings and also published in his books what he claimed were "verbatim transcripts" of the Uncle Don blooper. I have transcribed three of these tapes and compared them to a published example of the supposed blooper.

Uncle Don, the beloved longtime children's radio show host, had a distinctive performance style available on a number of "nostalgia" recordings, so it is possible, without being an audio expert, to estimate which, if any, of the blooper recordings seems best to represent the same man making an embarrassing mistake.

Each of the three versions of the blooper recording I've checked purports to be from an original Uncle Don broadcast. The first one—Version A—with extremely dim and scratchy sound, first has the supposed voice of Uncle Don telling a child to look for a birthday present behind the piano; then the speaker offers a spoken farewell, "Well, goodnight kiddies." This is followed by a sentence that sounds more like "Ahh, that ought to hold the little *youngsters*" than like any off-color remark. This recording came from the Michigan State University Voice Library, where it is credited to a broadcast on KBYU-FM at Brigham Young University in Provo, Utah.[10] Unfortunately, KBYU had no information about the source of the recording, nor could anyone at the station even verify whether it had ever broadcast such a program.[11]

The second recording, Version B, is from a twelve-inch LP recording entitled *Pardon My Blooper*.[12] First a narrator introduces the blooper, then we hear a song of good night to listeners. The song varies the wording to "Good night little *friends*," and the spoken words continue, "We're off? I guess that'll hold the little bastards for tonight." The "little bastards" remark is somewhat muffled and may be spoken by another person. Significantly, it begins with a sentence urging children to "Tune in again tomorrow . . ." and it ends with the words "for tonight," which were not spoken on Version A.

Blooper Version C is from a cassette tape entitled *All Time Great Bloopers*.[13] First the same narrator speaks the same introduction as in Version B, then we hear a voice that first says, "And this is your Uncle Don saying good night," then sings a song that says, "Good night little *kids*" (rather than little *friends*). On both Version B and Version C a voice asks, "We're off?" but what follows on C is a slightly differently worded and crystal clear "little bastards" remark, as follows: "Good, well that oughta hold the little bastards." This voice sounds as if it were dubbed in by someone else, and it is probably not Uncle Don at all. Version C also lacks the sentence asking listeners to "Tune in tomorrow."

Comparison of these three recordings, each alleged to be genuine, proves, in fact, the opposite, that none of them could be the real thing. It is not even certain that Version A contains the word *bastards* at all, and it seems obvious that Versions B and C that do contain the naughty word cannot both be authentic, unless we are to believe that "Uncle Don" made the same mistake more than once in closely similar phraseology. Even if he did say the bad words once after a program, there's no proof whatever that the words were actually broadcast. But perhaps there's a hidden clue to these mysteries, and to Schafer's method, in the narrator's introduction to the anecdote that's repeated in both of the commercial blooper recordings and in the version from a blooper book that we may label as Version D. In all three sources the narrator's part reads identically, "*A legend* is Uncle Don's remark after he had closed his famous children's program." Did Schafer mean here that a real event had become a legend, or was he admitting that the supposed event was really nothing but a legend? It should also be noted that the "little bastards" remark is worded slightly differently from any of the recorded versions. Uncle Don is said to have said, "I guess that will hold the little bastards."[14]

A colleague of Don Carney named Warren Abbot did claim to have heard Uncle Don utter the famous remark, but insisted that the remark was not recorded. He also claimed that "Don Carney apologized later over the air that it was only said in jest," but we have absolutely no other published or recorded verification of these claims. For the record, here is what Warren Abbot wrote under the title "Uncle Don: Yes, He Did" in the newsletter *Hello Again* for May 1971:

> Yes, Uncle Don did say it and I was in the studio that night and heard him. It happened at station WOR in New York and I was visiting in the control room and was watching him thru the studio window. This is what he actually said, "That ought to hold the little bastards until tomorrow." This was never recorded, to my knowledge. WOR or WABC, where I was chief engineer at the time, was not equipped to record anything. There are so many versions of the story that it is ridiculous. I even have one on the "Bloopers" recordings put out some time ago, where the announcer says that is is [sic] alleged that he said it. You can rest assure [sic] that it was not Don's voice on the recording, as Don Carney (that was his real name) and I were personal friends and worked together on radio for several years.[15]

Now we must evaluate one individual's claim that does seem to validate the Uncle Don legend, at least in part. This is a letter I received from Ed Winston of Rockville, Maryland, who wrote out for me in 1986 his memory of being a guest on Uncle Don's radio show on January 18, 1944, when he was five years old.[16] Winston wrote that he tried to claim his right to sing a song on the air because it was his birthday. He chose to sing "Home on the Range," but, Winston wrote, he incorrectly told Uncle Don that it was his "four and one-half" birthday, and Uncle Don covered the mike and signaled for it to be cut off, then supposedly muttered, according to Ed Winston, "That'll fix the little bastard." Ed Winston said he remembered this clearly from forty-two years earlier at such a tender age, and he assured me that Uncle Don's career shortly "came to an abrupt end." As we know, however, Uncle Don stayed on the air for five more years. I submit that since Ed Winston was wrong on the second point, he may well have remembered wrongly the first point. Also, of course, that isn't the way the legend goes, and there's still no corroborating evidence that the remark was actually broadcast.

The legend about the radio host cussing the kids, in fact, was being told concerning at least one other broadcaster at about the same time that Uncle Don was enjoying his greatest success. It was probably a standard story told to illustrate the hazards of live radio in the early days. A dated example confirms this; it is a column published in the *Los Angeles Examiner* on May 31, 1928.[17] The column is called "Cook-Coos by Ted Cook," and it was written by a popular humorist of the time whose column was syndicated in many of the Hearst newspapers. This particular column, after a couple of short witticisms, under the subhead "Embarrassing Moments" featured a letter signed just "J.K." The letter began, "I am a radio station Big Brother. I tell the little kiddies bedtime stories about Peter Weasel and such."

One night, this Big Brother confessed, he had "a heavy date," and in his haste to sign off when the program ended, he muttered over an open mike, "THAT ought to put the little this-and-thats to sleep!" The letter concludes, "Imagine my embarrassment when I found I had forgotten to switch off the microphone!"

So "Bozo the Clown's Blooper," previously "Uncle Don's Blooper," which has been a broadcasting legend for at least sixty years, probably tells us more about every broadcaster's nightmare than it does about actual broadcasting history. In my opinion, the evidence suggests that this entire cycle of stories is totally unverified and probably based solely on hearsay. If I'm correct in these assumptions, then the blooper records must be recreations at best, or stagings at worst, of a completely legendary incident. But the repeated playing of the records by blooper fans seems to have reseeded the Uncle Don legend itself, as well as cross-pollinating it with the legend about Bozo's blooper, or the clown who cussed the kids.

Uncle Don on the World Wide Web

A thorough and well-documented examination of Uncle Don's career and the alleged "little bastards" incident appears on the World Wide Web at this URL: http://www.snopes.com/radiotv/radio/uncledon.htm. Barbara Mikkelson and David P. Mikkelson characterize the incident as "perhaps the greatest apocryphal 'manufactured memory' in American popular culture." The Mikkelsons evaluate several claims of on-air profanity by Uncle Don and others, finding all of them to be unlikely for one reason or another. They point out that "even articles contemporaneous with Don Carney's career describe the story as apocryphal," as does Carney's obituary in the *New York Times*. As for the blooper recordings, which have sometimes been called "re-creations," the Mikklesons assert, "One cannot 're-create' an event that never took place."

Notes

An earlier version of this chapter was presented at the annual meeting of the California Folklore Society in Sacramento, April 21–24, 1992.

1. Jan Harold Brunvand, *The Mexican Pet: More "New" Urban Legends and Some Old Favorites* (New York: W. W. Norton, 1986), 184–85.

2. *Bozo*, of course, has become a generic term for a loser. For example, in a United Press Syndicate column published on March 3, 1992, Robert C. Maynard, commenting on the unlikely candidacy of Patrick Buchanan, whom he described as "a living joke," concluded, "If Bozo the Clown were to run a similar campaign, he might get as many votes. Maybe more." Uncle Don is remembered by many as an American icon; in a letter to the editor of the *New York Times* published on February 24, 1992, Henry Morgan, himself an old-time radio legend, nominated Uncle Don for a commemorative postage stamp, along with the likes of Kate Smith, the Happiness Boys, and others. Morgan was responding to the release of an Elvis stamp.

3. Jan Harold Brunvand, "Bozo Blooper Is without Foundation," for release the week of June 3, 1991.

4. Snead & O'Malley, Inc., *Chicago Tribune*, Oct. 27, 1986.

5. Hal Morgan and Kerry Tucker, *Rumor!* (New York: Penguin Books, 1984), 92.

6. Jan Harold Brunvand, "This-and-Thats about Blooper Legend," for release the week of June 17, 1991. Part of this column is incorporated in this chapter.

7. John Dunning, *Tune in Yesterday* (Englewood Cliffs, N.J.: Prentice-Hall, 1976), 621–23.

8. Frank Buxton and Bill Owen, *The Big Broadcast, 1920–1950* (New York: Viking Press, 1972), 246–47.

9. Harold Wentworth and Stuart Berg Flexner, *Dictionary of American Slang* (New York: Crowell, 1967), 44.

10. Maurice A. Crane, director of the MSU Voice Library, sent me a tape of this alleged Uncle Don incident in 1986.

11. Walter B. Rudolph, station manager, KBYU-FM, to Jan Harold Brunvand. Possibly the person who sent the original tape to the MSU Voice Library was mistaken about the source; another possibility is that KBYU had broadcast part of a commercial blooper record in a program about old-time radio.

12. *Pardon My Blooper,* Jubilee LP PMB-1. A cassette tape, also entitled *Pardon My Blooper* (Nostalgia Lane NLC 5026), has the identical recording. Neither the record nor the tape is dated.

13. A copy of *All Time Great Bloopers,* an undated cassette tape, was sent to me by Roger A. Bower of Littleton, Colorado, in 1986.

14. *Your Slip Is Showing,* comp. Kermit Schafer (New York: Grayson, 1953), 36, my emphasis. Carl J. White of New York City informed me in 1986 that the identical quotation also appeared in Schaffer's book *Blunderful World of Bloopers* (New York: Bounty Books, 1953), 103.

15. I am grateful to Jeff Elliott of Sebastopol, California, for sending me a photocopy of this issue of *Hello Again* in July 1992.

16. I am grateful to Carl J. White for putting me in touch with Ed Winston via correspondence we had in 1986 and 1987. White and Winston are coin bank collectors and both own Uncle Don banks.

17. Ron Goulart of Weston, Connecticut, included the Buxton and Owen debunking of the Uncle Don anecdote in his book *The Assault on Childhood* (Los Angeles: Sherbourne Press, 1969), 148. Goulart informed me in a 1986 letter he had discovered the 1928 Ted Cook column, a copy of which he kindly sent to me.

7

"Lights Out!": A Faxlore Phenomenon

On Saturday, August 14, 1993, a small news item—about six column inches—debunking a "faxed warning about gang initiations" appeared in the *Memphis Commercial Appeal*. The headline was "Officials Deny Faxing Gang Warnings," and the subhead read, "Untrue Documents Promote Hysteria." The documents were described as "heavily faxed" and claimed to be official police bulletins. They stated that "this is the time of year for gang initiations" and the specific threat was described as follows: "One of the methods used this year will be for gang members to drive with their lights off at night. When you blink your lights or flash your high beams, they will follow you home and attempt to murder you."

At a press conference, officials of Memphis and of Shelby County, Tennessee, said that these "fax driven rumors criss-crossed the county this week," that police were inundated with calls about them, but that no local law enforcement office had sent out the faxes, nor was there any evidence for such gang initiation practices.

Although it is clear in this news item that the "Lights Out!" rumor was already in active circulation, this is the earliest example that I have located. The next time I encountered the rumor was in an e-mail message from Chicago sent on September 9, and the next *published* report I found was in a suburban Chicago newspaper on September 11, four weeks after the Memphis report. But soon the "Lights Out!" rumor emerged in many cities and became a matter of national concern. The flap continued through autumn 1993 and even into the new year in some places. The rumor was driven nationwide largely by facsimile transmissions.

I collected three kinds of information about "Lights Out!": copies of the warnings themselves, letters from people reporting on the warnings, and further news stories.

The September 9 e-mail report came from someone at the University of Chicago who forwarded a memo credited to the Security Division of the First National Bank of Chicago. The first line, "Beware," was followed by two exclamation points; the capsule description of the initiation ritual, said to be planned for "the Chicagoland area," was followed by the bare elements of an illustrative story: "To date, two families have already fallen victim to this senseless crime." The memo concluded with an appeal for readers to "inform your friends and family not to flash their car lights at anyone!" This early example of the "Lights Out!" warning displays typical features of all subsequent versions: It uses somewhat sensational language, repeats the basic rumor (naming it as "Lights Out!"), and provides a validating reference (i.e., the bank's memo format); it also localizes the supposed criminal plans, alludes in a vague way to specific cases, and recommends a course of action.

Later versions of the warning—usually computer-written and often laser-printed—tend to have more exclamation points (sometimes coming before as well as after sentences), to have more words or whole lines printed in all caps or underlined (sometimes double-underlined, and sometimes both all caps and underlined), and often have handwritten additions such as "THIS IS NOT A JOKE" or "BE CAREFUL OUT THERE" or "URGENT!" A few examples were hand-lettered and photocopied or were retyped on a company's letterhead (including one from the City of Detroit Water and Sewerage Department). Most examples that I collected had been faxed; others were e-mailed, sent by U.S. mail, or posted as hard copy memos on bulletin boards.

Dates on these warnings range from early September to early December 1993, most coming in mid-September. Other cities mentioned in them are St. Louis, Detroit, Dallas, Atlanta, Norfolk, New York, Baltimore, Los Angeles, Sacramento, and Honolulu. (Articles in the press added Toledo, Columbus, Pittsburgh, Philadelphia, Washington, D.C., Minneapolis, Little Rock, Tulsa, Houston, San Antonio, Lubbock, Denver, Salt Lake City, San Jose, and San Francisco. Letters from readers added cities in New Jersey, Florida, Missouri, and the Northwest. Clearly, the "Lights Out!" rumor was flying coast to coast.) The institutions circulating the fliers were banks, businesses, law firms, universities, military posts, hospitals, and day-care centers. Several of the warning notices contain routing stamps or slips indicating that they were circulated throughout a whole office or company.

About mid-September the warnings began to name "Grady Harn of the Sacramento Police Department" as the source of the information. Also,

the weekend of September 25 and 26 was pinpointed as "Blood [or Bloods']
Initiation Weekend" when, supposedly, gangs, including the notorious
Bloods' Gang, would hold their murderous initiation.[1] A few of the fliers,
although unsigned, made first-person reference to "my step father" or to
another relative who had "called me" with this important information.
Some fliers admitted that "this information has not been confirmed," but
most fliers advised readers not to flash their lights at anyone, just in case.
One person who sent me a printed flier added in a note, "One of our stu-
pidvisers [at work] stood up and read this to us." After the supposed
"Bloods' Weekend" came and went without incident, the fliers—now mi-
nus the dates—continued to appear, mostly in fax machines.

During the 1993 autumn semester at Indiana University at Kokomo a
folklore class studied the "Lights Out!" rumor. The instructor, Susanne
Ridlen, forwarded to me a packet of the twenty items resulting from the
project, and these display the variations in the story in one community and
of the means by which it was transmitted.

The Kokomo students documented transmission of "Lights Out!" via
word of mouth, telephone (including long-distance calls), on both commercial and CB radio, via e-mail, fax, printed memos (distributed in schools
and workplaces), and in publications. Several Kokomo versions combined
"Lights Out!" with other car-related legends, and some people claimed that
the gang initiations included the cutting off of feet or of ears. The specific

gangs involved were said to be the "Crypts" and the Bloods, groups said to be moving to Kokomo either south from Chicago or north from Indianapolis. Other versions claimed an origin of the information from Mississippi, where such initiations supposedly had occurred. Motorists would be targeted either if they blinked (or "flickered") their lights or if they honked at a gang car driving without lights. Police were said to be warning motorists—via gas station attendants—not to flash their lights. Despite this, two (or three) people, according to the Kokomo rumors, had already died.

According to a story in the *Kokomo Tribune* on October 14 ("Police Shoot Hole in Gang Initiation Rumor"), "Lights Out!" was a baseless rumor thought to have reached Kokomo from Jackson, Mississippi, on September 19 in a message broadcast on CB radio. Both Indiana and Illinois State Police Gang Crimes Units were quoted in the news story as denying the rumor. (Similarly, the Salt Lake City Police Department on September 24 issued a news release calling the "Lights Out!" story "UNFOUNDED . . . UNSUBSTANTIATED AND WITHOUT MERIT." Many police departments across the nation issued similar denials.)

The letters (including e-mail, U.S. mail, and faxed correspondence) that I received from readers of my books commenting on the "Lights Out!" rumor add to the sketchy story a few more details that must have circulated orally, since they do not appear in the printed fliers. These letters all came from people who knew or suspected that the story was false. Most letters reported a chain of informal communication of the story—i.e., a co-worker whose girlfriend, a nurse, had heard about someone working on the other shift at the hospital or at a different hospital who had treated victims of the ritual. The initiations, according to some writers, "were supposed to test the mental toughness" of gang recruits. Sometimes the gang recruits would trace the offending cars via their license plates. The police were not publicizing the crimes, according to rumors, in order to lull gangs into a false sense of security in the hope that they could be caught in the act. A letter from Pennsylvania reported a variation in the story: "Cars full of Satan worshippers [were] driving around without their headlights." The writer had overheard his secretary warning her sister about the threat, and she had heard it from the driver of her van pool, who heard it from a friend who saw a sign warning people about this in a store window.

A Seattle reader in a letter dated September 24 (the Friday before "Bloods' Weekend") mentioned that on Thursday the twenty-third the flier appeared at her workplace, and "to my distress, every one of my twelve co-workers fell for it . . . despite my insistence that it couldn't possibly be true." Meanwhile in Salt Lake City in my own department at the university, here's what happened—or *nearly* happened—on the same days. On the twenty-third, a reader from Fort Lauderdale, Florida, faxed me a letter saying he was also faxing a copy of a memo that he suspected was based on a rumor; page two of the fax transmission was the "Lights Out!" warning itself, typed on the letterhead of a Florida Jewish community center. The secretary of my department pulled page one of the message and put it into my mailbox without reading it beyond the address. Page two—the warning memo—however, she read with alarm, and then took it with her on Friday to a full departmental meeting; or, not quite a full meeting, since I, as a partial retiree, had decided to skip town that afternoon. The secretary intended to read the notice to the assembled faculty to alert them not to flash their lights when driving home, but she was dissuaded from doing so by my colleague, Margaret Brady. Brady convinced her that the warning was just "one of those legends that people are always sending Jan." Our secretary still felt the story might be true, since her own daughter had also heard about it in Salt Lake City a few days earlier.

The news stories about "Lights Out!" may be taken in chronological order, insofar as dates can be determined from the clippings.

As mentioned above, the first clipping I have is from the *Memphis Commercial Appeal* of August 14. The second is from the *Daily Southtown*, a suburban Chicago paper, on September 11 ("Police Say Area Story of Gang Rite Is Hoax"). The lead reads, "It's a great story—just like most so-called 'urban legends.'" Besides describing the same "anonymous handbills," the author of this news story quotes police officials who deny it and adds that it sounds like something that might happen "in the frozen wastelands of Russia." The author also suggests the possibility of copycat crimes and concludes with the threat of prosecution against spreaders of the tale. Every facet of this fairly obscure little news item turns out to be typical of the stories in most papers.

Four days later, on September 15, Mary Schmich, a *Chicago Tribune* columnist, wrote about the rumor, calling it "urban faxlore." Schmich identified the Black Gangster Disciple Nation as the Chicago street gang blamed for the outrage, but she emphasized that the rumor was unsubstantiated and strongly denied by Chicago police. Schmich listed radio stations, colleges, hospitals, churches, and video stores as places where the warning had appeared. Because she had phoned me to discuss the rumor, Schmich was able to cite the earlier Memphis example of the story and also to compare "Lights Out!" to other urban lore about crime and violence.

(Schmich said that she was calling me at the suggestion of the folklorist Alan Dundes, who had not yet heard about the warnings but thought that I might have.)

At this point my phone began ringing off the hook, and I was preparing to leave on an extended trip, so I put a message on my answering machine saying, in effect, "No interviews, please." I decided to stay out of the spotlight and see what reporters might make of the rumor on their own or with the help of other folklorists whom they might contact.

Shortly after taking this vow of silence I started to see results. On September 18, two papers ran stories—the Little Rock *Arkansas Democrat-Gazette* ("Gang Initiation Rumor Baseless, LR Police Say") and the *San Jose Mercury News* ("Cops Try to Arrest Rumor of Gang Rite"). The enterprising Arkansas reporter located three of my books and compared "Lights Out!" to other urban lore, including an earlier local outbreak of "The Mutilated Boy" legend. The even more enterprising San Jose reporter managed to get a Memphis police spokesman and Alan Dundes on the phone. From Tennessee she learned that the story was known in Knoxville and Chattanooga as well; from Dundes (who now *had* heard the story and had a comment ready for it) she picked up the term *faxlore* and also the ideas that a fear of teenagers—especially gang members—was reflected in the story and that it might be inspired by acts of violence against tourists in Florida. In an unusual twist, the *Mercury News* withheld details of the warnings, fearing copycat crimes. This article also referred to the speed with which the rumor had blanketed Silicon Valley, where thousands of people are linked to e-mail and to computer bulletin boards.

In Salt Lake City (where I also dodged the press) another gang rumor was flying—that gangs were planning to rape a cheerleader as part of an initiation. Though police and school authorities denied the rumor, a September 18 article in the *Deseret News* reported widespread concern among students and parents, especially on the more affluent east side of the Salt Lake Valley. One television station was criticized for publicizing the story, even though the broadcast had made it clear that the rumors were unconfirmed.

Meanwhile, back in Chicago, on September 21, the student newspaper of the University of Illinois branch there was debunking the story again. One version of the warning photocopied on a state police letterhead was described as having a typeface that did not match the rest of the letterhead, a clue to its unreliability.

On September 22, the *Houston Post,* the *Houston Chronicle,* and the *Toledo Blade* ran articles on the rumor. The *Post* article ("Scary Gang

Rumor Has Its Fax All Wrong") was pretty standard, except for calling the warning "an electronic chain letter" and "an urban *myth*" (maybe I should have answered the phone after all). The *Chronicle* article ("HPD Tries to Stop Rumor about Gang Rites") had a novel touch—a color photograph of a grinning police chief holding up one of the fliers; the "Dragnet"-inspired caption read, "Just a phony fax, ma'am." The chief was quoted as saying, "I'd rather deal with the gangs than talk to any more hysterical people on the phone."

A sidelight of the Texas circulation of the rumor was revealed in a September 23 column in the *San Antonio Express-News*. Columnist Roddy Stinson, who a week earlier had dubbed his own city "the wide-eyed booby capital of the nation" for panicking over the "Lights Out!" urban legend (Stinson's term), now gave the booby prize to Houston, where the story had circulated earlier.

During "Bloods' Weekend" itself—September 25 and 26—the newspaper stories increased: I have clippings from papers in central New Jersey, San Francisco, Los Angeles, Salt Lake City, Minneapolis, and Pittsburgh. The New Jersey story mentions dozens of calls to police from fearful people, spurred by warnings traced to the Johnson & Johnson headquarters in New Brunswick and also circulated in area colleges, high schools, and in a large insurance company. The San Francisco article ("Rumors Fly on Computer Networks") also names hospitals as hotbeds of the story, but emphasizes computer rather than faxed transmission. Alan Dundes is quoted anew, this time with a different slant on the story. "There is an element of the car, which represents power, mobility, and sex," the Berkeley professor comments, adding that the rumor was probably fueled by recent shootings of foreign tourists in Florida.

The *Los Angeles Times* article of September 24 is the first publication to mention the mysterious Grady Harn of the Sacramento Police Department, who is named on many fliers; the *Times* checked with Sacramento and found that no one of that name serves on the police force there. Another innovation in the *Times* story is an unattributed claim that "the warnings are the work of a computer hacker who used facsimile telephone numbers to disseminate the messages." The fliers are described as "clumsily worded," which suggests, perhaps, poor social or communicative skills of the assumed hacker. Finally, the *Los Angeles Times* mentions that these phony warnings are "the latest examples of what sociologists call an urban myth." Although Los Angeles gang investigators are quoted in the story, the reporters who wrote the piece apparently did not attempt to interview any gang members themselves.

Both Salt Lake City newspapers now covered the story, each relating it to the earlier rumors about gang intentions to rape cheerleaders. One county sheriff in Utah said he had not been able to get off the phone for more than thirty seconds at a time between fielding calls about "Lights Out!" from citizens and from the press. In a technically garbled explanation of how the story may have started, a police official suggested that "the hoax note was faxed into a billboard computer system."

Probably "Bloods' Weekend" was when the Associated Press circulated an article debunking "Lights Out!" that was widely reprinted and quoted. (I do not have a dated copy of the AP release.) The AP story quoted Professors Ralph Rosnow and Gary Fine, co-authors of a book on rumor and gossip. Fine voiced the opinion that "*gang* in this particular rumor is a code word for poor, young black men."

In the Minneapolis news article of September 25 the suspected villain in the case was again described as a "hacker," but the paper associated "hacking" with *faxing* messages rather than with using computerized e-mail or a computer bulletin board. Articles published in Pittsburgh on September 25 and 27 added little to the picture except for speculating that the rumor came from "an unidentified originator in California."

In an interesting juxtaposition, the *Baltimore Sun* on September 27 ran a long story debunking the "Blue Star Acid" rumor that had cropped up there again recently with a sidebar story on "Lights Out!" The Baltimore version was that members of "the Los Angeles–based gang the Bloods were randomly shooting motorists as part of a nationwide initiation campaign."

At last the rumor was mentioned in the national press. In the September 27 issue of *U.S. News and World Report,* John Leo mentioned "Lights Out!" in passing in his column as "a new bit of urban folklore." The column was mostly devoted to comments on the shootings of foreign tourists in Florida. *Newsweek,* in a brief notice headlined "Big Fax Attack," mentioned Houston, Los Angeles, and Atlanta as sites of the rumor. In a syndicated column of September 29, William Raspberry of the *Washington Post* mentioned the rumor, although he indicated that just "people" (gangs were not mentioned) were driving with their lights off, hoping to entice victims to flash their headlights at them and thus become targets for violence.

The last weekend of September the magazine section of the *Dallas Observer* ran a detailed account entitled "Anatomy of a Rumor: How the Gang-Initiation Story Terrified Dallas." The author called it "something of a minor urban myth in several cities," and he did a creditable job of tracking local versions back to individuals who had picked it up while traveling, on the phone, via fax, and so forth. According to the reporter, one Dallas businessman said he was handed the warning "when he boarded an American Airlines return flight from Tampa."

From October to mid-December only a few further news stories appeared; the cities that were late to catch the rumor were Denver, Philadelphia, Allentown, Columbus, and Lubbock. With Lubbock, on December 14, my clipping file bottoms out. The Denver story was mainly about rumors of gang rapes at a mall, with "Lights Out!" mentioned only in passing. The *Philadelphia Inquirer* story was unrestrained in calling the rumor "a big, fat, stinking, Pinocchio-nose kind of lie" but adding, "and everybody believes it." Ralph Rosnow, who teaches at Temple University, was again quoted. The *Allentown Morning Call* story mentioned that the rumor had been retyped on Thomas Jefferson University security letterhead; both Professor Patricia Turner of the University of California at Davis and Alan Dundes were quoted in this story, evidently from original interviews by the Allentown writer. Turner made some interesting observations about the theme of the "demonized outsider" threatening a good samaritan on the road. Dundes repeated some of his earlier remarks, but also touched on the good samaritan theme.

In Columbus "Lights Out!" got only a short paragraph in a story that was primarily about another rumor—that groups are trying to raise funds to buy firearms for the homeless. Similarly, in Lubbock "Lights Out!" rated only a short mention in a full-page feature story about "those pesky rumors." The only unusual touch here was the remark of a local police sergeant about how he deals with the panicky public in such cases; he said, "I just try to sound authoritative and reassuring." By mid-December, then, the story was effectively dead in the nation's media, although a few individuals continued to write me letters about it.

Unexpectedly, "Lights Out!" emerged again in the national media in a fictional context as part of the new CBS-TV police drama "Traps" in which George C. Scott played Joe Trapcheck, a former homicide investigator who comes out of retirement to serve as a consultant in his old department. In the premiere episode, aired on Thursday, March 31, 1994, Traps has joined the "Headlight Killer Taskforce," which is working to solve a series of shootings related to people giving a "courtesy blink" to a car driving with its headlights out. Curiously, the episode also included another piece of urban folklore, where a photocopy machine is used to fool a suspect into revealing needed information; he is told that he's actually hooked up to a new type of polygraph.[2]

Reviewing the "Lights Out!" phenomenon, briefly, as *folklore*, it seems evident that although modern technology and communications facilitated the rapid dissemination of the rumor over an extremely broad area, the variations that developed were similar to those typically caused by oral transmission alone. Details were added and altered; the story was localized; authorities were invoked to support the story; supposed actual cases were cited; and so on. "Lights Out!" was similar to other recent rumors and legends, including "Blue Star Acid" (also fax and photocopy delivered), "The Assailant in the Backseat" and other car horror stories, "The Attempted Abduction" and other mall crime stories, and the like. *Faxlore* is a catchy term, but it is not clear that it should imply any essentially different kind of modern tradition.

Despite the sensational tone of the warnings, their informal channels of distribution, their poor English usage, and their lack of any specific verification, the message was taken to heart by many Americans. Thousands of people must have duplicated and distributed the fliers for them to have penetrated so widely. I believe the folklorists and sociologists who commented on "Lights Out!" were right in identifying themes like teenage and gang crimes, racism, urban problems, and attacks on foreign motorists as topics underlying the "Lights Out!" hysteria. (I'm not sure, however, where the sex, mentioned by Alan Dundes, comes in.) A well-known gang name, the Bloods, lent itself perfectly to intensifying the hysteria, as did another name, the Cryps (although misunderstood as "Crypts"). In Chicago a gang with the very word *Black* in its name—the Black Gangster Disciple Nation—was fed into this same racial fear, and in Kokomo the idea that the warning had come from Mississippi implies the same stereotype.

Press reports reveal other views of the rumor flap. Journalists tended to confuse terms like *myth, rumor, legend, chain letter,* and *hoax,* as well as to ignore the technical differences between fax, e-mail, and computer bulletin boards or computer newsgroups. Several newspapers mentioned copycat crimes, though none of the papers ever reported any actual "Lights Out!" crimes *or* copycats. In hope of determining the precise origin of the rumor—something folklorists seldom seek or find—journalists focused upon (indeed, may have invented) the hoaxing hacker character, presumably someone from California. No evidence for the existence of such a hoaxer was ever presented. An idea proposed by both law enforcement and newspaper sources is that the originator of the story should be found and prosecuted. Despite having this serious plan in mind, newspapers felt free to pun shamelessly in the wording of their stories and headlines: "just the fax," "a fax attack," "has its fax all wrong," "guns down the rumor," and others.

One persistent fear that both the general public and newspapers responded to was the idea of dangerous gang activity entering one's own community from some outside source, usually a nearby larger city that is thought to be awash with gang crimes. It still amazes me (as mentioned above) that no investigative reporter seems to have bothered to have contacted any local gang members to ask about initiation rituals in general and about "Lights Out!" or other auto-related customs in particular.

Finally, I reemphasize one theme of the warnings pointed out in only a single news article among the reports I collected. This is the good samaritan theme mentioned by Turner and Dundes. Flashing one's headlights at a car driving toward you at night without its lights on is a simple, common act of courtesy and safety. It's something most drivers have been taught to do, either by a driver's education teacher or simply by customary example from other drivers. (I'll be so bold as to call this a folk custom.) Some of the warning fliers allude to this custom by referring to it as "a courtesy flash." (I'll concede, however, that light flashing may also imply negative criticism in the minds of some drivers who flash or are flashed at.) Another strong message of "Lights Out!" then, is that something you, as a driver, have learned to do as a good and socially useful thing may, in this crime-ridden modern world, become an act of aggression toward another driver who represents an outsider to your standards of behavior—perhaps a younger person of a different race who belongs to a street gang—and this outsider will go so far as to murder you for daring to be courteous. In other words, the "Lights Out!" rumor says, "Forget about being a courteous driver any more, don't get involved, don't flash your lights, because IT MIGHT KILL YOU!!!"

Afterword

In a letter to the *Skeptical Inquirer* published in the July–August 1995 issue on page 61, Al Christians of Lake Oswego, Oregon, commented:

> A true incident may have inspired the rumors and faxlore described in your "Lights Out!" story. Around the beginning of 1993, a driver in Stockton, California, signaled to the driver of a lightless vehicle in the customary fashion. An occupant of the unlit car responded with gunfire and killed a schoolteacher in the back seat of the other vehicle. The story received prominent coverage in the region's media.

My response, published in the same journal, was this:

I learned about the Stockton, California, incident when my article was in press; after examining news stories, I concluded that it had no direct connection to the "Lights Out!" warnings. On September 18, 1992, a driver there used a hand signal to alert a driver behind him at a stoplight that his headlights were out. The driver of this second car, taking this as a sign of disrespect, shot at the first car, killing Kelly Freed, 29, a passenger, who was a longtime popular employee of a local school system, although not a teacher. In August 1993, at the sentencing, the prosecutor suggested that the convicted killer had acted "to save face with his fellow gang members"; however, the defense attorney denied that his client belonged to a gang. Never was a gang initiation mentioned in connection with this tragic case, and in February 1995, in articles about efforts to establish a Kelly Freed Teen Center in Stockton, no reference was made to gangs.

The differences in details between this actual crime and the supposed planned attacks described in the warnings, plus the fact that never in any news stories about the warnings—nor in any of the faxed warnings themselves—was the Stockton case mentioned, all suggest that the "Lights Out!" story developed independently.

Update: The Return of "Lights Out!"

Suddenly in November 1998 the "Lights Out!" rumor returned, circulating widely (and wildly!) on the Internet and in the form of faxes and fliers. This time there was no mention of officer Grady Harn, but in some versions the information was credited to "a police officer who works with the DARE program at the elementary school." Cities mentioned in these bogus warnings where the gang initiations were supposedly occurring included Los Angeles, California; Washington, D.C.; Boston, Massachusetts; Santa Fe and Albuquerque, New Mexico; Cleveland, Ohio; Midland, Texas; Ogden, Utah; and Vancouver, British Columbia.

So persistent did the rumors become over the holiday season that many police departments and newspapers issued denials. Among the published articles were these: "School Falls Victim to Urban Folklore" in the *Salt Lake City Deseret News* (December 21, 1998), "Fake Police Warning Is Faxed, E-mailed to Delaware" in the *Wilmington News Journal* (December 31, 1998), "Urban Legends Find Life on the Net" in the *Kansas City Star* (January 1, 1999), and "Police Say Gang Rumors Baseless" in the *St. Petersburg (Fla.) Times* (January 12, 1999). Despite such genuine warnings against the bogus warnings, the May 1999 issue of *Highways,* the official publication of the Good Sam Club carried a terse account of the mythical flashing-headlight gangsters in its "Street Smart" feature.

Notes

The first version of this essay was presented at the annual meeting of the California Folklore Society at the University of California at Davis, April 22–24, 1994. It was revised and published in essentially the same form as presented here in *Skeptical Inquirer,* March–April 1995, 32–37.

1. The Folklorist Ed Kahn pointed out to me the similarity to the much-feared Michelangelo computer virus supposedly set to strike DOS-based machines worldwide on March 6 (the Renaissance master's birthdate), 1992. Like the DataCrime (or Friday the 13th) virus of 1989, this threat proved to be much less destructive than predicted.

2. See Jan Harold Brunvand, *The Baby Train and Other Lusty Urban Legends* (New York: W. W. Norton), 139–45.

8

A Blast Heard 'round the World

The case of the roach in the toilet in Israel shows how easily gullible people will believe urban legends and how rapidly such stories spread, even internationally, with the aid of the mass media. The suckers who fell for "The Exploding Toilet" story during the summer and early autumn of 1988 were no less than two international news services and countless newspapers and broadcasters. In only a few hours a version of the story spread from the Middle East to the United States and other countries. Within days, and continuing for a few weeks, variations of the story appeared on computer networks and circulated among military personnel. A tabloid picked up the story and elaborated it from a skeletal news item to a more dramatic piece. Yet, even while professional news persons were circulating the story, a number of lay persons quickly realized that this was merely an old legend in a new guise. Their responses to the story, conveyed to me in letters and telephone calls, some in response to my books and newspaper columns, were the major source of data for this chapter.

The media version of "The Exploding Toilet" legend appeared first in the *Jerusalem Post* on Thursday, August 25, 1988, as the assumed reliable report of an event that had occurred in Tel Aviv one week earlier.[1] The five-paragraph story bylined "Michael Rotem" was headlined "Battle with Cockroach Ended in Hospital." According to the *Post* story, an unidentified housewife launched two comical mishaps involving her husband when she stepped on a cockroach, "threw it in the toilet," and "sprayed it with a whole can of insecticide" without flushing afterward. Her husband, according to the news story, the next to use the toilet, dropped in a smoldering cigarette butt; this "ignited the insecticide fumes," causing an explosion beneath him, which seriously burned what the *Post* referred to as "his sensitive parts." An ambulance was called, and when the paramedics heard how the man had become injured, "they laughed uncontrollably" and dropped the stretcher they were carrying him on down the steps of his house, causing further injuries; these were specified as "two broken ribs and a broken pelvis."

The *Post* story named the suburb where the couple lived and the hospital where the husband was taken. Both United Press International and Reuter's Service circulated the story on their news wires, hedging their reports somewhat in this fashion: "The incident, reported Thursday by *The Jerusalem Post,* occurred last week" (UPI), and *"The Jerusalem Post* reported yesterday" (Reuters). True enough, the paper *had* reported the story.

Newspapers around the world wasted no time printing the exploding toilet story. The *Seattle Times* even got the UPI version into its late Thursday edition with the headline "The Roach Wasn't the Only Casualty." After that, the lid was off.

As background, here is a summary of what is known about the traditional "Exploding Toilet" legend:

1. Other variations involve hair spray, perfume, alcohol, paint thinner, kerosene, or gasoline dumped in a toilet and ignited.

2. Sometimes the story begins with a motorcycle tipping over and spilling gasoline or with the wife painting a room and improperly disposing of paint thinner.

3. Invariably, this (and other "hilarious accident" legends) end with dropping the stretcher and adding to the man's injuries.

4. The urban legend about "The Exploding Toilet" has a prototypical rural form—a joke, not a belief tale—about an outhouse explosion.

Among many newspapers running the Israeli toilet story on Friday, August 16, 1988, were the *Boston Globe* ("In a Cockroach War, Unplanned Casualty"), the *Albany Times Union* ("Roach Gets Fiery Revenge"), the *Houston Post* ("Husband Pays for Wife's War with Roach"), the *Los Angeles Times* ("Next Time, Dear, Why Not Just Flush the Toilet?"), the *San Diego Tribune* ("Woman Bugged by Roach, but Spouse Suffers"), and the Phoenix *Arizona Republic* ("Fire in the Bowl! Bug-Bomb Backfires, Rescuers Crack Up").

Among other newspapers that employed punning headlines was the *Detroit News,* also in its Friday edition. This paper put the bogus story with the heading "Victim Is Butt of Bad Joke" on page one, directly adjoining a feature about the anniversary of Martin Luther King's March on Washington.

Much the same thing was doubtless going on in other countries. *The Dominion* of Wellington, New Zealand, for example, also carried the

Reuter's story on Friday, and I have clippings from several Australian and Canadian papers that ran the story. My data, however, is more complete for the United States than for anywhere else.

The reaction to the news reports was immediate. American readers and listeners, beginning early Friday, flooded newspapers and radio stations with calls identifying this as merely a new version of a familiar legend. Some of these people had read about the story in the preface to *The Mexican Pet* in which I quoted both an American and an English version.[2] (Another English version appears in Paul Smith's *The Book of Nasty Legends*: Here a wife had cleaned a toilet bowl with turpentine, mistaking the container for one holding bleach.[3])

Other people who contacted me had remembered my syndicated newspaper column that mentioned the story, which had been released to about thirty papers the week of April 27, 1987. But many of the callers had simply heard the exploding toilet story told orally before, and so they strongly doubted it when they saw it reported as fact in the newspaper.

Rex Springston, a writer for the *Richmond News Leader,* knew at once Friday that it was a legend when he heard the Tel Aviv roach story on National Public Radio's "Morning Edition" while he was driving to work. Springston quickly located both wire service reports at his office and then telephoned me to say he was challenging UPI and Reuter's on the stories. When he called a UPI foreign editor in Washington, Springston told me, the editor said that despite several calls from journalists disputing the story, the editor did not regard it as apocryphal because he had "learned of an insurance industry representative who had seen the story in an industry publication." Presumably, then, he said, "the incident did happen, but in the U.S. not Israel." Springston, however, went ahead and debunked the story in his paper's Sunday edition under the headline "Old Exploding Toilet Story Has News Faces Flushed."

Karen Swedin, a feature writer for the *Salt Lake City Deseret News* (which carried my column), pulled the Reuter's story from the news wire on Thursday, recognized it as an urban legend, and sent the item to me after making sure her paper would not run it. Other reporters also checked their sources, and many more of them called me from early Friday morning on through the weekend.

Richard Cheney in Los Angeles heard the story Friday on a local radio station. He called the station to say that he knew from my writings that "The Exploding Toilet" was a legend. Next Cheney called me, holding the telephone near his radio. While we chatted, a reporter for the LA station came on the air, retracted the story, and quoted both of us. A reader in San Francisco wrote to say that a television anchor on a local station while retracting the earlier story held up a copy of *The Mexican Pet* saying he had received numerous calls from viewers referring him to this book.

Pressed for verification, Reuter's at first stonewalled on the report; a spokesman for that agency in London was quoted in wire news stories Saturday saying, "The story is still genuine until we hear otherwise. There will be no follow-up until Saturday night after the Sabbath." The *Jerusalem Post* news editor, Yoram Kessel, contacted by foreign reporters Saturday, said, "It's the Sabbath. The country closes down. . . . There's no way to check it." By midday Saturday, however, both news services had issued statements saying that the incident was unverified; the UPI version mentioned that "essentially the same story, in a U.S. setting, appears in a book about urban myths."

Early the following week the *Jerusalem Post* officially retracted the story, and the wire services that had originally distributed it quoted the newspaper's statement as follows: "A good tale got so tangled in the telling that it assumed a newsworthiness it should never have had." The Tel Aviv bureau chief was quoted as saying that the reporter who wrote the original story had "heard the story secondhand from an insurance agent and failed to check it." The newspaper, it was reported, "had not yet decided whether to take disciplinary action" against the reporter.

Many newspapers that published the original accident story prominently on Friday printed a fairly innocuous retraction on Saturday or later. Some took the opportunity to indulge themselves in further punning headlines, along the lines of "Roach Tale Turns Out to Be Crawling with Errors, So Paper Steps on It" and "Paper Finds a Bug in Tale of a Roach." The *Philadelphia Inquirer* gave the original report five inches at the top of its "Scene" column (headlined "Bottom Up"), but used merely one inch of column space the next day for "Clearing the Record." The paper, however, also published a letter to the editor on September 19 in which a reader cited two of my books to show that such stories are often apocryphal. A similar letter was published a week earlier in the *New Castle (Penn.) News,* which had run the original cockroach story complete with a cartoon of a giant roach, but had never retracted it.

The original quasi-news story also made its way into computer networks and into a U.S. Navy safety bulletin, both of which must have brought the story to countless other readers. Navy personnel stationed on both coasts sent me the military reprint of the story, which was part of a longer message composed of accounts of other accidents, this particular one being credited to the Naval Safety Center in Norfolk, Virginia, which had secured the item from "a British exchange officer who had clipped it out of the *Daily Telegraph* he receives from home." These unclassified safety messages are transmitted to all navy ships and shore stations around the world.

The active oral circulation of "The Exploding Toilet" as an urban legend, even while a supposed authentic version from Israel was appearing in the news media, led to some odd coincidences. For example, a reader in Winnipeg, Manitoba, wrote to me in early September relating a standard version of the older legend that he had heard five years earlier; but now some friends were claiming they had recently heard the same story on a news program, which he at first could not positively identify. I had no sooner written back to the Winnipeg reader explaining things than he mailed me the debunking story clipped from his local newspaper, adding the comment, "I found my legend!"

Even more coincidental, a columnist in the *Bloomington (Ind.) Herald-Telephone*,[4] without knowing of the Israeli incident, had included a standard version of the old legend in his column for Sunday, August 28, which a reader of my column in Bloomington immediately clipped and sent to me. The Bloomington columnist claimed the story dated to the time when "Bloomington's ambulance service was in its infancy," but he must have had second thoughts about this when the paper received *my* columns for the weeks of September 19 and November 7 in which I debunked the Israeli story and touched on some of the material included in the present chapter.

Several newspaper editorial writers took a retrospective look at the whole episode of the unverified story out of Jerusalem getting such extensive press coverage. For example, David Bishop, ombudsman of the *Ann Arbor (Mich.) News* wrote in an early September column: "The story was harmless, but it does provide an interesting example of journalism's vulnerability." His own paper had not run the story, he said, because a news editor felt that "there was something fishy about this one." On September 6, John Brown, ombudsman of the *Edmonton (Alberta) Journal,* devoted his column to disentangling the various lines of transmission for the story and explaining as best he could why his own paper had fallen for it. Brown stated that nobody in the news pipeline "could be faulted for accepting the news in good faith," and he pointed out that "the news business has to operate on a good deal of trust. Time and expense dictate that." Brown said he felt that had the story supposedly happened in Edmonton, "it probably would not have passed The *Journal*'s system of checks." No one at the *Journal,* incidentally, had questioned the story, and the original piece appeared with the cheerful headline, "Oi Veh, What a Day!" on August 26. The paper did not get around to running the retraction from Reuter's until September 1.

Two Los Angeles newspapers published columns that reflected on the media's appetite for urban legends. The *Los Angeles Herald-Examiner* ran an unsigned editorial on September 11 comparing "The Exploding Toilet" story from Israel to other such legends and referring to "the dog days of summer [which are] traditionally . . . the silly season for journalists." The editorial recommended that journalists should "keep handy a few copies of the classic urban-legend compilations by Jan Harold Brunvand." At about the same date in September, Jack Smith of the *Los Angeles Times* headlined a column "All the News that Fits the Gullibility Gap," inspired by the *Times* itself falling for the story. Smith said of his fellow journalists that the episode showed "how much we love a good story, even if it isn't true," and he went on to discuss other "urban folk tales"—their subjects, their supposed verification by storytellers, and their nature as being improbable, yet "theoretically possible."

Most of the media audience for this much-published version of "The Exploding Toilet," however, probably never saw these editorial musings about the nature of urban legends. Instead, people simply read (or heard) about the Israeli incident and maybe its debunking and then perhaps retold the story to others. So variations cropped up as the published versions were repeated in oral tradition. A radio news broadcaster in Mesa, Arizona, for example, allegedly said that the incident had involved an *Iranian* woman whose husband broke his *collar bone* in the second accident. A man in San Diego wrote to say that he had heard the news report on the radio; he understood that the woman had returned to the toilet one hour after dropping in the roach to find the insect still alive, that she had emptied a full can (but not a *spray* can) of insecticide into the toilet, and that she closed the lid; the supposed result of her husband's dropping in a cigarette was "a flameball," and because of his encounter with the paramedics, the man broke his arm. This correspondent also told me that he understood the original Israeli source had been "a travelling insurance salesman," which seems to echo the old traveling salesman joke cycle.

When the story reached the tabloids there was a further revision. The *Weekly World News* version on September 19 provided the injured man with a name, "Saul Frankel," and later referred to him as "sore bottom Saul" and "sorry Saul." The headline on the tabloid story was "Man Bowled Over by Exploding Potty . . . Then Paramedics Laughed So Hard They Dropped Him on the Stairs!" a summary worthy of the folklorist's

Type Index. This tabloid story also quoted the man's supposed comment about the incident: "Next time I hope she just stomps the roach," which may echo the *Los Angeles Times* headline for the story and thus indicate the tabloid's source. As late as October 4, another tabloid, *The Sun,* was still carrying the Israeli item in a bylined story by one of its "writers" and with a credit to the *Jerusalem Post,* but no hint of that paper's subsequent retraction. In the February 1989 issue of *Penthouse* the original story was quoted from the *Boston Globe* with the comment, "Great balls of fire!"

To return to the background versions in older folk stories: One reader of my first column on "The Blast Heard 'round the World" (released September 19), James E. Myers of Springfield, Illinois, wrote to say that he was reminded of what he called "the very ancient farm story" about grandpa dropping his pipe into the outhouse hole beneath him where earlier his son had dumped gasoline. Myers recalled that the old man was picked up where he had been blown by the explosion some fifty feet away and was heard to remark that it was a good thing he had not let *that* one go in the house. This, of course, is one typical form of the old rural gag that preceded "The Exploding Toilet" as an urban legend.

Charles Wukasch of Austin, Texas, had written me a year earlier that the way *he* heard it, a hillbilly had brought a hand grenade home from the army to show the folks, and he pulled the pin and tossed it under the outhouse. Unfortunately, Grandpa was in the outhouse; Grandpa's punchline was the same in this Texas version as the one from Illinois. Another version from Texas had been sent to me years ago by Professor Kenneth W. Davis of Texas Tech University. He had heard it told about a small town

Weekly World News, September 19, 1987.

some forty miles northeast of Austin and concerning a young wife hoping to dispose of her old husband by pouring gasoline into the privy that he habitually used each morning while smoking his pipe. The man was blown some fifteen feet away and remarked later to his drinking buddies in a local bar that he was "as bare-assed all over as ary baby ever born."

When I heard this rural exploding-outhouse prototype for "The Exploding Toilet" told in Utah, in 1982, the event was associated with the town of Manti and a named individual about whom a whole cycle of local character anecdotes circulated. In the Manti version, his wife had poured turpentine down the outhouse after cleaning paintbrushes, and the man dropped his lit cigar butt down the hole, setting off an explosion. The man's comment—and the story's punchline—was, "It must have been something I et."

The age of these outhouse versions of the legend is suggested by a fragile yellowed clipping of a newspaper column that a woman from Liverpool, New York, sent me in 1991; she wrote that she had clipped it "over 50 years ago." The column is undated, but a reference in it to the current president, Franklin D. Roosevelt, proves it must have been published sometime between 1933 and 1945. Under the headline "The Tale of a 'Johnny' That Blew Up," the article tells about a wife who poured some naphtha left over from spring housecleaning down a hole in the family outhouse. Her husband, while using the privy, lit his pipe and tossed the match down the same hole. The resulting explosion blew the man fifty feet away and into a manure pile. Neighbors rescued him and asked how the accident happened. "I dunno," he replied, "It musta been something I et." When I quoted this version in a column written in February 1991, a reader from Auburn, New York, wrote, "I was born in 1925 and I heard that story as a small tyke. My mom told it as a hobo going by the O.H. and someone had poured in some gasoline, or whatever."

In the 1930s, many Americans still used outhouses, or at least remembered using them, and the idea of disposing of a waste product by pouring it down through a hole in the privy must have seemed logical to readers of that column. Whether hazardous wastes would remain volatile enough to cause a large explosion under an outhouse appears doubtful, but that questionable detail certainly did not prevent the tale from spreading.

Further proving the traditional circulation of the exploding-outhouse legend is a versified version of the story composed by the popular Canadian poet Robert Service. It's entitled "The Three Bares" in reference to a family's three-hole outhouse. The poem begins:

Ma tried to wash her garden slacks but couldn't get 'em clean
And so she thought she'd soak 'em in a bucket o' benzine.
It worked all right. She wrung 'em out then wondered what she'd do
With all that bucket load of high explosive residue.

Ma's solution to the problem is to dump "the liquid menace" into the center hole of the family's three-hole outhouse. Enter Grandpa, who takes his customary seat at the end of the row, lights his pipe, and drops the glowing match "clean through the middle seat." There's a huge explosion, which makes a "dreffel roar," as his grandchild Rosyleen describes it. When the smoke clears, they find Grandpa squatting in the duck pond, his whiskers singed and the toilet seat hanging around his neck. The last stanza of Service's poem is:

He cried: "Say, folks, oh, did ye hear the big blow-out I made?
It scared me stiff—I hope you-uns was not too much afraid?
But now I best be crawlin' out o' this dog-gasted wet. . . .
For what I aim to figger out is—WHAT THE HECK I ET?"

Service probably derived the title as well as the plot of his poems from Canadian folk tradition. A Newfoundland informant's description of a three-hole outhouse also refers to them as "baby 'bare' . . . mama 'bare' . . . [and] papa 'bare.'"[5]

Robert Service published "The Three Bares" in 1949; by that time I suspect that the exploding outhouse story was losing popularity, since indoor plumbing had become commonplace. The poem was reprinted in Service's *More Collected Verse,*[6] and certainly by then "The (Indoor) Exploding Toilet" legend had nearly replaced its rural prototype.

Most versions of the older rural jokes rationalize the depositing of a volatile substance into an outhouse in some way, mentioning things like killing off the fly maggots in the pit or suppressing the bad odor. Possibly the storytellers sometimes substitute gasoline for kerosene or turpentine in the story, knowing that only *that* fluid of the three is really volatile enough to be very dangerous. In the urban versions, few people seem to question whether insecticide, perfume, turpentine, or the like really has explosive qualities, although the motorcycle and gasoline version has become the currently most popular form of the story.

I have two references to early versions of the same rural gag from Australia, but have no way of knowing whether it originated there or was transmitted, either from England or the United States. W. N. "Bill" Scott in a book of tales refers under the heading "Country Dunnies" to a "gents" back behind a pub that the publican would clean out once a fortnight by pouring in a big bottle of "power kerosene" and igniting it.[7] Then in a column (November or December 1988) that Scott writes for the *Queensland Folk Federation,* he described being reminded, after reading about the Israeli news story, of a story he first heard at the age of about eleven (that would be 1934). In the columns, of which he sent me copies, Scott wrote: "The story that flashed like electricity around our little town one day was to the effect that the yardman had mistakenly used petrol instead of kerosene to perform his fortnightly task, and of course someone dropped a butt." Scott drops the story at that point, assuming that the aftermath is obvious.

A second Australian version came from a paper given by Ron Edwards at a folklore conference in Canberra and sent to me by Bill Scott. Collected from a returned soldier in 1960, the story refers to "The Exploding Dunny" episode occurring in an army training camp in 1940 when a slit trench used as a group toilet was being disinfected by application of kerosene. Someone tossed a match under a seat cover on one end, causing a fire that scorched someone else sitting on a seat at the other end.

None of the rural versions I have encountered anywhere, it should be pointed out, ever mentions the second accident involving laughing stretcher bearers and a nasty tumble.

Wherever and however the rural story originated, I am willing to believe that at one time people may have cleaned or disinfected or deodorized their outhouses using kerosene and that some kind of fire or explosion was at least a theoretical possibility. So far, however, I have not interviewed or heard from a single first-person witness to such a blast. I have, however, encountered two versions of the exploding toilet story claimed to be true. One was sent to me by a reader named Gordon Hogan, who recalled it in 1987 dating back to his boyhood days in Lewiston, Idaho, about 1928. Gordon and his brother had dirtied themselves and their clothes playing with some chunks of tar, and his mother cleaned them with gasoline and old rags, dumping the remaining gas into the toilet. As Gordon completed the story:

> Father was very regular in some of his activities. One was his morning ritual. Rise, put on his fuzzy wool robe, light the fire in the cookstove, get the paper, sit on the toilet, light his pipe, and drop the match in the toilet.
>
> What happened was not exactly an explosion in terms of blowing something apart. As he described it, there was a great WHOOSH and he was enveloped in flames.

Hogan furnished many details about the incident, and he wrote that although his father never repeated the story outside the family, Hogan "told the story many, many times, not having any idea that it was a myth." Incidentally, Gordon and his brother did not personally witness the flameball, of course, but the excitement downstairs awoke them that morning, and they immediately came down and heard what had happened directly from their father.

A second "true" example of the story seems to bring me full circle back to the stated source of the *Jerusalem Post*'s version of the exploding toilet, which was an insurance claim. This version comes to me on a photocopied page from an unnamed publication bearing the date June 29, 1979, in one upper corner and "volume 23, number 26" in the other. It is also "page 38" of its source publication, which is a typeset book or periodical of some kind. A handwritten comment on a Post-it note stuck on the sheet by the anonymous person who mailed the sheet to me simply says "Rec'd from brother in law who works for Fireman's Fund [an insurance company] and he says it is from their files." What this document purports to be is a factual account of a trial in which the plaintiff claims injury from a gasoline explosion occurring in the toilet of a private social club in San Francisco.

There are many particulars cited here in an account of a July 1973 trial. Court personnel and medical authorities are named, but the point of major interest for me as a folklorist is that the alleged events match quite closely the motorcycle versions of "The Exploding Toilet." That is, according to this reported court case, someone poured gasoline from a motorcycle engine down a toilet upon which someone else later sat while smoking and the resulting explosion blew him off the toilet seat. The results described were "first degree burns of the scrotum and the penis . . . and the plaintiff rendered psychologically impotent as a result of the subject accident."

I am reluctant to quote further from this document or draw conclusions from it without finding its actual source, but the details are convincing at the same time that the general plot outline is highly suspicious.

Returning to the highly popular motorcycle versions of the legend, let me mention that I rely on a colleague, the linguistics professor Adrian "Buzz" Palmer, to help keep me up to speed on such legends as they make the rounds in the nation's biker magazines. Buzz is an avid motorcyclist and an amazing vegetable gardener. One day I went to my campus mailbox and found a couple of nice zucchinis, a bag of Swiss chard, and a copy of the September 1991 issue of *Motorcyclist* magazine. There was a note attached from Buzz reading, "Another legend for you."

The magazine story was entitled "The New Bike, the Plate Glass Window, and the Commode." It was credited to "one of our editors [who] heard it from a paramedic who was teaching a seminar on emergency medical care." However, the editor of *Motorcyclist* commented that he'd seen the same story printed "half a dozen times in the last 30 years" and he appealed to readers to indicate where and when they think it may originally have happened. This version of the classic urban legend began with a new owner cleaning his bike on the patio. When he starts up his shiny cycle, the man loses control and crashes it through a plate glass window, suffering numerous cuts in the process. After the man's wife calls the paramedics and they rush him to the hospital, she cleans up the mess. She sweeps up the broken glass and uses toilet paper to soak up the spilled gasoline. The wife deposits the gas-soaked paper in the toilet. When the husband gets back from the hospital, he immediately uses the toilet, which his wife hasn't yet flushed. Sitting there still shaken from his recent experience, he decides to smoke a cigarette. After lighting up, he drops the match into the toilet, and the resulting explosion blows him right through the glass shower door. The same paramedics come to the man's rescue, and when they hear what has happened, they laugh so hard that they drop him off the stretcher. The story ends, "The bike is sold the next day."

The punchline of my own personal experience story is that when I placed this 1991 version of the story into my "Exploding Toilet" file, I found there yet another version that had been published in *Motorcyclist* magazine back in February 1984. This time the source was said to be "an insurance agent in Wisconsin" and the biker crashed into his TV set while trying to move his motorcycle into the living room out of the rain.

In this version, after dropping the man from the stretcher, paramedics also got into an accident with the ambulance on their second trip to the hospital. The conclusion of the 1984 version was, "The man sold the motorcycle the following day." This published version was headlined "Not That Old Story!" and on the margin of the photocopy in my file was written, "From Buzz Palmer."

Reviewing all the versions now at hand, I would suggest the following history for all of these various storylines:

First: The fairly common old rural practice of using volatile fluids to clean the outhouse pit, or of disposing of such fluids in same pit, may have suggested to people the possibility of accidents. Perhaps the practice sometimes led to actual accidents.

Second: Occasional similar domestic accidents occurred (as in the Lewiston, Idaho, incident reported by Gordon Hogan), but now involving an *indoor* toilet rather than an outhouse.

Third: Either version (outhouse or indoor toilet) may become embellished with a suitable punchline conclusion or may become attached to a cycle of local character anecdotes or both.

Fourth: Eventually the indoor toilet versions became modernized with references to things like spray cans or to the recurring household need for disposal of fluids like paint thinner, cleaning supplies, and fuels. Somewhere along the line the stories acquired the dropped stretcher ending, which is also found in several other hilarious accident legends. (Where the dropped stretcher legend itself comes from is a subject for another investigation.)

Fifth: Possibly, perhaps even *probably,* the San Francisco court case is authentic, and publicity or gossip about it entered the tradition, so that afterward in the oral versions motorcycle-related accidents became the most common first scene in exploding toilet legends. (Another possibility is that the San Francisco incident was a prank inspired by someone who knew a motorcycle version of the story or *possibly* the document sent to me is itself merely part of photocopy lore.)[8] At any rate, people in the insurance industry seem to have played some role in circulating exploding toilet stories, whether as conduits of actual fact or as tellers of urban legends.

This brings us full circle concerning the case of the exploding toilet in Tel Aviv: told by an insurance salesman to a journalist, published in the *Jerusalem Post,* circulated worldwide by news services, repeated and soon retracted in newspapers, broadcast and sent further by computer and via military information services, reelaborated by tabloids, and eventually— to some degree—reentering the oral tradition and there colliding with versions of the same story as that story had been going about by word of mouth from person to person all along.

◤

As the doubtful and debunked Tel Aviv news story faded from journalistic attention, a few publications continued to publish references to it. These included the following:

November 10, 1988—A column by Bob Swift, distributed by Knight-Ridder Newspapers, recalled "The Exploding Toilet" story circulating in August and compared it to other urban legends like "Stuck on the Toilet," "The Spider in the Hairdo," and "The Mouse in the Coke."

January 1989—*Postgraduate Medicine* ran a small item contributed by a doctor in Tennessee telling a standard gasoline-in-the-toilet story as true, and concluding, "We physicians need to continue to speak plainly to smokers about the health risks of smoking." The journal is published in Minneapolis; a reader in Alberta, Canada, sent the publication a letter chiding the editors for believing a legend.

February 18, 1989—An item from the *Seattle Times* was widely circulated in the press. The headline: "Exploding Toilets Flush Patrons at Seattle Courthouse." The accidental cross-connection of an air compressor with the water system of the King County Courthouse resulted in many explosions when the toilets were flushed. According to the article, "One woman reportedly passed out from shock." Numerous readers sent this item.

March 1989—A training/recruiting video for Peace Corps volunteers in Cameroon showed one man telling a story about someone putting watery gasoline into his pit latrine, then a hot coal blew it up. He mentioned killing maggots as a reason for dumping the gas.

March 21, 1989—*Weekly World News* had an item headlined "Pals' Explosive Prank Blows Teen Off Potty" that described an accident with spray air freshener supposedly occurring in England. A cubicle in a supermarket restroom had a door blown off.

June 14, 1989—The *Kansas Pesticide Newsletter,* under the headline "Misuse Hazardous to Health," reprinted an account of the exploding toilet in Tel Aviv, crediting it to "Fumigants and Pheromones." The headline implied that the important lesson of the story is proper use of insecticides. There was no indication that the story was anything but true.

Notes

The first version of this essay was presented at the seventh annual conference of the International Society for Contemporary Legend Research held at Texas A&M University, College Station, Texas, March 30–April 1, 1989. It was revised and published in essentially the same form as presented here in *Contemporary Legend* 3 (1993): 103–19.

1. The complete text of the *Jerusalem Post* story is quoted in Paul Smith's "'Read All about It! Elvis Eaten by Drug-Crazed Giant Alligators': Contemporary Legend and the Popular Press," *Contemporary Legend* 2 (1992): 41–71, along with the paper's retraction and several published responses to the incident.

2. Jan Harold Brunvand, *The Mexican Pet: More "New" Urban Legends and Some Old Favorites* (New York: W. W. Norton, 1986), 13–16.

3. Paul Smith, *The Book of Nasty Legends* (London: Routledge and Kegan Paul, 1983), 48.

4. The paper has since been renamed the *Bloomington Herald-Times.*

5. Gerald Thomas, "Functions of the Newfoundland Outhouse," *Western Folklore* 48 (1989): 224–25.

6. Robert Service, *More Collected Verse* (New York: Dodd Mead, 1963), 66–68.

7. W. N. Scott, *The Long and the Short and the Tall: A Collection of Australian Yarns* (Sydney: Western Plains, 1985), 198–99.

8. For a piece of photocopy lore based on "The Exploding Toilet," see Alan Dundes and Carl R. Pagter, *Never Try to Teach a Pig to Sing* (Detroit: Wayne State University Press, 1991), 394–96.

9

The Folklorists' Search for the Ghost in Search of Help for a Dying Person

In his 1975 best-selling book entitled *Angels: God's Secret Agents*, Billy Graham repeats an amazing story that he credits, without a date, simply to the *Reader's Digest*. The story is undoubtedly a folk legend given a Christian twist by Graham. Here is his version—the first story in his book—along with his brief commentary:

Help from Angels

Dr. S. W. Mitchell, a celebrated Philadelphia neurologist, had gone to bed after an exceptionally tiring day. Suddenly he was awakened by someone knocking on his door. Opening it he found a little girl, poorly dressed and deeply upset. She told him her mother was very sick and asked him if he would please come with her. It was a bitterly cold, snowy night, but though he was bone tired, Dr. Mitchell dressed and followed the girl.

As *Reader's Digest* reports the story, he found the mother desperately ill with pneumonia. After arranging for medical care, he complimented the sick woman on the intelligence and persistence of her little daughter. The woman looked at him strangely and then said, "My daughter died a month ago." She added, "Her shoes and coat are in the clothes closet there." Dr. Mitchell, amazed and perplexed, went to the closet and opened the door. There hung the very coat worn by the little girl who had brought him to tend to her mother. It was warm and dry and could not possibly have been out in the wintry night.

Could the doctor have been called in the hour of desperate need by an angel who appeared as this woman's young daughter? Was this the work of God's angels on behalf of the sick woman?[1]

The psychic investigator Joe Nickell in his 1995 book *Entities* comments on Billy Graham's lack of a verifiable source for the story; he compares earlier published versions and concludes (correctly, I believe) that "Rev. Graham has passed on a version of an old narrative about a ghost, presenting it as a supposedly true account suggestive of angelic visitation. No doubt he has done so in good faith (no pun intended)."[2]

Although the child's figure that summoned the doctor to the bedside of the gravely ill woman *could* be interpreted as an angel, the folk who tell this legend and similar stories make no such claim. In traditional versions the implication is simply that the helpful spirit is a ghost. For example, the story entitled "Help" in Ruth Ann Musick's book *The Telltale Lilac Bush and Other West Virginia Ghost Tales* follows essentially the same plot but stops with the doctor discovering the dead child's clothing in a closet.[3] (This version was collected in 1963 from a woman who heard it from her aunt who had heard it from a friend's grandmother. Musick notes, "The incident is supposed to have happened in Wetzel County.")

The West Virginia text names the doctor (Dr. Anderson) and the mother (Mrs. Ballard), as well as the woman's place of residence ("the old Hostler place"). The girl is wearing a blue coat and a white muff, both of which are later found in the closet "still warm and damp from perspiration." The sick mother says her daughter died three years before, and both mother and daughter had been stricken by pneumonia. As in Billy Graham's version, the doctor is awakened on a winter night by a knocking on his door; but in the West Virginia version instead of leading him on foot to her mother, the girl runs off after giving her message, and the doctor goes alone by horseback to the designated house.

These two versions suggest that the story is a migratory legend told with localized details. Musick's citation of Ernest W. Baughman's motif E363.1(a), *Ghost fetches physician for dying husband,* seems to confirm this.[4] Furthermore, Musick mentions a similar story in Helen Creighton's 1957 book *Bluenose Ghosts,* a version collected in Nova Scotia, in which "a long-dead mother summons a priest to give absolution to her profligate son who dies later that same night."[5]

Another story in which the ghost of a mother summons medical help, entitled "The Guiding Spirit," appears in "A collection of true stories from the files of FATE Magazine."[6] In this unique narrative, told in the first person, a nurse is summoned during a raging snowstorm to the bedside of a Mexican woman giving birth; the summoner is the woman's mother, who turns out to have died on the night of her own daughter's birth nineteen years previously. This story is given an exact date and location (December 17, 1950, Catron County, New Mexico) but it is attributed only to "M. M." of Auburn, California, and dated November 1954, presumably the date it appeared in the pages of *FATE Magazine* or was submitted to that popular periodical of the strange and paranormal. Without further verification, this would appear to be another version of the legend retold in the first person, perhaps by an editor of *FATE*.

From these references, it should be a simple matter to follow the leads and eventually find the source in folk tradition for Billy Graham's story. (Determining whether an *angel* was involved in the case would be more difficult.) However, the folklorist's search is not so simple, and, in fact, despite some progress during several years of research, I am still not sure where Billy Graham got the story and whether this Dr. S. W. Mitchell named by Graham ever had such an experience or, indeed, exactly when, where, or how Mitchell became associated with this legend. It is also problematic whether the similar story from Helen Creighton's collection (plus two variations of it from England and from Russia) represent a variant version of the same Dr. S. W. Mitchell legend or a separate, though similar, narrative.

Ernest Baughman's only citation for this general narrative motif (ghost summons help) is to a summary of a story given in Richard K. Beardsley and Rosalie Hankey's 1943 article "A History of the Vanishing Hitchhiker" published in *California Folklore Quarterly*. This short version, paraphrased in a footnote, reads as follows:

> [It is] a story supposedly told in London. . . . A woman dressed in white accosts a doctor from a taxicab as he is walking home late at night. He goes with her to an address she gives, where he discovers as he gets out of the cab that she has disappeared. When he rings the bell, he is told by the butler that there is no need for a doctor there. Out of curiosity he returns the next morning and learns that although his presence the night before is not remembered, it was indeed necessary. The master of the house had died. As he waits in a side room to examine the body, he sees a photograph of the woman in white; he is told that the picture is that of the master's wife, dead for ten years.[7]

The slight similarity of this story to "The Vanishing Hitchhiker" lies in the portrait identification motif, but this version *differs* from the other two "Ghost in Search of Help" legends in that the doctor is summoned by a woman not a girl, he comes in a taxicab, he does not actually render any help to the dying man, and he returns to the house the next day to learn who the ghost was. Beardsley and Hankey give no source for their London story; Hankey, however, collected one "Vanishing Hitchhiker" text in California, cited in an article a year earlier (1942), in which the hitchhiker is a white-haired old woman who says she needs a ride to her dying son's bedside.[8] The connection between "The Ghost in Search of Help" legend and "The Vanishing Hitchhiker" legend is not strong, since few of the hundreds of *other* versions of the hitchhiker story incorporates the ghost-as-helper motif.[9]

Let us turn to the earliest known example of the ghost-as-helper story. In 1964 William B. Edgerton, a Slavicist from Indiana University—as he wrote in a 1968 article in the *Journal of the Folklore Institute*—"came across several accounts of a 'miracle' that was said to have taken place somewhere in Petersburg [Russia] during December of 1890."[10] The account from the Russian newspaper begins, "There is a story going about town that is worthy of attention. The only question is whether it is true, and to what extent."[11] In this version, a priest carrying the holy sacraments arrives at a certain apartment and tells the young man who answers his knock that he was sent there by a woman to give the sacraments to a sick man there. The young man explains that he lives alone and is *not* sick, but the priest recognizes a portrait on the wall as that of the woman who had summoned him. The young man in great surprise says it is a portrait of his dead mother. He decides to take communion, and, the story concludes, "That evening he lay dead."

Six days later, as Edgerton reported, a Petersburg journalist published an article about his efforts to verify this incident. This account reads like a folklorist's attempt to track down variations of a contemporary legend, since the investigator found only "conflicting and mutually contradictory accounts." Nobody he interviewed had firsthand information about the incident, although many had heard it and believed it to be true. In the following weeks the same essential plot with slight variations appeared several times in the Petersburg newspapers.

The Russian version resembles both the one from London and the one from Nova Scotia, which, as Helen Creighton explains in *Bluenose Ghosts,* was claimed to be something that had actually happened in London to a FOAF of the storyteller and took place during "the early Edwardian period" (i.e., 1901–10). In Creighton's version, an Anglican rector living on the east side of London was planning his sermon late one Saturday night when the doorbell rang. At the door was an old woman wearing a bonnet, a shawl, and a "once black skirt now green with age." She convinced him to go to a certain house on the west side of London where he was urgently needed.

The rector took a taxicab to the address—a large mansion—and was admitted by a butler, who brought to him the master of the house. Hearing the rector's explanation, the man became frightened, confessed his wicked life, and agreed "to make his peace with God." The rector absolved him of his sins and urged him to receive communion the next morning. When the man did not appear in church, the rector returned to the mansion and learned from the butler that the master had died the night before. Invited inside to view the body, the rector recognized, in a painting hanging on the wall, the likeness of the old woman who had summoned him. It was a portrait of the master's mother, who had died many years before.

Edgerton in his article mentioned as a variant only the similar story reported from London in the Beardsley and Hankey article; he was not aware of the very similar London one published in 1957 by Creighton or of the "Dr. Anderson" version from West Virginia published in 1965 by Musick.[12] In a letter of February 4, 1993, Edgerton informed me, "I have found nothing more about this legend since I published [the article] twenty-five years ago."

Returning to Billy Graham's and Ruth Ann Musick's stories from the United States, we recognize in them several differences from the London and Petersburg stories: First, as Graham and Musick tell the legend, it is a *doctor* and not a *priest* who is summoned by the ghost of a *girl* rather than an *old woman*. There is no portrait identification in the doctor stories, but rather the identification of the spirit is based on the dead girl's clothing. Also, in the American stories the person needing help is the mother of the ghost, while in the English and Russian legends the mother herself summons help for her son or her husband. (However, in both stories, it should be noted, it is a *woman's* ghost that seeks help.) These two sets of variations might be thought of as two subtypes of a single legend that we might describe generically with the title "The Ghost in Search of Help for a Dying *Person*." Version A would comprise the three examples of the priest/rector[13] story from Russia and England, and Version B would consist of the doctor (or nurse) story in its various retellings from the United States. Another viewpoint, to which I am inclined, is to see these two stories as separate legends based on similar motifs: Legend A comprising the priest/rector story and Legend B comprising the doctor story. (In either hypothesis, the A story is found earlier in a reliably dated example.)

Who *is* this "Dr. S. W. Mitchell, celebrated Philadelphia neurologist," to whom Billy Graham attributes his version of the story, the one we are calling Legend B? Mitchell certainly is no ghost, for there are six further versions of the story, specifically naming him, given in popular, undocumented books published from 1959 to 1976.[14] All of these sources (at least three of them books written for juveniles) identify the main character as

Dr. Mitchell, and the story's plots are very similar, differing only in details that seem to derive from the writers' imaginations. Except for Ruth Ann Musick's story about "Dr. Anderson" and the *FATE Magazine* "nurse" version, the subject of all Legend B texts is Dr. Silas Weir Mitchell (1829–1914), a leading physician of his time and a prolific author of scientific works, fiction, and poetry. Writings by and about Mitchell are numerous.[15]

The doctor preferred to be called Weir Mitchell or S. Weir Mitchell. He was a distinguished member of the Philadelphia College of Physicians, prominent in the upper-class social life of the city, a lover of jokes and pranks, an avid fisherman, a friend of many intellectuals and politicians of his time, and a respected medical researcher. Mitchell's eclectic scientific interests—for which he gained an international reputation—included the effects of snake venom on humans, the treatment of battlefield wounds, and the diagnosis and treatment of nervous diseases, especially among women. He showed an early awareness of Sigmund Freud's writings and theories, leading one commentator in a 1952 book to describe Mitchell as a "psychiatric novelist."[16]

So popular and well known was Mitchell in his own time, both as a medical doctor and as a creative writer, that some of his admirers even wrote poems to him and about him. One such verse contained this stanza:

> At last some bright day at your door will appear,
> The famous neurologist, great Dr. Weir,
> A poet and writer of much versatility,
> Producing fine books with the utmost facility.
> Dr. Mitchell's opinion! You quake to receive it,
> He says you'll get well and you'd like to believe it![17]

As late as 1939, twenty-five years after Mitchell's death, the writer Christopher Morley alluded to him in his popular novel *Kitty Foyle*. An upper-class Philadelphia young man in the book says of his father, "He loves to think we're a literary family because Weir Mitchell was our doctor."[18]

Most of the writings about Mitchell mention his interest in spiritualism, usually including reference to some accounts he gave, either in correspondence or in published writings, of odd experiences of his or one of his friends involving what seemed to be supernatural incidents. For example, for a period after the death of a close friend, Mitchell could see, hovering off to the left, the face of the friend, "larger than life, smiling, and very distinct" until he turned his eyes to a different direction, and then the vision disappeared.[19] The author of a 1972 article in the *Journal of the*

American Medical Association reviews all the references to ghostly spirits found in Mitchell's biographical and fictional writings, but nowhere in this survey is there any mention of "The Ghost in Search of Help" legend.[20]

There is, however, a tantalizing allusion to the story in Mitchell's novel entitled *Characteristics*. Published in 1891, the novel is structured as a set of extended conversations within a close group of friends; when the subject of ghosts comes up, the leading character, named Dr. North, says:

> It is dangerous to tell a ghost-story nowadays. . . . A friend of mine once told one in print out of his wicked head, just for the fun of it. It was about a little dead child who rang up a doctor one night, and took him to see her dying mother. Since then he has been the prey of collectors of such marvels. Psychical societies write to him; anxious believers and disbelievers in the supernatural assail him with letters. He has written some fifty to lay this ghost. How could he predict a day when he would be taken seriously?[21]

In this passage Mitchell seems to be attributing to his fictional character a frustrating incident based upon an actual experience of his own. That is, Mitchell himself had playfully told or written up the traditional ghost legend in the first person, and then he was chagrined to find the public believing that he was presenting the story as the literal truth. There is but a single short and obscure published account of his telling the story. It was published in 1950 by R. W. G. Vail, then director of the New York Historical Society, who heard the story from someone who had heard it directly from the lips of Mitchell. The short account is worth quoting in full:

> One day in February, 1949, Dr. Philip Cook of Worcester, Mass., while on a visit to New York City, told me this story which he had heard the famous doctor and writer S. Weir Mitchell tell at a medical meeting years ago. (Dr. Mitchell died in 1914).
>
> "I was sitting in my office late one night when I heard a knock and, going to the door, found a little girl crying, who asked me to go at once to her home to visit a very sick patient. I told her that I was practically retired and never made evening calls, but she seemed to be in such great distress that I agreed to make the call and so wrote down the name and address she gave me. So I got my bag, hat, and coat and returned to the door, but the little girl was gone. However, I had the address and so went on and made the call. When I got there, a woman came to the door in tears. I asked if there was a patient needing attention. She said that there had been—her little daughter—but that she had just died. She then invited me in. I saw the patient lying dead in her bed, and it was the little girl who had called at my office.[22]

There is also one intriguing unpublished reference to Mitchell and the story of the ghost in search of help preserved in the S. Weir Mitchell papers, which are held in the library of the College of Physicians of Philadelphia.[23] This reference appears in a letter, and Mitchell was one who received and wrote a great many letters during his lifetime. As one biographer described his correspondence: "People wrote to tell him their dreams, their 'phobias, their mother-in-law's peculiarities. They wrote to praise, to question or to criticize—to thank, to request, or to remind. They asked about cats, rattlesnakes, colonial wines, Philadelphia alleys, fishing, history, Washington, pain in the wrist, visions before sleep and whether their ancestor had attended the University of Pennsylvania in 1802. They wrote of everything and Dr. Mitchell always answered."[24]

The letter in question, dated 1909, was among the papers on the doctor's desk at the time of his death in 1914; the writer wished to inquire whether the doctor had experienced a particular ghost visitation. The writer, Dr. A. Noel Smith of Dover, New Hampshire, said he heard the story from a stranger whom he had met in a hotel. The stranger claimed to have heard Dr. Mitchell himself tell the story at a meeting (so this is a classic FOAF attribution). Here is the full text of the photocopied three-page handwritten letter as I received it in December 1992 from the Library of the College of Physicians of Philadelphia:

[Printed Letterhead]

> A Noel Smith, M.D.
> 430 Central Ave.
> Dover, N.H.
> Telephone [no number given]

[Written in S.W.M.'s handwriting]
One of many about an early [illegible] ghost tale of [mine?]

2 Nov. 1909

S. Weir Mitchell, M.D.
My dear Doctor:—

Please pardon my intrusion upon your valuable time, but—as I should like the truthfulness, or otherwise, of what follows established, I have taken the liberty of addressing you.

A travelling man, a stranger, accosted me a few days since at one of our principal hotels, knowing that I was a physician, asking me if I believe in the supernatural, communication with the spirits of departed friends, etc.— I assured him that I had never experienced any personal observations or manifestations that would lead me to any such belief. He then related to me the following story, vouching for its authenticity.—He was a member of some organization, I think, in N.Y., and they had lectures now and then upon various topics. One evening it was announced that prominent men were present who would in turn relate their most wonderful experiences. You was [sic] the first called upon, and you stated that you could tell your most wonderful personal experience in a few words. You went on to say that you were engaged in writing late one evening in your library when somebody knocked three times upon the library door. This was thought to be very strange, as electric bells were in use. Upon opening the door, a little girl, about 12 years of age stood there, having a red cloak for an outer garment. She asked if you were Dr. Mitchell, and wished you to go at once to visit her mother professionally, as she was very ill. You informed her that you had given up general practice, but that Dr. Bennett lived diagonally across the street, and that you would direct her to his door, which you did. In a few moments the raps upon your door were repeated, and you found the girl there a second time. She could not obtain Dr. Bennett's services, and urged you to accompany her home; and you did so. She conducted you to a poor section of the city and up a rickety flight of stairs into a tenement house. She ushered you into a room where her mother lay ill upon a bed. You prescribed for the sick lady, giving her some general directions for future guide, and assured her that it was only at the very urgent and persistent efforts of her daughter that you were prevailed upon to come to her. The woman said that that was strange: that she had no daughter— that her only daughter had just died and her body reposed in a casket in the adjoining room. You then looked into this room & viewed the remains of a girl about 12 years of age, while hanging upon the wall was a red cloak.

I am curious to know, doctor, whether you ever had any such experience, or any approach thereto. Hence these words. Let me say right here that Mrs. Smith & myself enjoyed very much the reading together the "Red City" when running in the Century Magazine.

Thanking you in advance for your reply to this inquiry. I am

Yours Sincerely
A. Noel Smith

Although there is no record of Mitchell's reply to this interesting letter, nor have I yet found any other contemporary evidence of Mitchell's connection with the story, it seems likely from these last two accounts that he had actually told the story, perhaps more than once, at some point during his long and interesting life. However, we must also keep in mind, as a biographer wrote, that Mitchell "became a legend in his own time, the subject of countless anecdotes."[25]

In my opinion, after reviewing the twelve texts of two legends that have been summarized here, there was definitely an oral tradition of the priest/rector story going back at least to 1890 and told in at least three countries (Russia, England, and Canada). The doctor story is documented in Cook's 1949 memory and Smith's 1909 letter but is certainly older and probably goes back to something that Mitchell told about or wrote about as early as 1891. The doctor story has been collected from oral tradition only by Ruth Ann Musick in 1963. It is unclear where Billy Graham got the story, but his version and those published in six other popular books (by Colby, Duncan, Edwards, Ronan, Tyler, and in the *Reader's Digest* book *Strange Stories*) all seem to derive from the same original (perhaps an undiscovered article in an even earlier issue of *Reader's Digest*).

These later published variations on the doctor story are probably the work of writers and editors rather than from oral tradition. For example, Tyler's 1970 retelling added the unique detail that the girl's clothing smelled of mothballs. (She also refers to the doctor as "F. Weir Mitchell.") Edwards's 1961 retelling referred to Mitchell as an "aging physician," mentioned that he drank a glass of milk before going to bed, and specified that it was 10:30 P.M. when he heard the doorbell ring. Ronan, in 1974, specified December 1880 as the date of the incident, the year Mitchell was fifty-one years old and in the prime of life and at the height of his career, hardly the "aging physician" of Edwards's account.

All seven twentieth-century popular versions of the story contain some reference to the ghost's clothing being warm and/or dry; only Musick's folk version, which is different in a number of other details as well, reverses this to say that the clothes were "still warm and *damp* from perspiration." The 1909 letter referring to Mitchell himself telling the story makes no reference whatever to the condition of the ghost's clothing, nor does it mention the snowy weather, a consistent feature of every other telling of the story. One could speculate that either Musick's tale (from West Virginia) derives separately from an actual oral tradition or else its tellers began with a published account of the Mitchell story and then changed details (including the doctor's name) as they retold it. Only further texts from folk tradition would allow us to accept, modify, or replace these speculations.

Eventually, I hope, more information will become available about other early versions of "The Ghost in Search of Help" legend and its association with Dr. S. Weir Mitchell. In the meantime, I can report two more versions recently discovered that further establish at least the general story's vitality in folklore. The first of these is told in a Latter-day Saints context and was collected by a student of mine, Cindy Webb, who heard it from a returned Mormon missionary in autumn 1989:

> One day there was a missionary team walking in a park to take a break. A man came up to them and introduced himself as "Elias Snow". He asked them to come to his house immediately to teach his family the gospel. He gave them the address and then he was gone; they couldn't seem to find the direction he went. They proceeded to the address to see the family, and when they rang the doorbell a sickly woman came to the door. They told her they had been sent by Elias Snow, and she got a terrified look on her face and asked them to come in. As they were walking in they saw a picture of Elias on the mantle. The woman went on to explain that Elias was her husband and that he had died two years earlier. She was baptized into the church one month later.[26]

Clearly, this is a priest/rector legend, complete with the portrait identification and also incorporating the motif common in the Mormon "Three Nephites" legends of the sudden disappearance of the mysterious stranger. Conversion to Mormonism replaces making a confession and receiving absolution.

Finally, I received this summary version of the ghost searcher legend in a March 4, 1993, letter from David E. Bosley, an official in the U.S. embassy in Bangkok:

> While I was studying Chinese, one of the taped stories my class listened to for comprehension purposes was a tale of a Shanghai postmaster. The postmaster on one dark and snowy night is visited at his office by a waif sent on an errand by her parents. The postmaster is shocked that such a young child would be sent out to post a letter on such a dismal night. After accepting the letter and sending the child back to her home, the postmaster notices that the letter is overweight. He proceeds to the sender's home, found via the return address, and is confronted by the elderly parents. They tell him that their daughter died an untimely death years earlier.

This odd tale resembles the doctor versions of the legend, but presents us with new mysteries, including what was in the letter, to whom it was addressed, and why the ghost wanted so badly to post it. Perhaps most beguiling about this version is the suggestion that the postal system of old Shanghai was so accommodating that a postmaster, no less, would venture forth on a dark and snowy night to collect extra postage on a letter instead of merely forwarding it postage due. (I think it is safe to say that it does not snow often in Shanghai, so possibly that detail was added absent-mindedly by my correspondent in an attempt to make the story more dramatic.) As for that helpful postmaster, perhaps he was an angel.

I have no further conclusions about the history and relationships of the various versions of the two legends in question. I might add only that the several popularizers who have retold and revised the story of the ghost visiting Dr. S. Weir Mitchell in search of help have also effectively obscured the sources of their material, thus misleading decades of readers into thinking that this might actually be a verified instance of a spiritual intervention in the affairs of humans or even of an angelic presence. Published in popular pulp fiction about ESP and the like, little damage is done; but when Billy Graham and the *Reader's Digest* publish the story, it's another matter.

Notes

This essay was originally presented at the annual meeting of the American Folklore Society in Pittsburgh, October 17–20, 1996.

1. Billy Graham, *Angels: God's Secret Agents* (Garden City, N.Y.: Doubleday, 1975), 2–3.

2. Joe Nickell, *Entities: Angels, Spirits, Demons, and Other Alien Beings* (Amherst, N.Y.: Prometheus Books, 1995), 155. I am grateful to Joe Nickell for supplying me with copies of several published versions of the S. Weir Mitchell ghost story cited below. Neither Nickell nor I have been able to find Billy Graham's source in the *Reader's Digest*.

3. Ruth Ann Musick, *The Telltale Lilac Bush and Other West Virginia Ghost Tales* (Lexington: University of Kentucky Press, 1965), 28–30.

4. It should be noted that Musick has an extra digit in her motif citation, which she lists as E363.1.1(a) instead of E363.1(a).

5. Helen Creighton, *Bluenose Ghosts* (Toronto: Ryerson, 1957).

6. Corrine Kenner and Craig Miller, eds. *Strange but True: A Collection of True Stories from the Files of FATE Magazine* (St. Paul, Minnesota: Llewellyn, 1997), 150–51. I received a copy of this item from Joe Nickell.

7. Richard K. Beardsley and Rosalie Hankey, "A History of the Vanishing Hitchhiker," *California Folklore Quarterly* 2 (1943): 17n19.

8. Rosalie Hankey, "California Ghosts," *California Folklore Quarterly* 1 (1942): 175.

9. Louis C. Jones published two stories collected in New York in 1943 in which a ghost summons help. In one, the ghost of a woman's dead son sends her a housekeeper/companion; in the second, the ghost of a couple's son sends them an unspecified message. Both versions have the portrait identification motif, but neither involves a doctor or a priest. See "Hitchhiking Ghosts in New York," *California Folklore Quarterly* 3 (1944): 287–88. Commenting on these texts, Gillian Bennett recalled a story "heard at chapel in my childhood" in which a country doctor who

is also a Methodist lay preacher is summoned to the bedside of an old couple by the ghost of their dead daughter. The ghost hitchhikes in this version, but there is no portrait identification motif. See "The Phantom Hitchhiker: Neither Modern, Urban, nor Legend?" in *Perspectives on Contemporary Legend,* ed. Paul Smith, CECTAL Conference Papers Series no. 1 (Sheffield: Centre for English Cultural Traditions and Language, 1984), 56. This seems to be the doctor story, but also incorporates a ministerial motif in the context of a hitchhiker legend.

10. William B. Edgerton, "The Ghost in Search of Help for a Dying Man," *Journal of the Folklore Institute* 5 (1968): 31. A somewhat similar story appears in Patricia Alphonso's "'We Don't Wanna Hear the Scientific Reason': Teenage Lore of the St. Bernard Parish," *Louisiana Folklore Miscellany* 5 (1981): 33. In this version a woman in white takes a cab to a certain address and goes inside to get the cabfare; after a long wait, the driver knocks on the home's door and learns from the butler that his passenger was the ghost of a young man's mother returning for his funeral. There is no portrait identification. The informant claimed that "it was in the newspaper."

11. Edgerton, "The Ghost in Search of Help for a Dying Man," 32.

12. But see William B. Edgerton's "A Ghostly Urban Legend in Petersburg: Was N. S. Leskov Involved?" in *The Supernatural in Slavic and Baltic Literature: Essays in Honor of Victor Terras,* ed. Amy Mandelker and Roberta Reeder (Columbus: Slavica, 1988), 145–50, for the suggestion of a possible author for the original Petersburg newspaper's version of the legend.

13. The 1943 Beardsley and Hankey version attributed to London, although a priest/rector version in other details, is actually told about a *doctor.*

14. C. B. Colby, "The Doctor's Visitor," *Strangely Enough!* abridged ed. (New York: Scholastic Book Services, 1968), 147–48, originally published in 1959; Frank Edwards, "Dr. Mitchell's Mystery," *Strange People* (New York: New American Library, 1961), 50–52; Steven Tyler, "Stranger Then [*sic*] Science," *ESP and Psychic Power* (New York: Tower Publications, 1970), 102–3; David Duncan, "Caller in the Snow," *Strange but True: Twenty-two Amazing Stories* (New York: Scholastic Book Services, 1973), 94–96; Margaret Ronan, "The Girl in the Snow," *Strange Unsolved Mysteries* (New York: Scholastic Book Services, 1974), 99–101; and "Girl Who Fetched the Doctor," *Strange Stories, Amazing Facts: Stories That Are Bizarre, Unusual, Odd, Astonishing, and Often Incredible* (Pleasantville, N.Y.: Reader's Digest Association, 1976), 399.

15. See, for example, "Death and Career of Dr. S. Weir Mitchell, *New York Times,* Jan. 5, 1914; Beverley R. Tucker, *S. Weir Mitchell: A Brief Sketch of His Life with Personal Recollections* (Boston: R. D. Badger, 1914); and Joseph P. Lovering, *S. Weir Mitchell* (New York: Twayne, 1971).

16. David M. Rein, *S. Weir Mitchell as a Psychiatric Novelist* (New York: International Universities Press, 1952).

17. Anna Robeson Burr, *Weir Mitchell: His Life and Letters* (New York: Duffield, 1929), 187.

18. Christopher Morley, *Kitty Foyle* (Philadelphia: J. B. Lippincott, 1939), 158.

19. Burr, *Weir Mitchell,* 283–84; Ernest Earnest, *S. Weir Mitchell: Novelist and Physician* (Philadelphia: University of Pennsylvania Press, 1950), 157–58.

20. William K. Beatty, "S. Weir Mitchell and the Ghosts," *Journal of the American Medical Association* 220 (Apr. 3, 1972): 76–80.

21. S. Weir Mitchell, *Characteristics* (New York: Century, 1909), 208–9.

22. R. W. G. Vail, "A Philadelphia Variant of the Vanishing Hitchhiking Ghost," *New York Folklore Quarterly* 6 (1950): 254.

23. See Whitfield J. Bell Jr., *The College of Physicians of Philadelphia: A Bicentennial History* (n.p.: Science History Publications, 1987).

24. Burr, *Weir Mitchell*, 359.

25. Earnest, *S. Weir Mitchell*, 242.

26. The text, as told by Brent Hawkins of Salt Lake City, is deposited in the University of Utah Folklore Archive.

10

"The Missing Day in Time"

The majority of urban legends do not deal with the paranormal, the supernatural, or pseudo-science. A few do; for example, "The Vanishing Hitchhiker" is about a returning and usually prophetic spirit. Other legends tell of Satanic cult sacrifices, product trademarks that reveal contributions to the "Church of Satan," accurate prophecies of crimes and disasters, spirit images in films and videotapes, haunted airliners, sinking libraries and shopping malls, devilish bar codes and computer programs, and people being seriously injured or killed by microwaves supposedly emitted by tanning lamps or welding torches.

One fertile theme for such legends is the supposed conflict between science or government and religion, and one of the most detailed such stories is "The Missing Day in Time." The legend describes how the best tool of modern science—the computer—corroborated a biblical miracle. This legend circulates actively among fundamentalist Christians in varying versions, but it derives from older pseudo-scholarly religious speculations, both printed and oral.

The story of "The Missing Day in Time" is often told on a single-spaced one-page anonymous photocopied handout containing a few typographical errors, some punctuation mistakes, and a scattering of capital letters and exclamation points used for emphasis. The following typical text was received in church on Sunday, March 4, 1990, by a man in West Valley City, Utah, who sent it to me with the comment, "This might qualify as an urban legend":

THE SUN *DID* STAND STILL

Did you know that the space program is busy proving that what has been called "myth" in the Bible is true? Mr. Harold Hill, President of the Curtis

Engine Co. in Baltimore, Maryland, and a consultant in the space program, relates the following development:

"I think one of the most amazing things that God has for us today happened recently to our astronauts and space scientists at Green Belt, Maryland. They were checking the position of the sun, moon, and planets out in space where they would be 100 years and 1,000 years from now. We have to know this so we don't send a satellite up and have it bump into something later on in its orbits. We have to lay out the orbits in terms of the life of the satellite, and where the planets will be so the whole thing will not bog down! They ran the computer measurement back and forth over the centuries and it came to a halt. The computer stopped and put up a red signal, which meant that there was something wrong either with the information fed into it or with the results as compared to the standards. They called in the service department to check it out and they said, "It's perfect." The head of operations said, "What's wrong?" "Well, they have found there is a day missing in space in elapsed time." They scratched their heads and tore their hair. There was no answer!

One religious fellow on the team said, "You know, one time I was in Sunday School and they talked about the sun standing still." They didn't believe him; but they didn't have any other answer so they said, "Show us." He got a Bible and went back to the Book of Joshua where they found a pretty ridiculous statement for anybody who has 'common sense'. There they found the Lord saying to Joshua, "Fear them not; for I have delivered them into thine hand; there shall not a man of them stand before thee." Joshua was concerned because he was surrounded by the enemy and if darkness fell they would overpower them. So Joshua asked the Lord to make the sun stand still! That's right—"The sun stood still, and the moon stayed . . . and hasted not to go down about a whole day." Joshua 10:8,12,13. The space men said, "There is the missing day!" They checked the computers going back into the time it was written and found it was close but not close enough. The elapsed time that was missing back in Joshua's day was 23 hours and 20 minutes—not a whole day. They read the Bible and there it was—"about (approximately) a day."

These little words in the Bible are important. But they were still in trouble because if you cannot account for 40 minutes you'll be in trouble 1,000 years from now. Forty minutes had to be found because it can be multiplied many times over in orbits. This religious fellow also remembered somwhere [sic] in the Bible where it said the sun went BACKWARDS. The space men told him he was out of his mind. But they got the Book and read these words in II Kings: Hezakiah, [sic] on his deathbed, was visited by the Prophet Isaiah who told him that he was not going to die. Hezekiah asked for a sign as proof. Isaiah said, "Do you want the sun to go ahead ten degrees?" Hezekiah said, "It's nothing for the sun to go ahead ten degrees, but let the shadow return backward ten degrees." II Kings 20: 9–11. Isaiah spoke to the Lord and the Lord brought the shadow ten degrees BACKWARDS! Ten degrees is exactly 40 minutes! Twenty-three hours and 20 minutes in Joshua, plus 40 minutes in II Kings make the missing 24 hours the space travelers had to log in the logbook as being the missing day in the universe! Isn't that amazing? Our God is rubbing their noses in His Truth!"

The above article was copied from "The Evening Star", Spencer, Indiana. It is verified by Mr. Harold Hill, who gave permission for reprinting, February 22, 1970.

Besides anonymous handouts like this, I've collected "The Missing Day in Time" from periodicals, religious tracts, letters to editors, and from people who heard it in sermons or lectures. Most versions describe the discovery of the missing day, the scientists' dilemma, the religious man's advice to search the Bible, the first account in Joshua of "about a whole day," and the second account of an additional forty minutes found in 2 Kings resolving the scientific problem. Harold Hill is generally cited as the person relating the story, and the *Evening Star* (or *Evening World*) of Spencer, Indiana, is given as the source of his article. Only rarely is a date for the report suggested (in this case, 1970).

The "Missing Day in Time" legend is told vividly and dramatically; its style echoes oral delivery, which makes sense, considering the statement that Harold Hill "*relates* the following." The "space men" and the "religious fellow" are both quoted, and we have the visual detail that "they scratched their heads and tore their hair." Laypersons' not scientists' terms appear in references to a satellite that could "bump into something" and also in the suggestion that the whole system could "bog down." Some naivete about computers is suggested in the notion of running one "back and forth over the centuries" and in having the computer "put out a red signal." Expressions of religious feeling in the story conclude with the idea of God "rubbing their noses" in "Truth" (spelled with a capital *T*). The biblical quotations are accurate, although it is not specifically stated in Joshua 10 that if darkness fell his enemies "would overcome him." (In fact, in verse 11 the Lord casts great stones upon the enemy, killing more "than the children of Israel slew with the sword.") The passage from 2 Kings, although placed in quotation marks, is actually paraphrased. It is not explained how "about a whole day" was calculated to be exactly twenty-three hours and twenty minutes.

Typical of traditional narratives (which I consider this story to be), within the consistent structure of the basic story, other texts display variations, both in details and in wording. Sometimes, for example, the satellites are sent "out" and sometimes sent "up"; the periods of "100 years and 1,000 years" are rephrased as "centuries and millennia." The "head of operations" who is consulted may be called "the *IBM* Head of Operations," and the computer may "put up a red flag" instead of "a red signal" or it may simply "signal" or have "ground to a halt." Greenbelt (often misspelled as two words) is occasionally said to be in Indiana, and the numerical references to biblical passages are occasionally wrong. The word *approximately,* which paraphrases the biblical phrase *about a whole day* may appear in quotation marks as if it is part of the actual wording. The scientists are sometimes said to be "dumbfounded" or "baffled" instead of literally tearing their hair, and God in one text rubs their "minds" in the Truth instead of rubbing their noses in it.

Did the Sun Stand Still? an undated tract, one of many in this genre, includes a text of virtually the same story as found in the photocopies, prefacing it with the usual credit to Harold Hill and specifying that "the great computers at the Green Belt Maryland Space Research Center" had confirmed the two miracles.[1] Irwin H. Linton, identified as a "member of the U.S. Supreme Bar Association" and author of "A Lawyer Examines the Bible," is also quoted in the tract. According to the tract, Linton had described an earlier similar discovery of the missing day. In this account "an agnostic astronomy professor at Yale University" is converted by another faculty member, here referred to as "that old saint, Professor Totten." The agnostic astronomer, supposedly, had stumbled upon the missing twenty-four hours and turned to Totten for advice; "the wiley Totten" sent him to read "the Great Book," where the astronomer found first the passage in Joshua then the lacking forty minutes in 2 Kings. In the tract the story concludes, "We are told that the professor dropped to his knees and cried out as doubting Thomas of old: 'My Lord and My God!'"

In another undated tract, entitled *Apologetics,* Yale University's Totten is identified as "a godly professor of Military science" and "a great Bible scholar."[2] His encounter with the "ungodly professor that was an instructor in Astronomy" resulted in this professor (or "instructor") confessing after he found the final forty minutes that "he had to believe in a God that had that accurate a 'Book.'" It should be noted that the episode pitting Totten against the astronomer has the same two-part structure, as well as the same figures for hours and minutes, as the computer story; furthermore, it quotes supposed actual conversations between the skeptical inquirer (i.e., the astronomer in the Yale version or the computer scientists in the NASA version) and the true believer. However, this Yale version of the story ends in a conversion rather than an observation about God rubbing anyone's nose in Truth.

There is no mention in the *Apologetics* tract of Harold Hill or of the space scientists' rediscovery of the missing day, but Immanuel Velikovsky's *Worlds in Collision* is cited as corroboration of the story of the sun standing still in the book of Joshua. Also, mention is made of "copious references" for information to works written by Dr. Harry Rimmer, including a book entitled *Harmony of Science and Scripture,* about which more below.

A tract issued by Osterhus Publishing House in Minneapolis also includes Harold Hill's computer story and a reference to the Yale professor.[3] In fact, "two eminent men of science" are named: "Prof. C. A. Totten of Yale University and Sir Edwin Ball, British astronomer," but the anecdote about Totten's encounter with the ungodly astronomer is lacking. Reference is made to Totten's book *Joshua's Long Day,* in which "full details are given." None of these sources supplies a date either for Totten's publications or his tenure at Yale, leaving the impression that he is a current or at least a fairly recent faculty member.

Who are Harold Hill and Professor Totten, and when did they make their momentous discovery of the missing day, a finding that seems to be described only in religious tracts and anonymous photocopied fliers? In December 1986 I consulted Von Del Chamberlain, then director of the Hansen Planetarium in Salt Lake City. He wrote to me as follows:

> About 1970 a story started in church circles about a computer program at NASA which was used to calculate the movements of planets back in time. . . . The "only explanation" for this was to be found in the Bible. I heard this story repeated, with variations, from pulpits, and I have heard that it is sold as an engraving on wood plaques.
>
> While I was working at the Smithsonian's National Air and Space Museum, I attempted to trace this story to its origin and finally talked to Mr. Harry Hill, President of Curtis Engine Company in Maryland. He claimed that one of his staff was the key person involved while on contract with NASA, but Hill would not reveal any names. I also talked with several people at NASA, and it was apparent that no computer program of the type described existed.

Harold Hill, an electrical engineer, told his own story in a Christian inspirational book entitled *How to Live like a King's Kid.*[4] The book's premise is that the Bible serves humankind as "The Manufacturer's Handbook" for living on earth. Hill's book has twenty-eight chapters with intriguing titles like "How to Be Ecstatically Happy in Traffic" and "How to Fix Expensive Machines—Fast," but the relevant one here is chapter 13, "How to Find the Missing Day."

Harold Hill's account of the missing day incident is essentially the same as that in the fliers and tracts; he says he told the story often in his lectures to "high school and college groups on my favorite subject, 'Science, Philosophy, Evolution, and the Bible.'" There are, however, some variations: Hill begins with a reference to "way back in the sixties," and the scientists are doing "statistical preparation for the moon walk." Besides the orbits of the sun, moon, and planets, they are "looking into the trajectories of known asteroids and meteors." The computer, as usual, "put up a red flag" and "one religious fellow" directs the scientists' attention to the two biblical passages.

Somehow, Hill writes, a tape recording or someone's notes made from one of his lectures came into the possession of Mary Kathryn Bryan, a columnist for the Spencer, Indiana, newspaper. After she reproduced the story (no date is mentioned in Hill's book), and after news services repeated it, Hill says he was flooded with letters and calls asking for more information. The form letter he used to reply is reproduced in his book.

The letter states that after nearly five thousand inquiries, Hill wishes to refer those who want to learn more to the accurate account of his information published in the *Spencer Evening World,* to which, he writes, he can add nothing. He admits that "since the incident first came to my attention, I have misplaced details regarding names and places but will be glad to forward them to you when they turn up. In the meantime, I can only say that had I not considered the information to be reliable, I would not have used it in the first place." The rest of the form letter is an account of Hill's religious conversion and his philosophy of life.

In corroboration of his claim that the biblical accounts of a long day are accurate, Hill cites the same Book Fellowship Tract, *Did the Sun Stand Still?* mentioned above as well as "the eminent scientist" Professor C. A. Totten of Yale University and his book *Joshua's Long Day.* Hill's chapter concludes with what he calls a "book report" on Totten's work credited to V. L. Westberg of Sonoma, California, and dated August 1970. For the first time in the sources here discussed, Totten's book is given its actual year of publication, 1890. In his brief review Westberg summarizes Totten's mathematical calculations of the exact year of the missing day and critiques Totten's theory attempting to explain it as a physical reality, but these technical matters go beyond my consideration of the missing day as a legend.

In Hill's book, neither the author nor Westberg makes reference to the incident in which Totten converts an ungodly astronomer. This seems odd, since Hill surely read about the incident in the Book Fellowship tract, and Westberg presumably read it in Totten's book, to which the tracts refer.

NASA's Public Affairs Office at the Goddard Space Flight Center in Greenbelt, Maryland, has issued a terse press release in response to queries about Harold Hill and the missing day. The release states that the center "has no knowledge of the use of its computers supposed by Mr. Harold Hill and attributed to our scientists. Goddard does not apply its computers to the task of projecting thousands of years into the future or past, as this would be irrelevant to the operational lifetime of satellites, which rarely exceeds a dozen years." The release concludes by saying that Hill "worked briefly at Goddard early in the 1960s as a plant engineer, a position which would not place him in direct contact with our computer facilities or teams engaged in orbital computations."

The *Bible-Science Newsletter* of Caldwell, Idaho, another source mentioned in Hill's book, published five short items concerning Joshua's long day and Hill's computer story.[5] In 1970 issues of the *Newsletter,* which are summarized in a May 1978 Bible study supplement, the editors provide a detailed and fairly objective review of most sources I've mentioned here, as well as some I've not been able to locate (such as a 1970 article in *The Ministry,* a Seventh-Day Adventist publication, and a book that Totten is said to have drawn from by "J. B. Dimbleby of South Hackney, England" called *All Past Time;* oddly, the 1978 *Newsletter* does not mention Hill's own 1974 book). A clue in the study guide that I *could* follow up on appears in this short paragraph: "Because the 'computer story' bears a marked resemblance to Totten's ideas, it is not unexpected that some people believe that Harold Hill obtained his material from Totten's book. A champion for creationism several generations ago, Harry Rimmer, also accepted the calculations of Totten."

Harry Rimmer, whom I mentioned above, had been credited for material used in the *Apologetics* tract from Minneapolis. His book *The Harmony of Science and Scripture,* first published in 1927, appeared in numerous later editions,[6] one of which I suspect either Hill or his source for the computer story consulted in constructing that story; Hill, however, did not mention Rimmer in his chapter about the missing day and he or his source might merely have borrowed the Rimmer material as it was paraphrased in the Book Fellowship tract or some other religious publication.

In his book Rimmer takes on no less than the defense of complete acceptance of the literal truth of the entire Bible. On page 294 he reaches the missing day problem in his chapter "Modern Science and the Long Day of Joshua." Rimmer quotes two "eminent men of science," first Sir Edwin Ball, the astronomer who "found that *twenty-four hours had been lost out of solar time*" (my emphasis). This key phrase appears either verbatim or in the variation "elapsed time" in most versions of the computer story. (Hill's own account says "a day missing in solar time.")

Rimmer's version of the dramatic encounter between Totten and the "accomplished astronomer" (nothing about his being "ungodly" or "agnostic" here) is described as being "a condensed account of his [Totten's] book," written in 1890. Guided, and goaded, by Totten, the Yale astronomer finds the two passages accounting for the partial day and the missing forty minutes, then "he laid down the Book and worshipped its Writer, saying, 'Lord, I believe!'"

Finally, we must look into Charles A. L. Totten's book *Joshua's Long Day and the Dial of Ahaz: A Scientific Vindication*. It has been reprinted several times, and I located the edition of 1968 with a foreword by Howard B. Rand, which also includes Rand's essay "When the Earth Turned Over."[7] Totten wrote here an extremely detailed and complete review of relevant scriptural passages, discussed military aspects of the battles, demonstrated the complex mathematical calculations of when the biblical "long days" occurred, and gave a summary of worldwide mythology concerning other such "long days." But Totten modestly mentioned that he "does not pretend to explain *how* the Day in question was lengthened, but accepts it as a literal fact fully corroborated by history." Totten's conclusion based on his calculations (or those performed by others) is that "the conjunction of Joshua's Long Day was upon Wednesday the 1,194,006th day, i.e., 173,932 weeks and 6 days before June 17th, 1890."

Rand's contribution to the 1968 edition was an attempt to give a scientific explanation of how the long day could have occurred on a spinning earth. He postulates a giant meteor shower as the cause, remembering the great stones cast down on the battlefield by the Lord, but also mentions the possibility of a comet or of interspace visitors.

The most notable aspect of Totten's book and Rand's addition is that neither one makes any mention whatever of an encounter between an astronomer at Yale University and Totten in which the missing day was discovered in the Bible. Either that anecdote appears elsewhere in Totten's numerous writings or Rimmer (or someone else) made it up. Totten's journal, *Our Race: Its Origin and Its Destiny,* was published from 1890 through 1915; the description of his encounter with the ungodly astronomer may be found somewhere in the journal's pages, which I have not been able to examine.

Far from being "a scientist of standing," as Rimmer termed him, "Professor" C. A. Totten was merely a lieutenant who taught military science and tactics at Yale from 1889 to 1892. He was an anti-Semite and a crackpot besides, whose favorite theory was the racial purity of the Aryan race and whose favorite pastime was predicting imminent apocalypse. Dan A. Oren in his book on Jews and Yale writes that "Totten was detailed [to Yale] by the War Department (as part of the conditions for Yale's receiving Connecticut land grant monies through 1893)." According to Oren, Totten "packed" the undergraduates into his military courses in which he also put forth his religious and racial theories, proving them in part through the exegesis of nursery rhymes. Oren speculates "that students may have attended the course as much to laugh at the man as to learn from him."[8]

Totten, however, had his supporters. The *New York Times* on June 26, 1891, mentioned Rev. Frederick L. Stevens, "one of the most enthusiastic of Lieut. Totten's disciples in the university." Stevens, according to the *Times,* "was recently removed to the Insane Retreat in this city in a condition of hopeless dementia."[9] The author of another *Times* article on March 13, 1892, ridiculed Totten's latest prediction that the Anti-Christ would arrive on March 29, mentioning in passing that he had enrolled 196 students in his current class.[10] On March 30 the *Times* reported again on "Lieut. Totten's Vagaries," the author remarking that "the long-sought star hiding behind the sun, which Lieut. Totten prophesied would appear to-day, when the last week of Antichrist begins, did not, so far as is known, put in an appearance." In an interview, Totten stuck to his general predictions and issued some further vaguely worded prophecies of impending doom.[11]

Obscure as he was in the history of science, and obviously unsuccessful as a prophet of doom, Totten did manage to launch his missing day theory (which was perhaps partly borrowed from earlier writers) into the future. The dramatic form in which the theory was presented—as an encounter between Totten and a Yale astronomer—may have been reported somewhere by Totten himself or perhaps was invented by Rimmer or another ardent apologist for a literal reading of the Bible. This reported incident is the likely source of Hill's missing day story, either because Hill himself or someone who told the computer story to him read it in Rimmer's 1927 book or in a religious tract summarizing Rimmer's work.

Once repeated and shaped by Hill's lectures and then brought to a wider public via the 1970 Indiana newspaper column and its reprintings, the computer version of "The Missing Day in Time" story is still being continually re-recreated in oral and printed tradition just as any urban legend is modified. The generalized and often unreliable citations of supposed supporting references in the texts representing this tradition seem sufficient to convince some modern fundamentalists that the story provides a credible example of how science has proven some claims of religion to be literally true, even though the story sounds much too good to be true.

As Michael A. Covington, a computer scientist at the University of Georgia, wrote me on August 4, 1990, concerning this story, "If the report were genuine, some other scientist would have replicated it by now, since vast numbers of people do astronomical computing nowadays."

Perhaps the best statement about the whole subject is one found in *The Interpreter's Bible*, volume 3, published in 1953. Concerning the passage in Joshua 10:13, this commentary suggests that "it is profitless to try to rationalize this and many other miracles of the Bible."[12]

Afterword: The Star *and the* World

In 1999, after many years of his newspaper being queried about "The Missing Day in Time," David N. Benson of the *Auburn (Ind.) Evening Star* tracked the confusion to its source and uncovered much interesting new evidence of the story's early circulation. Benson's lengthy and well-researched article appeared in the May 5, 1999, issue of his newspaper, and I am grateful to him for sharing his information plus sending a copy of the article (which richly deserves wider circulation).

According to Benson, Mary Kathryn Bryan's report of the missing day story appeared in "Mary Kay's Kollum" in the *Spencer (Ind.) Evening World* on October 10, 1969. She got a typewritten copy of the story in 1969 from the wife of a Baptist minister in Spencer, and evidently the source was a tape recording of a talk given by Harold Hill, possibly at a Christian camp in Oklahoma the year previously. Bryan's column triggered a long series of letters and calls to the *Evening World* requesting further information and clarification. The inquiries continue to this day, and the newspaper still sends out a form letter of explanation with a copy of the original column and a denial from NASA. "Every year, *The Evening World* runs an anniversary story," Benson's article notes. Harold Hill died in 1987 without ever retracting his story about the missing day or finding his original notes on its source. Mary Kathryn Bryan retired from the newspaper in 1973 and told Benson that although she no longer has her copy of the story, she remembers that it was typewritten and mimeographed.

How the *Evening World* of Spencer got confused with the *Evening Star* of Auburn is a mystery; Benson's theory is that when *The Bible-Science Newsletter* reprinted the missing day story in 1970 a writer or editor may have been misled by the name of the Washington, D.C., newspaper the *Evening Star* (later the *Washington Star-News* and then the *Washington Star*). The *Newsletter* had credited its story to a contributor from Maryland who may well have been familiar with the Washington paper.

Besides grappling with these details, Benson was also successful in locating and interviewing NASA officials of the time who clarified the minor role that Harold Hill played in the operations at Greenbelt, Maryland, and who confirmed the utter impossibility of the incident described in "The Missing Day in Time." Finally, Benson provides a list of Internet sites where the legend is either presented as fact or denied, remarking, "You can find others by searching the Internet using 'Curtis Engine' and 'Evening Star' as keywords." Benson's article (in a slightly different form that includes a version of the legend copied from another Web site) may be consulted in the archives of his newspaper's Web site under the date May 5, 1999, at this address: http://evening-star.kpcnews.net.

Notes

An earlier version of this chapter was presented at the Fifteenth Anniversary Conference of the Committee for the Scientific Investigation of Claims of the Paranormal (CSICOP), in Berkeley, California, May 4, 1991.

1. *Did the Sun Stand Still?* tract no. 1211 (North Syracuse, N.Y.: Book Fellowship, n.d.), seven pp.

2. Harry Conn, *Apologetics* (Minneapolis: Men for Missions, n.d.), nine pp.

3. *The Missing Day/Behind the Missing Day* (Minneapolis: Osterhus Publishing House, n.d.), four pp.

4. Harold Hill, as told to Irene Burk Harrell, *How to Live Like a King's Kid* (Plainfield, N.J.: Logos International, 1974).

5. *Joshua's Long Day,* in *Five Minutes with the Bible and Science: Daily Reading Magazine,* supplement to *Bible-Science Newsletter* 8.5 (May 1978): 1–2.

6. Harry Rimmer, *The Harmony of Science and Scripture,* 4th ed. (Berne, Ind.: Berne Witness Company, 1937).

7. Charles A. L. Totten, *Joshua's Long Day and the Dial of Ahaz: A Scientific Vindication,* Study no. 2 of the Our Race Series—The Voice of History (1890; Merrimac, Mass.: Destiny Publishers, 1968).

8. Dan A. Oren, *Joining the Club: A History of Jews and Yale* (New Haven, Conn.: Yale University Press, 1985).

9. "A Clergyman Insane: He Is a Graduate of Yale and One of Lieut. Toten's [*sic*] Disciples," *New York Times,* June 26, 1891, 1.

10. "No Rest for Totten," *New York Times,* Mar. 13, 1892, 4.

11. "Lieut. Totten's Vagaries," *New York Times,* Mar. 30, 1892, 1.

12. I am grateful to Joseph Duffy for help with finding some of the references cited in this chapter. After I spoke at the 1991 CSICOP meeting, Tom McIver referred me to his article "Ancient Tales and Space-Age Myths of Creationist Evangelism," *Skeptical Inquirer* 10 (Spring 1986): 258–76, in which "The Missing Day" was discussed, including a text broadcast by the television evangelist Jimmy Swaggart. Responses to McIver's article appeared in *Skeptical Inquirer* 11 (Fall 1986): 108, and 15 (Summer 1991): 350–51. McIver later supplied several further references to "The Missing Day," and I continue to find the story in active circulation among fundamentalist Christians.

11

Some Oddities of Military Legendry

In the last section of his 1959 book *American Folklore,* Richard Dorson made an enthusiastic pitch for the collection and study of military folklore. "Volumes of floating lore," effused Dorson, "swirl through the armed services . . . [and] the experiences of war spew up countless exploits and escapes enshrined in legend."[1] The typical subjects of GI legend, as illustrated in Dorson's examples (besides "exploits and escapes") were military snafus, greenhorn pranks, and horrors—legend topics still found today in GI folklore.

In the decades since Dorson's Korean War–era survey, few attempts have been made to enlarge the canon of American military legends. An exception is Bruce Jackson's 1990 essay on personal war narratives in which he discusses, among others, the story of the hippie (or the old woman) spitting on a Vietnam veteran.[2]

In this chapter I briefly identify and provide examples of five seldom described categories of military legends. The materials were collected not from fieldwork or from my own military career of one year, two months, and twenty-two days in the U.S. Army (but who was counting?) but rather from wartime writings and from responses by military personnel and veterans to a request in one of my newspaper columns for examples of characteristic GI stories.

The categories that emerged are homefront stories, training stories, troop transport stories, survival stories, and technological stories.

Homefront stories are often tales about civilian misunderstanding of and contempt for military personnel, such as "The Spitting Hippie" story already mentioned. Here's a typical homefront story from World War II that I call "The War Profiteer." It was reported in *Time* magazine on March

23, 1942. *Time*'s report, sent to me by a reader who had kept the clipping because he had also heard the story told, began:

> The story went around the U.S. last week. Everybody who told it swore that it was true. Everybody had got it from a friend of a friend of a friend.
> . . .
> Riding on a bus, a woman passenger was heard to say: "Well, my husband has a better job than he ever had and he's making more money, so I hope the war lasts a long time."
> Another woman got up and slapped her face. "This is for my boy who was killed at Pearl Harbor. And this"—another slap—"is for my boy in the Phillipines." [*sic*] At the next stop, the woman who was slapped got off.

In other versions of the legend, a man does the slapping or a woman overhears the remark in a bakery, after which she buys a lemon cream pie and throws it into the face of the person who said it.

A similar World War II homefront story is "The Accuser Rebuffed." The mother of a boy fighting in Italy begins to criticize an apparently healthy young man standing next to her on a crowded bus. "Why aren't you in uniform like *my* son, fighting for your country?" she asks. After tolerating her abusive language for a while, the young man replies, "Why don't you ask your son to look for the arm I lost in Salerno?" and he shows her his empty sleeve.

In yet another variation on the theme, several bus riders snicker at a young man who is tenderly caring for the young woman accompanying him whose hands are in a muff: he feeds her a snack, lights her cigarette, wipes her nose, and so on. Finally, angered at the crowd's attitude, the young man removes the muff and shows that the girl's hands are missing: "That's what the Japs did to her in a prison camp," he says.

Similar legends refer to Vietnam war veterans. In one, an angry crowd at a Fourth of July parade cheers on a young man who knocks down and kicks another man who has not saluted the flag as it was carried by. In some versions of the story, the attacker stabs the man who failed to salute. Then the crowd realizes that the man who didn't salute is blind, and he explains that he was blinded in combat in Vietnam.

In another story, an injured Gulf War vet telephones his parents from the hospital to ask if he may bring home with him a comrade who is blind and a multiple amputee. The parents say no, that this would be too much of a burden on them. Their son then kills himself, since he was describing his own injuries and realized that his parents would be unable to accept him again.

The category training stories was suggested by the following letter from a reader:

> Dear Professor: I went through Infantry Basic Training in 1944 with a group who were almost entirely unsophisticated 18–year-olds. Short truths, like the following, were passed around in great numbers:
>
> First, to insure that you alternated your two pair of shoes, a staple was pounded into the heel of each shoe in one pair. (Some camps used a paint mark instead.) On odd-numbered days, you had to wear the marked pair.
>
> At Camp Wheeler, Ga., and also at Fort Jackson, S. C., I heard about a poor soul who had both his left shoes marked. Too frightened to make a fuss, the soldier supposedly alternated wearing two lefts and two rights all through training.
>
> Another story I heard in those days was about poison ivy during bivouacs. New training cycles began every two weeks, and if you missed any part of the training, you were put back into a subsequent cycle. The last two weeks of each cycle was spent on bivouac, doing field problems.
>
> The poor soul in this story contracted such a bad case of poison ivy during bivouac that he had to be hospitalized. When he emerged from the hospital, he would be put back into another cycle, and soon he was bedded down in the same poison ivy patch as before.
>
> He did this all one spring and summer and was waiting hopefully for the first frost to kill the poison ivy plants and end his agony.

Another training story from the same era was sent by a reader who began: "This supposedly took place just before World War II, when many thousands of draftees had to be trained but only a relatively few experienced officers were available." He continued:

> An artillery crew that had been training for some time were being reviewed by a senior officer. Each time they went through the firing drill the officer noticed that at the moment the gun was fired one of the team would stand off to the side with his arm extended straight out and with his fist clenched.
>
> The officer asked the purpose of this procedure, but all the men knew was that it was part of the drill.
>
> The officer was curious, so he continued his inquiries around the post. But no one seemed to know the reason for this apparently meaningless gesture.
>
> Finally a World War I veteran reviewed the gun drill, looked closely at

the man with the arm extended and fist clenched, and then exclaimed, "Why, of course! He's holding the horses!"

In the motorized Army, that part of the drill became obsolete, but it was still included in the training exercise.

A story about a training snafu involving an airplane was sent by a retired U.S. Air Force colonel, who said the story has kicked around in the service for about thirty years. It concerns a command pilot and his young first lieutenant copilot who are starting a flight in their C-46. The lieutenant's wife had recently left him, and the older man was trying to cheer him up while firing up the big bird, taxiing to the runway, and talking through their take-off checklist.

"Just before they were airborne," wrote my informant, "the commander glanced at the copilot and said in a pleasant voice, 'Cheer up!'" Dutifully, the lieutenant (thinking he had said "*Gear* up!") hit the lever retracting the landing gear, and slowly the aircraft sank into the runway, shattering the propellers and ripping the belly apart."

The next category, troop transport stories, was suggested by a passage dated June 23, 1943, in John Steinbeck's book *Once There Was a War*:

> A troopship is a nest of rumors, rumors that go whisking from stem to stern. . . . The story starts and is repeated, and everyone, except perhaps the permanent crew, believes each for a few hours before a new one takes its place.
>
> It might be well to set down some of the rumors so that when heard they will be recognized for what they are, the folklore of a troopship.[3]

Steinbeck included examples of troopship rumors in his book, and several of my readers with military backgrounds confirmed this as an active category of military legends by sending their own examples of such stories.

A naval reserve commander wrote me about shipping out from San Francisco during World War II when he was a brand new ensign. During the first big storm, his ship groaned and banged in a terrifying way. My informant wrote, "The ship pitched into the stormy seas, shuddered to regain her proper position above the surface, only to plunge again." All the while the ship made horrendous noises that badly frightened the younger sailors.

According to an on-board rumor, the ship had run aground earlier in the war, then limped home for major repairs. Now in its weakened state, it could break apart at any time. But my informant and his fellow landlubbers later learned that *all* ships are extremely noisy during heavy weather and also that disaster rumors are common at sea. Steinbeck, in fact, had described the same rumor. The front end of his ship, as he heard on the grapevine, was "weak and only patched up . . . very likely to fall to pieces."[4]

The same reserve officer who wrote me also knew one skipper during the Korean War who liked to start rumors:

> He would come into the chart house and ask the Quartermaster to break out the charts for some interesting place, such as Hong Kong. Then he would stroll up the main deck to the fo'csle, down the other side to the fantail, and back up to the bow.
>
> Never did he make that circuit before some sailor would stop him with "Say, Captain, I hear we're going to Hong Kong."

A retired army officer sent me several stories he heard on a troopship to Europe in 1944. Two were about German submarines that were either closely following the ship waiting to attack or were being guided to it via radio signals transmitted by spies planted on board. Steinbeck also mentioned rumors about lurking submarines and spies on board. He reported a story he heard about an American sub surfacing next to the convoy that was said to have narrowly escaped being blown out of the water because it was mistaken for the enemy.

Troop transport stories were told about airplanes as well as ships. I received the following telegraphic account of a traditional military *air* transport prank from a veteran of naval aviation:

> Transport plane. Troops sitting in web seats. Pilot walks to the back to use bathroom.
>
> A little later the copilot backs out of the cockpit unreeling two strings. He hands them to a soldier and says he too needs to use the bathroom.
>
> Copilot explains that soldier should pull right string to guide plane right, pull left string for left turn. Time passes, but nobody comes back.
>
> Guy gives one a little pull, and the plane banks! Pulls other string, and plane banks the other way! (Strings are really tied to flight engineer who steers aircraft accordingly.)
>
> Pilots return, thank the dupe, and reel up string as they reenter cockpit.

Survival stories are accounts of places or persons that survive a military attack in some seemingly miraculous way.

The Japanese surprise attack on Pearl Harbor on December 7, 1941, produced many sensational but unverified local stories. Most concerned the supposedly traitorous actions of Japanese living in Hawaii or else described a nonexistent enemy invasion of the islands. Gwenfread Allen's book *Hawaii's War Years: 1941–1945* contains a chapter debunking "rampant rumors" of the time, including:

> That Japanese people in Hawaii were warned about the raid via codes in Honolulu newspaper ads.
> That directional arrows were cut in the cane fields by Japanese farm workers to guide attackers to Pearl Harbor.
> That paratroopers had landed.
> That water supplies had been poisoned.[5]

None of these rumors contained a shred of truth. But one story *not* discussed in Allen's book did become a genuine survival legend among members of the Latter-day Saints church. According to the story, one of the Japanese pilots attempted to bomb the Mormons' Hawaiian temple, mistaking it for a likely target. But when he tried to release his bombs, they would not drop from their racks. However, when he flew on to his assigned target, the bombs fell without a hitch. Supposedly, after the war the pilot learned what the building really was, and the apparent miracle so impressed him that he joined the Mormon church.

Whether or not a miracle really spared the Mormons' sacred edifice, the story has reached mythological proportions among the LDS. The historian Kenneth W. Baldridge of Brigham Young University at Hawaii sent me a copy of his own detailed investigation of the story.[6] Baldridge points out that standards of military strategy and discipline refute the idea of a straying pilot, and besides, he wrote, "I've never talked to anybody who has met the man."

There were two main sources cited to support the straying bomber story: One was a supposed eyewitness and the other was a former Mormon missionary who claimed to have met the converted pilot in Japan. But Mormon records (which are extremely detailed and accurate) do not include a Pearl Harbor pilot who became a church member. Mormon folk who believe the story only know a friend of a friend of a supposed witness or participant. Besides, no civilian targets were bombed in the Pearl Harbor attack, and certainly the element of surprise would have been lost had a pilot chosen to strike something that lay fifteen minutes of flying time from the planned target.

As a Mormon "faith-promoting story," there are different theories for why the building was spared. The simplest attributes it to a mechanical failure. But the mechanism functioned perfectly when the plane was over the correct target. Other stories mention a mysterious force field that kept the plane from approaching the temple, a protective cloud that shrouded it from attack, or a peculiar drowsiness that overcame the pilot when he tried to drop a bomb.

Baldridge wrote, "In the gamut of stories, no two seem to be alike. In checking out a possibility, I receive a new story instead of a confirmation of the one I am checking."[7] That must frustrate a historian, but it's a familiar experience for a folklorist.

Another survival story was sent to me by retired navy Senior Chief Petty Officer John R. Olson of Jacksonville, Florida, from whom I learned the legend about how AGOI ("A Guy Over In") some other unit survived a direct shot to the head during combat. Olson called his story "The Magic Bullet" and suggested the acronym AGOI rather than the folklorist's term FOAF when referring to certain bizarre military stories that are always attributed to someone in a different unit from the storyteller's own: "AGOI—a guy over in—[D Battery, Third Platoon, C Company, etc.] was on patrol or in his bunker when an enemy sniper fired at him. The bullet punched through his helmet, but due to the extremely long range of the shot it deflected between the outer steel shell and the fiberglass inner liner. The bullet then rattled around inside the helmet before falling harmlessly out."

Occasionally, wrote Olson, the story was embellished with the comment, "The guy said it sounded just like a bee or a hornet." Sometimes, according to the story, the man actually believed that there *was* a bee in his helmet. When he yanked off his helmet, the bullet clipped off a piece of his ear. Olson recognized "The Magic Bullet" story as an updating of similar yarns told in earlier wars. These often described bullets magically stopped by a Bible or by a packet of letters from the man's wife or girlfriend that he carried in his shirt pocket.

The reason for the tale's updating, Olson suggested to me, is that in the Vietnam War most line troops wore body armor or flak jackets. Thus, there was less logic to the old bullet-in-the-heart scenario. Any bullet that could penetrate the armor would surely also make it through some sheets of paper in a man's pocket. It made more sense, then, for the well-aimed bullet in the story to be directed at the head, where a hit was usually fatal—except, of course, to AGOI.

Paul Fussell, in his book *Wartime: Understanding and Behavior in the Second World War*, discusses other survival stories. He notes that, among military personnel, these stories have the function of "fostering irrational hopes and proposing magical outcomes."[8] In his chapter on wartime rumors, Fussell mentions a magic bullet story. In this one, which was included in an episode of the television series "M*A*S*H," a bullet or piece of shrapnel strikes a soldier without doing harm and is thereafter carried as a good luck charm.

Fussell quotes one World War II soldier who saved a stray bullet that had bounced harmlessly off his helmet and who later said of it: "For years I carried this bullet about as the One with My Name On it, possession of which, according to army superstition, guaranteed immortality, at least for the duration."[9]

My examples of technological stories have come out of the high-tech world of recent wars, though I'm sure prototypes must have existed in earlier military engagements. During the 1983 invasion of Grenada, for example, one story goes that an American army unit was pinned down in a house and the radio was broken. But a quick-witted soldier supposedly used the telephone in the house to call back to Ft. Bragg and request fire support, charging the long-distance call to his phone credit card. During the Gulf War, according to a similar story, a soldier in an armored unit was able to call home from his tank while his unit was engaged in battle and describe the details of combat to his wife.

Another Gulf War story may be more a joke than a legend, since I'm not sure whether anyone ever really took it seriously. The story claims that on an island in the gulf controlled by enemy forces the Iraqis had put up wooden decoys of military vehicles and installations, hoping to fool the American bombers. Supposedly, after air force intelligence recognized the trick, the bombers retaliated by dropping decoy wooden bombs onto the decoy targets.

Perhaps the oddest military legend of all that I have encountered, and one that defies neat classification, is "The Tale of the Truck," a wholly implausible story, but still one that's often told as true. It combines horror, patriotism, and whimsy and may actually be just a military prank that survives in the form of a quasi-legend told during training.

When I first heard the story during a radio interview, I thought that Denver talk show host Alan Dumas was putting me on with "The Tale of the Truck." Dumas said that a former marine had called him with the strange story. The caller claimed that the metal ball on top of flagpoles was called "the truck." Inside the truck, he said, on all official U.S. government buildings, such as those on military posts, two things were kept, a match and a bullet. These items supposedly were there so that the last American survivor facing an enemy attack could burn Old Glory before the invaders got their hands on it and then shoot himself so he wouldn't be captured.

Dumas told me he "voiced skepticism" on the air about the story, but subsequently he got three more calls confirming it. First a former navy chaplain called saying he'd heard the same story; next a teenage girl called to say that her army reserve father had told it to her; third, another marine phoned in to say that a question about the contents of the truck had actually been on an exam he took in basic training.

I dutifully took notes on the story and on Alan Dumas's sources. A short while later I heard from Dr. Whitney Smith, executive director of the Flag Research Center in Winchester, Massachusetts. He wrote on May 16, 1991, to ask whether I knew any flag-related legends, and he gave this example:

> A number of ex-military people have telephoned to inquire what is inside the finial—the decorative symbol at the top of the pole which is part of the regimental flag carried by troops.
>
> In fact, the finial is solid metal, but the legend is that it is hollow and contains *three* objects—a grain of rice, a match, and a *silver* bullet.
>
> The story goes that a soldier surrounded by the enemy can break open the finial and gain some strength from eating the rice. He then uses the match to burn the flag so it will not fall into enemy hands.
>
> Finally, he commits suicide with the bullet—whether to prevent his own capture or out of shame at having burned the flag is not made clear.[10]

This version makes a bit more sense, because it would be much easier to reach the finial on a regimental flag than the top of a flagpole on a government building. But what about the rice, the silver bullet, and especially that odd meaning for the word *truck?* The *Oxford English Dictionary* at least explains the meaning: "a circular or square cap of wood fixed on the head of a mast or flag-staff, usually with small holes or sheaves for halliards." This definition of *truck* is listed in the OED as a "nautical" usage, with the first sample quotations, from 1626, mentioning "the trucke or flagge staffe." There are several other such references in the *OED*. For example, in *Two Years before the Mast*, Richard H. Dana Jr.'s 1840 classic, he wrote, "We painted [the ship] both inside and out, from the truck to the water's edge." Or, more colorfully, in an 1899 citation, "The second mate ordered me to go up and reeve the signal halliards in the mizzen truck."

The range of quotations in the *OED* suggests that the word *truck* was applied first to various wheels or rollers used to move equipment around and was later used for the pulley guiding the rope that hoists a flag up a flagpole. When a finial shaped like a ball or ornament was added to the pole, it too was called a truck. But where did the details about grains of rice, matches, and silver bullets stored inside the truck come from? A reader of my column came up with a plausible explanation; he was the same man who sent me a version of "The Magic Bullet"—retired Senior Chief Petty

Officer John R. Olson of Jacksonville, Florida. Olson wrote, "Dear Doc: I've heard 'The Tale of the Truck,' but I thought it was true. Just goes to show that even the old chief can be fooled (not very often, though)."

Olson reasoned that the elements of the story must be symbolic, since they are so obviously impractical: the match would not likely light after a long period inside the hollow truck, where condensation would form in changing weather conditions; the bullet would have to be the right caliber for the last soldier's weapon; and the grain of rice would not provide enough energy to make much of a difference.

But the rice is easily understood, Olson reasoned, if it's taken as a symbol for sustenance. While bread in *our* culture represents all food, hence any sustenance ("Give us this day our daily bread . . ."), *rice* is the Asian staple food and, as such, is highly symbolic to those peoples. Olson suggested to me that "The Tale of the Truck" contains this symbolism and portrays military values consistent with an origin among U.S. Marine Corps personnel serving in the Pacific region. He wrote: "A naval vessel does not burn its colors; a warship goes down with the colors flying; the captain at the helm and the gunners at their battle stations. The marines would be more apt to find themselves in a last man situation ashore, and you have to consider the Marine mystique. As an old 'gunny' sergeant told me when I was a young seaman, 'The enemy has never seen the back of a live marine's uniform.'"

Now that, I believe, makes pretty good sense out of an oddity of military legendry.

Notes

An earlier version of this chapter was presented at the annual meeting of the American Folklore Society in Jacksonville, Florida, October 15–18, 1992.

1. Richard Dorson, *American Folklore* (Chicago: University of Chicago Press, 1959), 268.

2. Bruce Jackson, "The Perfect Informant," *Journal of American Folklore* 103 (1990): 400–416. See also Jerry Lembcke, *The Spitting Image: Myth, Memory, and the Legacy of Vietnam* (New York: New York University Press, 1998).

3. Steinbeck's wartime dispatches were serialized in the *New York Herald Tribune* in 1943 and first published in book form in 1958. I quote from *Once There Was a War* (New York: Penguin, 1977), 9.

4. Ibid., 10.

5. Gwenfread Allen, *Hawaii's War Years: 1941–1945* (Honolulu: University of Hawaii Press, 1952), 47–56.

6. Kenneth W. Baldridge, "In Search of a Tale: A Personal Account (Was There an Attempt to Bomb the Hawaii Temple, or Wasn't There?)," paper presented at the meeting of the Mormon Pacific Historical Society, May 21, 1988 (originally written in April 1978), fourteen-page computer printout.

7. Ibid, 11. An account of Baldridge's conclusions appeared as "Exploding an LDS Myth," *Latter-day Sentinel,* May 17, 1989, 4.

8. Paul Fussell, *Wartime: Understanding and Behavior in the Second World War* (New York: Oxford University Press, 1989), 48.

9. Ibid., 49.

10. In a follow-up letter dated June 6, 1991, Smith clarified for me that the truck itself is placed just below the finial: "It has holes or other hardware for the hoisting of a flag. The finial is pure decoration."

12

Some News from the Miscellaneous Legend Files

My book *The Vanishing Hitchhiker* concluded with a chapter entitled "Urban Legends in the Making."[1] I described the items in this section as "fragmentary rumors and stories," and I attempted to differentiate these from the "established legends" that circulate "among the public at large in well-wrought versions."[2]

In retrospect, however, it is clear that I was wrong. The ten stories that I referred to as being "in the making" ("The Economical Car," "The Exploding Toilet," "The Man on the Roof," and so forth) did not "emerge" later as *real* urban legends, since, as I learned, they already possessed all the traits of the genre, being apocryphal, anonymous, supposedly true plotted stories widely told in different variants over a considerable time period.[3] Only lack of information about these particular stories made them seem to me to be emergent legends. Still, it is possible, as the Finnish folklorist Leea Virtanen phrased it, that "our environment is bristling with narratives that are potential primordial cells for folklore."[4] In this chapter I am seeking some of these narrative cells, specifically in the daily news.

People frequently send me what one recent correspondent called "candidates for legend-hood." These are stories that readers think might eventually become new urban legends. I receive masses of mail from readers of my books and syndicated newspaper column. I keep these letters in a series of miscellaneous files labeled "cars," "crime," "animals," "sex," and so forth. (In 1993 I systematized my files and created a type index that was published in *The Baby Train and Other Lusty Urban Legends*.[5])

Some of these nominated items for legend status are odd personal experiences of the writers; others are stories clipped from the tabloids. But most are news clippings from the legitimate press, and it is these that I am reviewing here. Often I receive multiple copies of the same wire service stories, suggesting widespread opinion that they might be legends rather than news. Certainly this material demonstrates an affinity between human interest news stories and modern legends.

Things people send me are an index to what they believe modern legends are like. It's true that these beliefs are conditioned by what people have read, which prompted them to write to me, but the letters also indicate that most writers recognize actual legends in oral tradition; now they are wondering about another odd story they've come across. These people are suggesting that the news stories they send might eventually generate urban legends.

Journalists themselves sometimes respond to the news qualities of urban legends. Bob Greene, for example, devoted a 1988 column to an "urban horror story" of New York City. He included variant examples of the trick he had heard about of leaving a sign saying "No Radio" in a parked car to discourage thieves.[6] Similarly, Jim Knippenberg of the *Cincinnati Enquirer* described how "cicadas invade urban folklore," citing local legends of the 1987 Midwestern seventeen-year cicada plague.[7] One of his stories, which he called a "widespread gem," was about a "weird lady" who baked a cicada pie and sent it to school with her child. But these two local stories probably have not been told much, if at all, nationally.

Other columnists sometimes compile lists of news "oddities" that resemble legends, such as in two "Our Towne" columns written by Jack Thomas of the *Boston Globe*.[8] These columns contained such items as that a Seattle zoo was feeding donated Easter bunnies to the lions and that a Dallas wrecking company had razed the wrong house. But there are no actual legends circulating on these themes.

Some columnists have parodied urban legends, such as the following example from Gerald Kloss's column, "Slightly Kloss-Eyed," which appears in the *Milwaukee Journal*:

> This happened to my nephew's doctor's wife's plumber's cousin, who's a 275-pound defensive tackle for a pro football team. He was sitting at home one morning when he suddenly got the urge to put a new washer in the laundry tub faucet down in the basement.
>
> But the basement was so stuffy that he decided to shuck his clothes and work in comfort. After banging his head against the laundry tub, he went upstairs and came back down wearing a football helmet. He worked at the faucet for a minute before he heard someone saying "Ahem!" in the corner of the basement. It was a female meter-reader who had entered while he was upstairs getting his helmet.

She smiled at the naked man in the football helmet and quipped, "I hope you win the game Sunday, mister."

He shrugged and replied, "Thanks for your support, lady. You can talk about all the money we make, but we're really playing for all you fans out there, and you sure can count on us to put out a 100% effort. Our running game's shaping, and if our pass defense holds up, I think we've got a good chance of going all the way."[9]

A *Harvard Lampoon* publication, *Mediagate,* went so far as to parody a whole *book* of urban legends, and also, again, to suggest that legends spring from news events. The following listing is quoted from a fake publisher's notice, headlined "Bookman Publishing's Catalog for Fall '87": "*The Embarrassing Fart and More New Urban Legends* by Jan Harold Brunvand. Yet another set of rumors, tall tales, and fourth-hand hearsay compiled by the author of *The Vanishing Hitchhiker.* Includes more recent urban legends such as the Senile President, the Adulterous Evangelist, and the Smelly Gym Sock in the Big Mac. 233 pages hardbound. $34.95."[10]

Parodies of urban legends occur among lay individuals as well, as shown by this item posted to a computer newsgroup: "I think Jan Harvey Brunvald, alleged author of 'The Choking Doberman' is an urban legend. Has anybody ever actually seen this guy?"[11]

The material quoted so far, written by people who are aware of urban legends, echoes actual legends that deal with themes like crime, food contamination, nudity, cleverness, reversals of fortune, and the like. But these published stories are really insider jokes, not popular folklore. What do the clippings of *genuine* news stories that are sent to me reflect?

Most news clips I receive are straight accounts—presumably objective and factual—of events that demonstrate the similarities between news and modern legends. First, consider a traditional textbook definition of the major elements of a good news story, which poses the question, "What is News and Why?" The author labels the primary news value of any story as being its "oddity . . . or the WOW factor"; then he lists seven further elements that define news: "Immediacy, Proximity, Prominence, Conflict, Suspense, Emotions, and Consequence." Demonstrating these elements in one hypothetical case, this journalist suggested that a story about a local house fire late in the day in which a prominent family lost two children while a dog rescued a third would deserve a banner headline on page one of the local newspaper.[12]

By way of example, I quote the following letter that was sent anonymously to several Salt Lake City news media:

Currently there is a six year old little girl in Primary Children's Hospital with no hands.

She apparently took a hammer to the family car and to punish her her father took the same hammer to her hands. By the time they got her to the hospital she had lost two fingers (they fell off) and then her blood vessells, bone and nerves were so badly damaged that they had to amputate both hands.

The mother will not press charges because "he was in charge of discipline", and the hospital is being forced to return this child to these two crazy people.

For God's sake, can't the media do something.[13]

There was no such child, no crime, and no cover-up, according to a reporter who checked the tip out thoroughly before releasing the letter to me. Although the letter reflects details found in some actual child abuse cases, no case at the named hospital or elsewhere even remotely matched the situation of the rumored scandal. The story does, however, contain two typical legend motifs: legal helplessness of a wronged innocent and alleged suppression of information by authorities.

If the story were true, it would certainly be hot news; and, whether true or not, if it had variants circulating through the community (and perhaps it does), it would also be a legend. So this example might be the emergent form of a legend, "The Hammered Child." At any rate, the story definitely belongs in my miscellaneous file.

Most of the actual published news stories that I'm sent are not just allusions to legends or hot tips that turn out to be unverifiable. Here are eight summarized examples from my recent mail; all of these stories, as published, contained names, dates, places, and other positive verification:

Fake steroids were sold to athletes via the black market. One male athlete bought, and used, birth control pills, thinking them to be steroids.[14]

Living worms in uncooked fish were consumed along with homemade or carelessly prepared sushi and sashimi.[15]

Two automobile accidents occurring two years apart at the same site were nearly identical in their details, police said.[16]

The elderly victim of a pit bull attack was further injured when the ambulance carrying her to a hospital was involved in an accident.[17]

Two men who died the same day were mistaken for each other; the wrong one was cremated, and the other was displayed in a coffin at the wrong funeral.[18]

An innocent man was apprehended by police because a bank withdrawal slip he picked up to use had a stick-up note written on it by someone else.[19]

A burglar tidied up the place he broke into, emptying trash, doing dishes, folding laundry, and so forth.[20]

A federal agent's gun barrel caught a bullet shot at him and saved his life.[21]

These eight news stories are universally *odd,* and most of them contain some streak of humor, usually black humor. Several of them get their news value from the element of coincidence, applying to the topics of crime, death, injury, or horror. My summaries tend to highlight their binary plot structure, with the second half of each story balancing or taking a step further the situation that is stated in the first half. Summaries of *actual* urban legends phrased in the same way would read like this:

A woman becomes pregnant despite taking birth control pills; she learns that her daughter has been stealing her pills and substituting baby aspirin.

A couple reports the theft of their car to a mob-related neighbor, who makes one phone call and arranges the quick return of the car.

The difference, of course, is that these last two plots represent widely told apocryphal stories circulating in versions that have somewhat varying details; the first summary is based on "The Baby Headache" and the second on "The Helpful Mafia Neighbor." Therefore, these two stories are "legends," while the former list of eight stories are genuine news items— not yet legends, at least to my knowledge.

There does not seem to be much difference between the two groups of stories, although I certainly cannot predict which—if any—of the news stories may become elaborated, repeated, and folklorized. The differences between them rest on selection, oral circulation, and variation, not on particular plot elements.

Some journalists cross the line from reporting facts to repeating folklore when they introduce undocumented anecdotes into news stories. Readers may accept such stories as true, unless their consciousness has been raised by hearing other variations told or by reading about urban legends. Here are six examples of such anecdotes, none of which has any solid verification in the otherwise factual news stories in which they appeared:

A friend of a Honolulu columnist swears it is true that a teamster asked to take a urine test for drug use brought a sample from his wife instead; the teamster was supposedly found to be pregnant.[22]

Eskimos from the Northwest Territories staying in a Montreal hotel, the *Washington Post* reported, are said to have brought a seal with them, which they butchered in the bathtub and cooked in their room.[23]

A Detroit paper mentions that "a long-forgotten pope" in the nineteenth century had decreed that muskrat meat could be lawfully consumed by Michigan Catholics on the meatless days of the liturgical calendar.[24]

According to an article from Milwaukee on the destructive nature of jealousy, a wife is said to have destroyed a new white Mercedes, thinking it belonged to her husband's ex-wife, but it was actually a present for her.[25]

In a letter to the *New York Times* the author disputes that Blue Star Acid scares are based on rumor and describes how "a highway patrolman" (date and place not identified) tasted some suspected cocaine that was really crystal LSD and became seriously ill.[26]

A friend of a friend of a Kansas City columnist carried an old purse to hold the dog droppings when she walked her dog; a mugger kicked the dog and snatched the purse. He was caught and charged with cruelty to animals.[27]

In these six examples we have elements like humor, irony, crime, horror, and above all oddity. Although several of these anecdotes are prefaced with a FOAF-like reference—"A friend . . ." or "said to be true"—we do not have evidence of the variant versions that we demand of a legend.

The regular column entitled "Ariadne" in *New Scientist* on November 26, 1988, touched on the question of what constitutes a "good" urban legend in discussing a story that I consider to be an emerging legend. It's about someone hearing an odd chirping sound coming from their attic. In Ariadne's version, the SPCA rescue squad is called to remove the creature that is chirping. But they find in the attic *not* a stranded bird or insects but only a smoke alarm that is audibly signaling its weak battery, which they remove. This is Ariadne's comment: "This story needs a fire in it somewhere before entering the legend stakes, perhaps started by one of the rescue squad and unnoticed because the smoke detector was out of action. Then there could really be a rare bird in the attic all the time, only discovered, charred, when the fire was extinguished. The SPCA could sue the man for cruelty."[28]

Occasionally a journalist attempts to track down an emergent legend, as Elaine Viets did in the *St. Louis Post-Dispatch* in January 1989.[29] As I recounted in chapter 5, Viets heard a bizarre story, presumably local, about a man hitting a deer with his car, putting the stunned animal into the back-seat, but getting into a series of hilarious scrapes when the deer revived and his hunting dog became involved in the mad attempt to subdue the deer. Allegedly the man stopped the car, ran to a telephone booth to dial 911, but was trapped there by his own dog, which he had accidentally hit on the head with a tire iron during the struggle. Supposedly a police tape of his emergency call existed. Viets was at first unable to verify the story, and I told her in a telephone conversation that it seemed to have too many holes in it to be true, plus it contained elements reminiscent of several urban legends, such as the one I call "The Deer Departed." Eventually Viets got to the root (or almost) of the story.

A tragic airline crash supplies a final example of news and legend interacting. Journalists in this instance first passed on a remarkable story and then debunked it. This occurred after Northwest Flight 255 crashed at Detroit Metropolitan Airport on August 16, 1987, killing 154 of the 155 people on board. The lone survivor was four-year-old Cecelia Cichan, whom news reports described as being spared only because she was "clutched in the lifesaving arms of her dead mother."[30] The *London Daily Mirror*, for example, headlined the story, "Mum's Dying Cuddle Saves Girl," and countless other papers worldwide gave it similar coverage.

In mid-December, however, when files of the National Transportation Safety Board's investigation of the accident became available, it was revealed that the girl had been found thirty-five yards away from the body of her mother and six to eight feet away from any other bodies. Trained journalists working on the scene were at a loss to explain how the fantasy details crept into the reports, though once the anecdote was *printed,* journalists were reluctant to publish the truth. As the Michigan State University professor of journalism Stephen Lacy commented, "This is, of course, a marvelous story, even if it is not true."[31]

That comment fits very well with one of my own shorthand definitions of urban legends: "True stories that are too good to be true." Suggesting once again how close legends may seem to news at times, Lacy also said: "Reporters have a tendency not to check out non-controversial, human interest things, and apparently no one did until now. Then it sort of gets into the folklore."

Precisely! I have concluded, not surprisingly, that the legendlike qualities of many news stories include such things as human interest, oddness, coincidence, and pathos applied to such subject matter as animals, children, accidents, scandal, and crime. Some of my clippings and similar news stories may indeed represent "urban legends in the making," though it is most difficult to attach any specific well-known legend to any particular event reported in the media. However, the similarity between human interest news and modern folk narrative seems sufficient reason to collect and catalog both kinds of stories, even if we must store the clippings temporarily under the heading "Miscellaneous." At least, if legends about them *do* emerge, we will have some data on their genesis.[32]

Notes

The first version of this chapter was presented in a panel on emergent legends at the annual meeting of the American Folklore Society in Philadelphia, October 18–22, 1989. It was revised and published in essentially the same version as presented here in *Western Folklore* 49 (Jan. 1990): 111–20.

1. I may have been unwittingly echoing Alexander Woollcott's phrase when he called the disappearing woman story "a fair specimen of folklore in the making," but that was not my intention. See *While Rome Burns* (New York: Viking Press, 1934), 93.

2. Jan Harold Brunvand, *The Vanishing Hitchhiker: American Urban Legends and Their Meanings* (New York: W. W. Norton, 1981), 175–85.

3. This statement may be taken as my concise definition of a legend, at least for the purposes of this book.

4. Leea Virtanen, "Modern Folklore: Problems of Comparative Research," *Journal of Folklore Research* 22 (1986): 221–32.

5. Jan Harold Brunvand, *The Baby Train and Other Lusty Urban Legends* (New York: W. W. Norton, 1993), 325–47.

6. An undated copy of Greene's syndicated column was sent to me from the Chicago area in October 1988; the headline is "A Clear Signal for the Criminal Mind." Greene quotes variations of the wording on "No Radio" car signs, and he cites examples from published sources as well as personal observation.

7. Jim Knippenberg, "Aw, Come On," *Cincinnati Enquirer,* June 16, 1987.

8. Jack Thomas, "Odd Items from All Over," *Boston Globe,* Dec. 26, 1988, and "More Odd Items," *Boston Globe,* Dec. 29, 1988. The Newton, Massachusetts, reader who sent the clippings had marked his envelope, "Urban legends enclosed!"

9. Gerald Kloss, "Trapped by an Insurance Salesman, and Other Urban Legends," *Milwaukee Journal*, "Green Sheet," Sept. 9, 1987.

10. Harvard Lampoon, *Mediagate* (New York: Atlantic Monthly Press, 1988), 229.

11. The posting is dated March 1, 1989; its return address indicates that it came from someone at Microsoft, the Seattle-based software company. The name "Brunvand" (or "Brunvald," "Brunvard," "VonBrun," and so forth) is often cited in newsgroup exchanges concerning suspicious stories that are going around. The term *urban legend* appears to be well known on the electronic grapevine.

12. Carl Warren, *Modern News Reporting*, 3d ed. (New York: Harper and Row, 1959), 13–29.

13. The typed letter, dated February 3, 1986, begins, "Dear Sirs" and concludes, "I can't sign this because I'm only a private citizen and not supposed to know about this. Please do something."

14. Steven R. Churm, "Business in Counterfeit Steroids Booms as Demand for Drug Grows," *Los Angeles Times*, Dec. 26, 1988.

15. Associated Press and United Press International reports of this incident were released on April 27, 1989; both quote the *New England Journal of Medicine* as well as a spokesperson from the U.S. Centers for Disease Control.

16. I have a clipping of an Associated Press report datelined Pensacola, Florida, dated April 10, 1988, taken from an unidentified Texas newspaper that headlined the story "Fatal Bridge Accident Has Eerie Similarities to Crash in July '86."

17. Trish Power, "Survivor of Dog Mauling Badly Injured in Accident," *Miami Herald*, Aug. 20, 1988.

18. Phil Blumenkrantz, "Funeral Mixup Turns Families' Grief to Horror," *New Haven (Conn.) Register*, May 20, 1988. The sender of this clipping commented, "This may be an urban legend come true!"

19. Shelby Siems, "What's It Like to Be Arrested as a Bank Robber?" *Foster's Daily Democrat* (Dover, N.H.), May 6, 1988. The sender of this clipping commented, "The urban legend possibilities are countless."

20. "Tidy Housebreaker Cleans Up in Gilroy," *San Francisco Chronicle*, Oct. 22, 1987. The sender of this clipping had earlier submitted Herb Caen's *San Francisco Chronicle* column of February 20, 1986, in which a similar story was related: a white woman abducted by a black man and taken to his apartment was forced to wash his dishes to prove that she respected blacks. Caen commented, "If 'washed his dishes' is some kind of euphemism, nobody's letting on."

21. Frank Burgos, "Gun Barrel Catches Bullet, Saves Life of Federal Agent," *Miami Herald*, Oct. 22, 1987. The Atlantis, Florida, police officer who sent the clipping commented, "I am convinced that the incident took place substantially as described. . . . It strikes me that this is a likely candidate to become an urban legend."

22. Dave Donnelly's column in the *Honolulu Star-Bulletin*, September 4, 1986, begins, "With all the news of urine tests for drugs in the papers, I'm reminded of a story . . ."

23. The news story, datelined Yellowknife, Northwest Territories, is by Herbert H. Denton and headlined "Cultures Clash over Game Hunts in Arctic." It appeared in the *Washington Post* on December 17, 1987. The seal-in-the-bathtub incident,

which fills the two lead paragraphs, is said to have taken place "a few years ago." It is credited to a Canadian Broadcasting Corporation commentator.

24. Christopher Cook, "Muskrat Love," *Detroit Free Press Magazine,* Jan. 29, 1989, 18. The muskrat-eating habits of French settlers in southeastern Michigan, and folklore surrounding the practice, are discussed by Dennis M. Au in "God Bless dee Mushrat: She's a Fish!" *1987 Festival of American Folklife* (Washington, D.C.: Smithsonian Institution and National Park Service, 1987), 73–76, and "Let Them Eat Muskrat," *The Digest* 8 (1988): 4–6.

25. Ed Foster-Simeon, "Insecurity Colors Jealousy's Worst Suspicions," *Milwaukee Journal,* July 10, 1988. Attributing the story to "Laura," who sought revenge against "Brandon," the writer concludes, "psychologists throughout the country report that stories like Laura's are not only very real but also alarmingly common."

26. The letter from Paul Tullis of Berkeley, California, dated December 12, 1988, appeared in the *New York Times* on December 24, 1988, in the same section as a letter from me in which I identified an LSD tattoo story discussed in an earlier *Times* article as an urban legend. In a third letter published the same day a reader reported that virtually the same LSD tattoo legend was told during a guided tour of the FBI headquarters in Washington, D.C.

27. George H. Gurley Jr., "Pit Bulls: Scourge of Dogdom," *Kansas City Times,* June 9, 1988. The reader who sent the clipping commented, "Enclosed is of 'Dead Cat in Package' genre."

28. "Ariadne," *New Scientist,* Nov. 26, 1988, 104.

29. Elaine Viets, "A Man, a Deer, a Dog, and 911," *St. Louis Post-Dispatch,* Jan. 3, 1989, and "Year's Wildest Tale: Man, Deer, Dog," *St. Louis Post-Dispatch,* Jan. 10, 1989.

30. This quotation is from a United Press International report datelined Detroit that appeared in the *Salt Lake Tribune* on December 14, 1987; it was headlined "Mother's Arms Didn't Shield Jet Crash's Lone Survivor."

31. The *London Daily Mirror* headline and Lacy's comments are quoted by John Castine and Joel Thurtell in a Knight News Service report in the *Cincinnati Enquirer,* "'Marvelous Story' False, Reports Show," published November 22, 1987.

32. Elliott Oring considers similar matters and some further examples in "Legend, Truth, and News," *Southern Folklore* 47 (1990): 163–77.

13

The Heroic Hacker:
Legends of the Computer Age
ERIK BRUNVAND

The computer hacker has been depicted in the popular press as a socially maladjusted teenager whose goal is to wreak malicious havoc on unsuspecting computer users. In the culture of the computer programmer, however, the hacker takes on a far different aspect. The true hacker is raised to heroic status with tales of amazing feats circulated through computer networks in the form of stories and legends. The persona of the true hacker comes through clearly in hacker legends collected from the Internet.

◪

You have probably read about computer hackers in the newspaper and seen stories on the evening news about gangs of teenage hackers breaking into computer systems and causing tremendous damage. If so, then your impression of what it means to be a hacker is likely to be negative. The popular press tends to depict the hacker as a criminal or at least as a young man who enjoys causing lots of people lots of trouble. He is usually a teenager and very smart, but also a social outcast; the overall impression is of a dangerous intellect typically seen only in spy movies. In the media's version, the goal of a hacker is often simply to cause computer systems to crash, but sometimes the goals are more directly criminal. Stealing long-distance phone service, credit card numbers, financial information, or other valuable forms of information are all targets of these dangerous individuals.

The term *hacker* has a different meaning, however, among computer programmers. Although the media version of a hacker certainly exists, by far the majority of programmers do not engage in criminal activity. To the working programmer, *hacker* is much more likely to be used as a term of respect for another's programming abilities than as an insult. A well-known on-line lexicon of programming terminology, known as either *The Jargon File* or *The Hacker's Dictionary*,[1] defines a hacker as follows:

> hacker n. [originally, someone who makes furniture with an axe] 1. A person who enjoys exploring the details of programmable systems and how to stretch their capabilities, as opposed to most users, who prefer to learn only the minimum necessary. 2. One who programs enthusiastically (even obsessively) or who enjoys programming rather than just theorizing about programming. 3. A person capable of appreciating hack value. 4. A person who is good at programming quickly. 5. An expert at a particular program, or one who frequently does work using it or on it; as in 'a UNIX hacker'. (Definitions 1 through 5 are correlated, and people who fit them congregate.)

Because the understood definition of *hacker* relates to a specific attitude toward programming as well as a level of programming talent, not all programmers, not even all good ones, are considered hackers. *The Jargon File* goes on to say: "It is better to be described as a hacker by others than to describe oneself that way. Hackers consider themselves something of an elite (a meritocracy based on ability), though one to which new members are gladly welcome. There is thus a certain ego satisfaction to be had in identifying yourself as a hacker (but if you claim to be one and are not, you'll quickly be labeled bogus)."

Implicit in the notion of a meritocracy is that some members of the group represent higher or lower levels of ability within the basic qualifications for group membership. As a programmer, to be known as a "true hacker" is a compliment indeed.

As with any community, programmers have their own heroes. If a hero is a figure who is larger than life, one who is endowed with greater skills and powers than ordinary persons, then a hacker hero is one who exhibits tremendous abilities in the aspects that hackers value. The heroic figures in hackerdom are those whose programming feats amaze even skilled programmers. A hacker of this magnitude can, through his or her programming prowess, make the computer do things that seem magical even to one skilled in the art of programming. Legends of these feats are circulated throughout the community. In this case the communication media are an integral part of the community's identity. E-mail, newsgroups, the Internet, and the World Wide Web comprise the virtual home of the hacker community. Physically disparate, but connected intimately through these high-speed electronic networks, the hacker community tells legends of their heroes' exploits around the high-tech equivalent of a campfire: a glowing computer display.

To understand the heroic qualities of legendary hackers, it is important to understand a little about the culture from which they come. The culture of computer hackers is very young. Although there are analogous communities of people skilled in similarly complicated disciplines, the computer hacker culture is connected intimately with the electronic stored-program computer. Computers of this type have existed only since the 1950s. The qualifier *stored-program* is important. Although it seems obvious today, the idea that a program that controls the actions of the computer can be stored in the same type of memory that is holding the data that the program was working on was in fact a major leap of understanding for the early computer designers.

Computers are built from electronic components that, while complex in their manufacture and their organization into systems, are essentially nothing more than very small, very fast switches. Switching theory—the science of studying systems built from switches—is far older than computer science. A telephone system is an example of a switching network; calls must be routed through a switching network to find the desired receiver. Railroads are another example of a switching network. Consider the problem of making sure that two trains will not try to use the same piece of track at the same time in opposite directions. A railroad system employs switches that control where the trains go and which section of track they will use.

Both of these examples are related to the early stages of hacker culture, but the railroad example is of particular importance. The first computer hackers are generally agreed to have been students at MIT in the 1950s who were part of the Tech Model Railroad Club (TMRC).[2] This club had (and probably still has) a huge model train layout that was the focus of the club activities. The subcommittee of the club responsible for the complicated wiring of the switches that controlled where the trains went were hackers waiting to emerge. The switching network of the TMRC railroad was essentially a special purpose computer, but one where the programming was done either by changing wires or by real-time control of the switch settings by the operator.

When these railroad switch hackers discovered the computers that were being installed at MIT in the 1950s, some of them immediately realized that these large, cumbersome calculating machines were exactly what they had been struggling to create with the model railroad layout. Some became enthralled with trying to figure out what they could make the computers do. This exploration, for the type of person who would come to be called a hacker, arose simply out of an intense desire to explore the limits of the technology; if the explorations resulted in programs that were useful to others, so much the better. From the beginning, the hackers found themselves outside the traditional scientific community that was also trying to understand what could and could not be done with these new devices. The hackers, however, understood how far the technology could really be pushed.

It was the hackers, working in the early hours of the morning—because that was the only time they could get access to the machines—who first demonstrated that a computer could do the then unthinkable task of playing a game of chess. Hackers first demonstrated that the computer display could be used in an interactive way. Rather than simply use the display for static status information, you could cause the machine to draw shapes that looked like spaceships and play games by causing the ships to move around on the screen and interact with other shapes. Hackers were also the first to use the computer in an interactive way for entering text. To an engineer of the day, using valuable computer time to simply enter text in an interactive text editor was unthinkable. Hackers understood that interacting with the computer, instead of treating it as a hands-off behind-glass computation resource, was the way of the future.

Because they were operating outside of the official engineering and scientific culture of the day, hackers developed an outlaw persona from the start. It's important, though, to make a distinction between an outsider and a criminal. Prototype hackers were not criminals; they were simply operating outside the bounds of the established culture. Working mainly at night, without formal scientific backgrounds or training, early hackers were exuberant, fearless, unconventional explorers of this new world of computing.

◢

The early history of hackers is centered around MIT in the 1950s and 1960s. Naturally curious and intelligent MIT students who had been exploring the phone switching network and the control systems of the TMRC were drawn to the computers of the MIT Artificial Intelligence Lab. The director of the lab, Marvin Minsky, was sympathetic to the hackers' desire to explore, and he was impressed enough with their accomplishments that he allowed them to have direct access to the machines, even though the true hackers among the group had by then dropped out of school to spend more time hacking. Legendary hackers from this time include Peter Deutsch, Bill Gosper, Richard Greenblatt, Tom Knight, and Jerry Sussman.

This was the "golden age" of the computer hacker. The machines were large, slow, and cumbersome to use; it took an extraordinary effort to make them complete even the simplest computation.

As computers spread to other parts of the country, so did the hacker culture. Centers of hacker culture developed in the mid-1960s at other universities, such as Carnegie Mellon and Stanford. The Stanford Artificial Intelligence Lab (SAIL), under the direction of John McCarthy, for example, became the center for West Coast hacker activity. When the SAIL machine was finally shut down in 1991, hackers sent an e-mail good-bye message to the Internet as if the SAIL machine was itself sending a last farewell to its friends.[3] Even commercial research centers were home to hackers. ATT, Xerox, and others all had highly skilled programmers working for them. Legendary hackers from this second wave of activity include Ed Fredkin, Brian Reid, Jim Gosling, Brian Kernighan, Dennis Ritchie, and Richard Stallman.

The third wave of hacker activity was born in northern California without a direct connection to the MIT hackers. It started with the Homebrew Computer Club in the San Francisco Bay area. This was a group of electronic hobbyists with a common interest in the then radical idea of

Royal McBee CGP-30 drum-based computer. (Courtesy of the Computer Museum of America at Coleman College).

building their own computers. Because of the size and cost of the early computers, the first hackers were restricted to using a small number of machines built by large companies and installed at universities or industrial research centers. This third wave of hackers wanted their own machines so that they could not only program at home but also build and modify their own computer hardware. It was this group of legendary hackers, which includes Lee Felsenstein, Steve Dompier, Steve Wozniak, Steve Jobs, and Bill Gates, who formed the foundation for the entire personal computer industry of today.

◼

In addition to the legends of hacker feats based on the exploits of real-life hackers, there are also stories that circulate through computer networks that are not connected to any person in particular. These stories feature a semianonymous hacker, perhaps named, but not identifiable as a real person. It is a story of this type that I offer as an example of one of the best-known hacker legends: "The Story of Mel, a Real Programmer."

I first saw this story in 1984 when it was sent to me through e-mail while I was a graduate student at Carnegie Mellon University. At the time it was not attributed to any author in particular and was sent to me by a friend as a great story about the good old days of hackerdom. The story is told in the first person as the storyteller remembers an encounter with a True Hacker named Mel. This is, to my knowledge, the most widely circulated hacker legend on the Internet and is often pointed to as the best way to begin to understand the culture of the hacker. It is formatted in free verse rather than in prose and sounds to my non-folklore-trained ears a bit like an epic poem.

The story was first posted to a Usenet newsgroup on May 21, 1983. The author, Ed Nather, originally wrote and posted the story in prose format. At some point as it was passed from person to person through the Usenet it was modified into free verse form. It is this free verse form that is by far the most common variant of the story as it continues to circulate through the Internet today.

The introduction to "The Story of Mel" gives the motivation for the reminiscence as a rebuttal to an article that makes light of current academic thought in computer programming by asserting, "Real Programmers write in FORTRAN." The article to which "The Story of Mel" refers is one published in the computer magazine *Datamation* in 1983 entitled "Real Programmers Don't Use Pascal"[4] Pascal is a computer language designed by Nicklaus Wirth to promote so-called structured programming, which forces the programmer into a logical system structure that makes the program easier to understand and debug.[5] FORTRAN is a computer programming language designed for engineering and scientific code and is perhaps the oldest computer language still in wide use today. As such it is a fairly primitive language compared with Pascal and extremely primitive compared with even more modern programming languages. Constructs that are easily expressed in modern programming languages—like Java,[6] for example—would require a hacker's skill to code in FORTRAN. The main point of "The Story of Mel" is that today's programmers may think that programming in FORTRAN is hard, but one programmer didn't even need FORTRAN to perform amazing feats. The first few stanzas set the stage for the story to follow:

> A recent article devoted to the macho side of programming made the bald and unvarnished statement:
>
> Real Programmers write in FORTRAN.
>
> *Maybe they do now,*
> *in this decadent era of*
> *Lite beer, hand calculators, and "user-friendly" software*
> *but back in the Good Old Days,*
> *when the term "software" sounded funny*
> *and Real Computers were made out of drums and vacuum tubes,*
> *Real Programmers wrote in machine code.*
> *Not FORTRAN. Not RATFOR. Not, even, assembly language.*
> *Machine Code.*
> *Raw, unadorned, inscrutable hexadecimal numbers.*
> *Directly.*
>
> *Lest a whole new generation of programmers*
> *grow up in ignorance of this glorious past,*
> *I feel duty-bound to describe,*
> *as best I can through the generation gap,*
> *how a Real Programmer wrote code.*
> *I'll call him Mel,*
> *because that was his name.*

Mel is most likely a fictional programmer, although the story is told as a true account and uses real machines and real languages as examples. This story is obviously written to be read by computer programmers; as such, it is full of technical terms and jargon. The feats that mark Mel as a Real Programmer described later in the story are amazing only to someone who knows something about programming. I have included as an appendix to this chapter the entire "Story of Mel" along with extensive annotations that should make it more accessible to nonprogrammers.

Mel lived in the golden age of hackers when computers were simple enough to be programmed by writing directly in the binary language of the machine. Digital computers process all information in binary notation. The nature of the switches used to build computers is such that the most fundamental operation a computer can do is simply recognize the difference between the representation of a 1 and a 0. If 1s and 0s are all the machine can understand at the most basic level, then programming directly in the language of the machine involves writing down long strings of 1s and 0s. There is a slight simplification of this notation that allows these numbers to be written in base 16 instead of base 2 (the "hexadecimal numbers" referred to in the first stanza), but the result is largely the same: a sea of mysterious numbers that is all but indecipherable to the nonhacker.

To make these programs easier to write and understand, they can be abstracted into a symbolic form. The first abstraction is assembly language, in which machine operations are described in words and those words are translated into binary numbers by a program called an assembler. A further abstraction would be a programming language like FORTRAN. Operations are first described in a more abstract way in FORTRAN statements, then the FORTRAN program is translated into assembly language by a compiler, and finally the assembly language is translated into machine code by an assembler. With every abstraction, however, there is a loss of control. For complete control over the inner workings of the machine, direct expression in machine language may be required. Even in the days in which "The Story of Mel" is set there were assemblers available, but Mel's amazing feats required the absolute control that comes from programming directly in the machine's language.

The story describes how Mel used these numbers to control a cumbersome computer from the late 1950s to play blackjack and how at the request of management he reluctantly added a control to adjust the odds and let the customer win. However, he got the control backward, so the computer won instead of the customer. Sometime later the narrator of the story is assigned to track down that control and fix it so that the customer will win, as originally intended. In the end, the teller of the story discovers some of the amazing tricks used by Mel in writing his programs and decides to give up trying to modify the program. He does this both because finding and changing the targeted part of the program would be very difficult and also because of his awe and respect for the code of a Real

Programmer and his feeling that as the work of a Real Programmer the code should not be altered.

◢

"The Story of Mel" embodies many of the themes and ideas found in other hacker legends. Mel, like other legendary hackers, is a type of prowess hero whose heroic qualities are a result of his extraordinary programming abilities. The hero of prowess is defined by Tristram Potter Coffin and Hennig Cohen: "The values they embody reflect the standards, attitudes, and potentials of his society, and most of these heroes are historical."[7] In the society of the programmer the valued skills are related to the ability to make the computer obey commands. Control over the activity of the computer, especially in ways that are unusual, unexpected, obscure, or particularly clever, are the hallmarks of a hacker.

Like heroes of prowess in other societies, the hacker who has such strength in one area may have balancing flaws in other abilities. The legendary hacker, for example, is likely to be described as inept at dealing with other humans. The tendency to work long or odd hours, a disregard for personal appearance, and an inability to communicate effectively with other people who are not themselves hackers are also part of the persona. Thus, the heroic hacker is weak in exactly the traditional aspects of a hero in other societies. Instead, the hacker's prowess is based on more arcane knowledge: power over the logical yet inscrutable computer.

One quality of the traditional hero that is present in the hacker hero is virtue, embodied in the Hacker Ethic. According to *The Jargon File* the Hacker Ethic is "the belief that information-sharing is a powerful positive good, and that it is an ethical duty of hackers to share their expertise by writing free software and facilitating access to information and to computing resources wherever possible."

Another example of the Hacker Ethic can be seen in the license agreement of the interactive text editor Emacs written by Richard Stallman. Emacs is completely extensible and includes a fully functional version of the LISP programming language so that customizations to the editor can be written as LISP programs. Emacs is distributed free of charge by GNU, the organization founded by Stallman, and includes a novel licensing agreement called the "GNU General Public License" or the "copyleft" agreement.[8] According to the copyleft agreement, by using the Emacs program you agree to share what you do with other hackers. As Stallman writes: "The legal meaning of the GNU copyleft is less important than the spirit, which is that Emacs is a free software project and that work pertaining to

Emacs should also be free software. 'Free' means that all users have the freedom to study, share, change, and improve Emacs. To make sure everyone has this freedom, pass along source code when you distribute any version of Emacs or a related program, and give the recipients the same freedom that you enjoyed."[9]

Another feature of traditional hero legends found in hacker legends is a historical setting. Like the romantic notions of medieval times and the chivalry of the knights, hacker legends tend to be told about the old days of the computer world. Given that "the old days" were only the 1950s at the earliest, it is perhaps surprising how much of a historical feel these stories have. The computer industry has moved so rapidly from its birth and computer programmers are getting started at a younger and younger age, so that the early years seem like distant memories to today's programmers. The machines of the 1950s and 1960s could be thought of as the dragons of the past: mean and unforgiving. The hackers who could tame them are the equivalent of the dragonslayer. A hacker legend about the old days might talk about programming "the bare metal," meaning writing programs in the most fundamental machine language as Mel did, without benefit of higher level programming tools, or about the single programming insight that inspired the legend. The legends are also likely to focus on the hardships that early hackers overcame to make computers obey their commands.

The feats of the heroic hacker are sometimes referred to in magical terms. Computers seem to be operating largely by magic to many people, so it is not surprising that the person who wields inordinate skill over that machine might be thought of as a magician of sorts. In a hacker legend, the better the hacker, the more magical the feats. Even the terms used by programmers in their profession have a magical aspect to them. Well-regarded programmers in a company are likely to be referred to as "wizards" or "gurus" by not only their peers but also by management. I have seen computer professionals for major international companies whose business cards give their position as "UNIX Wizard,"[10] or "C Guru."[11] Comments (nonprogram text meant for documentation) in a hacker's program are likely to refer to particularly obscure commands sequences as "magic" or, if they are particularly obscure even to a hacker, as "deep magic."

Another legend about the magical aspects of hacking, this one about hacking hardware rather than software, is told about a machine at MIT.[12] In this legend the storyteller comes across a mysterious switch on the side of the MIT AI Lab's PDP-10 computer. The switch has clearly been installed by a hacker and not a computer technician and is labeled by hand with one position marked "magic" and the other "more magic." The switch is currently in the "more magic" position. The switch is flipped to the other position and the machine crashes instantly. The storyteller and another hacker follow the switch to its source, but the wires don't seem to go anywhere that could influence the machine in any way. So they boot the machine and try again. Again, as soon as the switch moves from "more magic" to "magic," the machine crashes. The story ends:

> This time we ran for Richard Greenblatt, a long-time MIT hacker, who was close at hand. He had never noticed the switch before, either. He inspected it, concluded it was useless, got some diagonal cutters and diked it out. We then revived the computer and it has run fine ever since.
>
> We still don't know how the switch crashed the machine. There is a theory that some circuit near the ground pin was marginal, and flipping the switch changed the electrical capacitance enough to upset the circuit as millionth-of-a-second pulses went through it. But we'll never know for sure; all we can really say is that the switch was magic.
>
> I still have that switch in my basement. Maybe I'm silly, but I usually keep it set on 'more magic'.

Part of the appeal of the hacker legend to the programmer is perhaps the very obscurity of the feats described in the legends. "The Story of Mel," for example, goes into great detail about the programming style of the hero, but one would have to be at least a little bit of a programmer to understand what was so amazing. A related aspect is that the hacker of legend is often able to perform some feat with the computer that other programmers, or even the computer designer, didn't think was possible.

An example of this is a legend that is told about the designer of a microcontroller chip called the 8051. A microcontroller is like a microprocessor but smaller, less powerful, and designed to be included in other devices. The "computer controlled" fuel injection of your car, for example, is controlled by a microcontroller, and probably by the 8051, it being the most commonly used microcontroller for cars. The story goes that the designer of the 8051 was having trouble with his car. He took it to a garage, where the mechanics connected a diagnostic system to the computer control of the engine. Thinking to impress them, the designer told them that he had invented the chip they are checking. They proceeded to bombard him with questions about the chip that he could not answer. The questions indicated that the mechanics had written new code for his chip to improve the performance of the car that made use of the 8051 in ways that he, the designer of the chip, could no longer understand. The theme of the hackers surpassing the designer by extending things in ways that were never imagined must surely have parallels to other legends in other cultures.

Another legend about doing the impossible is told about third-wave Apple hacker Andy Hertzfeld. According to *Byte Magazine:*

> Besides everything else he did to help get the first Macintosh out the door, Andy Hertzfeld wrote all the first desk accessories. Most of these were written in assembly. However, to show that desk accessories could also be written in higher-level languages, Hertzfeld wrote a demonstration puzzle games desk accessory in Pascal.[13] Like its plastic counterparts, users moved squares around until the numbers 1 to 9 were in order. As time began to get short, the decision was made that the puzzle, at 7KB [7KB = 7168 bytes], was too big (and too game-like) to ship with the first Macintosh. In a single weekend, Hertzfeld rewrote the program to take up only 800 bytes. The puzzle shipped with the Mac.[14]

There are, of course, programmers who do fit the media's picture of the computer hacker. These programmers use their skills to cause trouble, crash machines, release computer viruses, steal credit card numbers, remove copy-protection, distribute pirated software, and make free long-distance calls (the phone system is so much like a computer system that it is a common target for computer criminals). These people may also call themselves "hackers," leading to more confusion. Hackers in the original sense of the term, however, look down on such activities. Among the programming community, and to a large extent even among the illegal programming community, these people are called "crackers" and their activities are known as "cracking."

The cracker definitely does not follow the Hacker Ethic. Even among legitimate hackers there are those who add to the Hacker Ethic the belief that system-cracking for fun and exploration is ethically okay as long as the cracker commits no theft, vandalism, or breach of confidentiality. Hackers who use their skill for these latter purposes have crossed over and become crackers.

Crackers have their own lore, their own heroes, and their own set of ethics distinct from those of hackers. They also garner much more attention in the popular press.

◢

Mel is perhaps the best example of a True Hacker and a Real Programmer who embodies a hacker's virtue. Mel's legendary status is well illustrated in another hacker legend from the Internet, this one about the problems of making code fit into the guidance computer of a satellite before lift-off. The story ends with the following summation:

> The solution was both clever and bletcherous. The overflow bit became part of the opcode. To get the extra opcodes, the program would add-to-memory an accumulator value that would cause an overflow when added to the instruction that was in memory. Since the instructions were in ROM they didn't get modified, but the added bit of the overflow gave 8 more opcodes.
>
> I only presume that these opcodes were powerful enough that the extra instructions required to generate them cost less than the instructions they replaced. I have long since lost the article reprint we used. Dave Parnas, who taught the course, had a great time with this particular machine . . .
>
> All I know is: Mel would have *loved* it![15]

Appendix

The Story of Mel: A Real Programmer[16]

A recent article devoted to the macho side of programming made the bald and unvarnished statement:

Real Programmers write in FORTRAN.[17]

Maybe they do now,
in this decadent era of
Lite beer, hand calculators,[18] and "user-friendly" software[19]
but back in the Good Old Days,
when the term "software" sounded funny
and Real Computers were made out of drums[20] and vacuum tubes,[21]
Real Programmers wrote in machine code.[22]
Not FORTRAN. Not RATFOR.[23] Not, even, assembly language.[24]
Machine Code.
Raw, unadorned, inscrutable hexadecimal numbers.[25]
Directly.[26]

Lest a whole new generation of programmers
grow up in ignorance of this glorious past,
I feel duty-bound to describe,
as best I can through the generation gap,
how a Real Programmer wrote code.[27]
I'll call him Mel, because that was his name.

I first met Mel when I went to work for Royal McBee Computer Corp.,[28]
a now-defunct subsidiary of the typewriter company.
The firm manufactured the LGP-30,[29]
a small, cheap (by the standards of the day)[30]
drum-memory computer,

and had just started to manufacture
the RPC-4000, a much-improved,[31]
bigger, better, faster—drum-memory computer.
Cores cost too much,[32]
and weren't here to stay, anyway.
(That's why you haven't heard of the company,
or the computer.)[33]

I had been hired to write a FORTRAN compiler[34]
for this new marvel and Mel was my guide to its wonders.
Mel didn't approve of compilers.

"If a program can't rewrite its own code,"[35]
he asked, "what good is it?"

Mel had written,
in hexadecimal,
the most popular computer program the company owned.
It ran on the LGP-30 and played blackjack with potential customers
at computer shows.[36]
Its effect was always dramatic.
The LGP-30 booth was packed at every show,[37]
and the IBM salesmen stood around
talking to each other.
Whether or not this actually sold computers
was a question we never discussed.

Mel's job was to re-write
the blackjack program for the RPC-4000.
(Port? What does that mean?)[38]
The new computer had a one-plus-one
addressing scheme,[39]
in which each machine instruction,
in addition to the operation code
and the address of the needed operand,
had a second address that indicated where, on the revolving drum,
the next instruction was located.[40]

In modern parlance,
every single instruction was followed by a GO TO![41]
Put that in Pascal's pipe and smoke it.[42]

Mel loved the RPC-4000
because he could optimize his code:[43]
that is, locate instructions on the drum
so that just as one finished its job,
the next would be just arriving at the "read head"[44]
and available for immediate execution.
There was a program to do that job,
an "optimizing assembler,"[45]
but Mel refused to use it.

"You never know where it's going to put things,"[46]
he explained, "so you'd have to use separate constants."[47]

It was a long time before I understood that remark.
Since Mel knew the numerical value
of every operation code,[48]
and assigned his own drum addresses,
every instruction he wrote could also be considered
a numerical constant.[49]
He could pick up an earlier "add" instruction, say,
and multiply by it,
if it had the right numeric value.[50]
His code was not easy for someone else to modify.[51]

I compared Mel's hand-optimized programs[52]
with the same code massaged by the optimizing assembler program,[53]
and Mel's always ran faster.
That was because the "top-down" method of program design[54]
hadn't been invented yet,
and Mel wouldn't have used it anyway.
He wrote the innermost parts of his program loops first,[55]
so they would get first choice
of the optimum address locations on the drum.[56]
The optimizing assembler wasn't smart enough to do it that way.[57]

Mel never wrote time-delay loops,[58] either,
even when the balky Flexowriter[59]
required a delay between output characters to work right.[60]
He just located instructions on the drum
so each successive one was just past the read
head when it was needed;[61]
the drum had to execute another complete revolution
to find the next instruction.
He coined an unforgettable term for this procedure.
Although "optimum" is an absolute term,
like "unique," it became common verbal practice
to make it relative:
"not quite optimum" or "less optimum"
or "not very optimum."
Mel called the maximum time-delay locations
the "most pessimum."

After he finished the blackjack program
and got it to run ("Even the initializer is optimized,"[62]
he said proudly),
he got a Change Request from the sales department.[63]
The program used an elegant (optimized)[64]
random number generator[65]
to shuffle the "cards" and deal from the "deck,"
and some of the salesmen felt it was too fair,

since sometimes the customers lost.
They wanted Mel to modify the program
so, at the setting of a sense switch on the console,[66]
they could change the odds and let the customer win.

Mel balked.
He felt this was patently dishonest,
which it was,
and that it impinged on his personal integrity as a programmer,
which it did,[67]
so he refused to do it.
The Head Salesman talked to Mel,
as did the Big Boss and, at the boss's urging,
a few Fellow Programmers.[68]
Mel finally gave in and wrote the code,
but he got the test backwards,[69]
and, when the sense switch was turned on,
the program would cheat, winning every time.
Mel was delighted with this,
claiming his subconscious was uncontrollably ethical,
and adamantly refused to fix it.

After Mel had left the company for greener pa$ture$,
the Big Boss asked me to look at the code
and see if I could find the test and reverse it.
Somewhat reluctantly, I agreed to look.
Tracking Mel's code was a real adventure.[70]
I have often felt that programming is an art form,
whose real value can only be appreciated
by another versed in the same arcane art;
there are lovely gems and brilliant coups
hidden from human view and admiration, sometimes forever,
by the very nature of the process.
You can learn a lot about an individual
just by reading through his code,
even in hexadecimal.
Mel was, I think, an unsung genius.

Perhaps my greatest shock came
when I found an innocent loop that had no test in it.
No test. None.[71]
Common sense said it had to be a closed loop,
where the program would circle, forever, endlessly.[72]
Program control passed right through it, however,
and safely out the other side.[73]
It took me two weeks to figure it out.

The RPC-4000 computer had a really modern facility
called an index register.[74]

It allowed the programmer to write a program loop
that used an indexed instruction inside;
each time through,
the number in the index register
was added to the address of that instruction,
so it would refer to the next datum[75] in a series.[76]
He had only to increment the index register
each time through.
Mel never used it.

Instead, he would pull the instruction into a machine register,[77]
add one to its address,
and store it back.[78]
He would then execute the modified instruction
right from the register.[79]
The loop was written so this additional execution time
was taken into account—
just as this instruction finished,
the next one was right under the drum's read head,
ready to go.
But the loop had no test in it.[80]

The vital clue came when I noticed
the index register bit,[81]
the bit that lay between the address
and the operation code in the instruction word,[82]
was turned on—[83]
yet Mel never used the index register,
leaving it zero all the time.[84]
When the light went on it nearly blinded me.

He had located the data he was working on
near the top of memory—[85]
the largest locations the instructions could address—
so, after the last datum was handled,
incrementing the instruction address
would make it overflow.[86]
The carry would add one to the
operation code, changing it to the next one in the instruction set:[87]
a jump instruction.[88]
Sure enough, the next program instruction was
in address location zero,[89]
and the program went happily on its way.

I haven't kept in touch with Mel,
so I don't know if he ever gave in to the flood of
change that has washed over programming techniques
since those long-gone days.
I like to think he didn't.

In any event,
I was impressed enough that I quit looking for the
offending test,
telling the Big Boss I couldn't find it.
He didn't seem surprised.

When I left the company,
the blackjack program would still cheat
if you turned on the right sense switch,
and I think that's how it should be.
I didn't feel comfortable
hacking up the code of a Real Programmer.

Notes

An earlier version of this chapter was presented at the annual meeting of the
American Folklore Society in Pittsburgh, October 17–20, 1996.

1. *The Jargon File,* v3.2.0 is available at http://www.tuxedo.org/jargon (May 10,
1999), as well as many other places on the Web.
2. Steven Levy, *Hackers: Heroes of the Computer Revolution* (1984; New York:
Dell, 1994), 17–38.
3. "Take Me, I'm Yours: The Autobiography of SAIL," Jan. 1991, http://
www.cs.utah.edu/~elb/folklore/SAIL (Feb. 27, 1997).
4. Ed Post, "Real Programmers Don't Use Pascal," *Datamation* 29.7 (July 1983):
263–65. Although the magazine is dated July, it must have been available in May
since "The Story of Mel" is a direct response to this article.
5. See Nicklaus Wirth, *Algorithms + Data Structures = Programs* (Englewood
Cliffs, N.J.: Prentice Hall, 1976).
6. It takes a great deal of programming skill to write the programs that make a
language like Java so powerful. Java was designed by Jim Gosling, now at Sun
Microsystems.
7. Tristram Potter Coffin and Hennig Cohen, *The Parade of Heroes: Legendary Figures in American Lore* (New York: Anchor Press, 1978), 52.
8. Available at http://www.gnu.org/copyleft/copyleft.html (May 10, 1999).
9. Richard Stallman, Frequently Asked Questions (FAQ) file about GNU Emacs,
http://www.cs.utah.edu/~elb/folklore/faq7.txt (May 10, 1999).
10. UNIX is a computer operating system developed by hackers at ATT and
favored by hackers even today over other operating systems.
11. C is a programming language also developed by hackers at ATT and also
one of the programming languages that hackers seem to prefer over others. For a
biblical-style account of its development, see Ian Chai and Glenn Chappell, "The
C Programming Language," Mar. 1989, http://www.cs.utah.edu/~elb/folklore/C-
bible.html (May 10, 1999).
12. "A Story about Magic," http://www.cs.utah.edu/~elb/folklore/magic.html
(May 10, 1999). See also Karla Jennings, *The Devouring Fungus: Tales of the
Computer Age* (New York: W. W. Norton, 1990), 84.

13. Recall that the inspiration for "The Story of Mel" was an article entitled "Real Programmers Don't Use Pascal."

14. "Noted and Notorious Hacker Feats," *Byte Magazine,* Sept. 1995, 151–62.

15. Posted to newsgroup alt.folklore.computers, Apr. 1991, http://www.cs.utah.edu/~elb/folklore/satellit.txt (Oct. 14, 1996).

16. "The Story of Mel, a Real Programmer" was first posted to Usenet on May 21, 1983. Usenet is a descendent of the Arpanet, the first computer network. The Arpanet was born with five sites in 1969 (before video games [Pong didn't appear until 1972], before hand-held calculators [1972], before home VCRs [1975], and before personal computers [1976–77]) as a way to let researchers funded by the Defense Department's Advanced Research Projects Agency (ARPA) collaborate. The original five sites on the Arpanet were Bolt, Beranek, and Newman—a Cambridge-based company that built the original Arpanet Interface Message Processors (IMP) that were used as the special-purpose computers that passed data on the Arpanet—UCLA, Stanford Research Institute, the University of California at Santa Barbara, and the University of Utah.

The first public demonstration of the Arpanet came in 1972. By then the Arpanet had expanded to thirty-seven nodes across the country. The public demonstration was at the International Conference on Computer Communications and was a great success.

As the Arpanet grew, other networks were developed that used the technology developed on the Arpanet. One of these, Usenet, was a collection of computers connected by phone lines but without the expensive IMPs that made the Arpanet run. Usenet was slower, but anyone could connect with a modem. Usenet came into being around 1979. Although there had been special-interest e-mail lists on the Arpanet almost since its inception (the SF-lovers list for science fiction fans was one of the first), it was on Usenet that the idea of interest-specific electronic bulletin boards or newsgroups really blossomed.

17. Ed Post wrote "Real Programmers Don't Use Pascal" as a humorous piece in response to the recent development of the computer programming language Pascal and the concept of structured programming. At the time of the introduction of Pascal, most scientific programmers used FORTRAN.

FORTRAN, which stands for FORmula TRANslation, began in the late 1950s as a mechanism for describing scientific expressions at a higher level than the direct machine instructions of computers. It was, and still is, designed to get the maximum computation speed from a given program. This makes it somewhat "unfriendly" for programming more symbolic or structured applications.

The intent of Pascal was to define a richer set of programming structures that could easily handle nonnumeric data, such as text, strings, and symbols. Also, Pascal has a different view of how the control flow of the program should be described. Instead of being able to jump from any point in the program to any other point (instructions that perform this type of control change are called "goto" statements because they go to another part of the program), Pascal requires that the control be structured into a fairly strict hierarchical organization.

Post's main point was to poke fun at Pascal as an academic language because "real programmers" would use a more fundamental language like FORTRAN, which is harder to use and faster.

18. Electronic hand calculators first appeared in 1971, with the influential HP-35 pocket calculator arriving soon afterward in 1972. This signaled the end of the slide-rule era in engineering.

19. *User-friendly* has a couple of different meanings. Software called "user-friendly" very often isn't. Often the extra window dressing put onto a piece of software to make it user-friendly serves mostly to make it harder to use. For Real Programmers, adding extra code simply to make the program easier to use is wasted effort. People who value the contribution of the code should have to spend the effort to learn how to use it.

20. "Drums" refers to drum memories, which are magnetic data storage devices much like the familiar hard disks of today but shaped like cylinders instead of platters. In the fifties and sixties the state of the art in magnetic encoding of data didn't allow for very dense storage on the magnetic surface of the medium. So, to increase the surface area of the storage medium, to increase the speed at which the magnetic material passed by the read head of the device, and to keep the speed at which the heads encountered the magnetic medium constant, these devices were shaped like cylinders with the magnetic coating on the outside surface of the cylinder and the cylinder rotating along its long axis at very high speeds. These are analogous to the wax cylinders used with early phonographs.

21. Vacuum tubes are electronic devices used to amplify electronic signals and to act as electronically controlled switches. Digital computers are constructed at their most basic fundamental building blocks as electronically controlled switches. The very first electronic computers used relays for these switches (in the 1940s). Vacuum tubes were used for the switches from the late forties to the late fifties. The first commercial computer to use transistors for the switching elements was the IBM 1401 in 1959. Individual transistors gave way to integrated circuits in which hundreds, and eventually millions, of transistors were fabricated on a single silicon substrate, or chip. Integrated circuits have been used since the midsixties.

22. Machine code refers to the lowest level of program instructions. Machine codes are the instructions actually interpreted by the hardware of the computer. These instructions are almost always simple add and subtract operations on internal computer registers, simple load and store operations on the computer's memory (used to bring data from the memory into the internal registers), and a few basic control-flow operations that test values in the internal registers of the computer and decide whether to alter where the next machine instruction is fetched from in memory.

Machine code instructions are usually represented as strings of 1s and 0s that are interpreted by the binary logic of the computer. For example, a machine code instruction used to add the contents of two registers and put the result in a third might look like this:

$$1010 \ 0011 \ 0100 \ 0001$$

The 1010 indicates that this operation is to add two numbers, the 0011 is 3 in binary, indicating that the first argument should come from register 3, the 0100 is 4 in binary, signifying that the second argument should come from register 4, and the 0001 is 1 in binary, indicating that the result of the addition should be stored into register 1. This is an extremely simple example. A real machine code instruction would have many more bits and be quite a bit more difficult to explain.

The purpose of so-called high-level languages is to be able to express an addition in a convenient text form and to have the compiler translate that form into the machine code for you. Programming directly in machine code requires a special type of talent.

23. Rational FORTRAN (RATFOR) is a dialect of FORTRAN that provides a richer set of control-flow possibilities. RATFOR is not a new language, rather it is a translator that translates Rational FORTRAN into FORTRAN. It allows the programmer to use features not found in the normal FORTAN language and then translates those features into standard FORTAN automatically.

24. Assembly language is the machine code of a particular computer written as text rather than as bits. For example, consider the machine code for addition in note 21. An assembly language version of that instruction might be this:

ADD R3 R4 R1

This is essentially the same machine language instruction, but text has been used instead of the actual bits that the machine sees. Programs written in the assembly language of a particular machine are translated into machine code by a program called an assembler.

25. Hexadecimal means base 16. Binary is a base 2 number scheme because there are only two symbols used: 1 and 0. Decimal numbers are a base 10 scheme because there are 10 symbols used: 0 1 2 3 4 5 6 7 8 9. After 9 the numbers are represented using positional notation, where the higher order symbols represent multiplying by the base. 15 for example is $1 * 10 + 5 * 1$.

Hexadecimal is base 16, which means that numbers are represented using 16 different symbols: 0 1 2 3 4 5 6 7 8 9 a b c d e f. After counting to f, the same positional notation is used. In hexadecimal notation (or hex), 15 is $1 * 16 + 5 * 1$ or 21 in base 10.

Hex is used in computer notation as a convenient way of expressing bit values. If you group a binary number into groups of four bits there are exactly sixteen possible values for each of those groups. You can easily express each group of four bits as a single hex digit. For example, the previous machine code example was, in binary:

1010 0011 0100 0001

In hex, this same number would be expressed as:

A341

where each hex digit corresponds to a group of four bits in the binary word.

26. Writing a program "directly" in machine code means writing hex digits that correspond to the desired machine code bits for each instruction you want the machine to execute. Since it takes many, many machine code instructions to execute even the simplest program, this would be tedious, to say the least.

Even now tools that extract the raw unformatted data from a memory or from a disk are likely to return a file full of "raw, unadorned, inscrutable hexadecimal numbers." Few programmers can create programs by writing those numbers directly.

27. To a programmer, "code" refers to the text of the program you are writing. The "source code" is the program text in the language that the programmer is using (i.e., FORTRAN). The "object code" is the machine code produced usually by the operation of the compiler on the source code. "To code" is to write a program. If

a programmer tells you she is "coding up an application" she is writing a program to perform a specific task.

28. The Royal McBee Company is a real company. I have found out little about it except that the machines named in this story are real machines built there in the late fifties and early sixties.

29. The LGP-30 computer was first sold in 1959. A number of these machines were in use in various military installations from 1959 on. The Army Ballistic Missile Agency (now called NASA), for example, had ten of these computers in 1961.

30. The LGP-30 contained 113 vacuum tubes and cost $50,000 in 1959.

31. The following table shows the addition and multiply times for the LGP-30 and RPC-4000 computers. These are taken from records of the computers used by defense contractors in the sixties. Note that the RPC-4000 computer makes a significant improvement in add times, but has the same multiply and divide times as the older LGP-30. In contrast, your PC at home is likely to have identical add and multiply times of about 10 nanoseconds, or .01 microseconds.

Add Time Microseconds	Multiply Time Microseconds	Divide Time Microseconds	System
8,000	17,000	17,000	LGP 30
500	17,000	17,000	RPC 4000

32. Core memory is a type of random-access memory that stores bits by changing the magnetic field of a small magnetic doughnut. These torus-shaped magnets (or cores) can be magnetized or demagnetized by passing a current through a wire that is strung through the center of the core. By passing a current through a different wire, also strung through the core, you can sense whether the core is magnetized or not. Core memory was faster, denser, and more robust than magnetic drums, although initially more expensive. Magnetic core memories were used in computers from the early sixties through the seventies.

33. Core memory ended up being so much faster than magnetic drums and disks that it quickly became the main memory of choice for computers beginning in the early sixties. Initially expensive, core rapidly became more cost effective than drums. Companies that didn't make the switch soon enough were not likely to survive. By the same token, semiconductor memory in the late seventies offered the same dilemma. It was faster, smaller, and denser, but originally much more expensive. Some companies didn't believe that semiconductor RAM would catch on. You haven't heard of these companies either.

34. A compiler is a program that takes the original program text (source code) and translates it to machine code so that the computer can understand it. Initially compilers simply translated the program statements into the direct machine code versions. As compiler technology advanced, however, the source programs could get further and further away from the machine code (become more "high-level" languages) and the job of the compiler to translate these more abstract expressions into the simple machine code that the machine could execute became more and more complicated. Modern compilers are very complex programs indeed.

35. One of the great leaps of understanding in the early days of computing is

attributed to John Von Neumann and his colleagues, who realized that a computer could use memory for storing the program it would execute, not just data. Before the advent of the "stored-program" computer, the program would be communicated to the machine by setting huge numbers of switches on vast panels that controlled the operation of the machine. Once the switches were set, the machine would execute the indicated operations on the data that was stored in the machine's memory. Needless to say, setting switches so that a new program could be run was a serious undertaking. By storing the program the same mechanism that allows the computer to retrieve data from the memory can be used to retrieve the next instruction to execute.

Once you have the program stored in the machine's memory, that program can be thought of as stored data. Then the program currently running can modify the program data so that subsequent instructions are executed. This is known as "self-modifying code" because the program modifies itself by writing data in the section of memory that holds the program. Because of the small memories in early machines, this was a common programming practice. It has since fallen out of favor because it makes programs very difficult to understand and debug. It's difficult to tell if a program is doing the right thing if the program itself might change. Compilers, in general, forbid self-modifying code by specifically not generating it. If you want to write this type of code, you have to do it by hand.

36. Computer shows are large conventions where manufacturers of computer hardware and software show off their latest and greatest products to potential customers. In the early days the highlights of these shows were as likely to be new hardware designed by a couple of scruffy teenage hackers as from a big company like IBM or Royal McBee. The original Apple II computer that essentially started the home computer revolution was introduced at the West Coast Computer Fair in 1977.

37. Typical computer shows are organized in large convention centers where each company rents some space and puts up a booth. The size and placement of the booth are usually good indicators of the size and placement of the company in the computer world. However, the star of any particular computer show is likely to be a small booth tucked into a corner somewhere with a ground-breaking, but undiscovered product.

38. To "port" a program is to translate it to another language, another system, or in some way modify the program to run under another set of circumstances. If you have a program that runs on a Macintosh, for example, it would have to be ported to run on an IBM PC. Porting is assumed to involve modifying only small parts of the program, as little as necessary to get the program to run on the new system.

Computer programs are often designed to be portable by isolating the machine-specific part of the code to one well-defined part of the program. The theory is that to port the program to a new system, only that machine-specific part will need to be modified. In practice, this theory is often wrong and there are many subtle changes that need to be made in other parts of the program.

39. An addressing scheme is the mechanism by which the computer figures out the location in memory (the address) of the next instruction to be executed in the program. The address of the next instruction is usually either the next sequential location in memory or another location encoded in the current instruction. To

decode the "somewhere else" address from the machine code you would need to know the addressing scheme of the machine.

40. I don't have any examples of actual LGP-30 code, but based on this description, an ADD instruction might look something like this:

ADD 100 104

where the 100 is the memory location of the argument to the addition ("add the contents of memory location 100 to the current sum held in the internal register of the computer"), and the 104 is the address of the next instruction to execute ("when you are finished with the addition, find the instruction at memory location 104 and execute that instruction next").

41. A "goto" instruction is one that changes where the program will find its next instruction. Most programming languages (unlike the LGP-30 machine language) execute instructions in the same sequence in which they are written in the program. That is, when the machine finishes one instruction, it fetches the next sequential instruction in the machine's memory and executes that one. The goto is an instruction that forces the execution to jump, or "go to," an instruction somewhere else in the memory that is not in sequence.

The influential computer science pioneer (and legendary figure himself) Edgar Dijkstra considered the goto statement a bad idea because it makes understanding the orderly flow of control in the program more difficult (clearly Dijkstra is not a hacker). This was published in a famous (to computer scientists) letter: "GOTO Statement Considered Harmful," Letter to the editor, *Communications of the ACM*, Mar. 1968, 147–48.

42. The Pascal language, developed by Nicklaus Wirth in the midseventies, had as its goal to support exactly the type of "structured programming" that Dijkstra was advocating. Pascal does not have a "goto" statement and also forces the programmer to carefully structure the control flow of the program so that it can be more easily understood and reasoned about.

The first major reference to Pascal by its creator is Wirth, *Algorithms + Data Structures = Programs*.

43. *Optimum* is an absolute descriptor meaning the best that can possibly be, but *to optimize* has come to mean "to improve." The process of optimizing code is to take a computer program and improve it by making it faster or smaller or both.

44. Like on a hard disk, bits stored on the drum are encoded as magnetized spots on a magnetic coating on the surface of the drum. The "read head" is the piece of the drum that senses the magnetic spots and reports the values to the computer. It "reads" the values on the disk in much the same way that a tape recorder reads the magnetic information on a cassette tape and reports them to an audio amplifier.

The drum rotates at high speed below the read and write heads. The read head is restricted to reading only the spot that is currently directly under the read head. So, to read a specific spot on the drum, the read head must wait patiently for the desired spot to rotate around and come under the head. Although the drums might have spun quite quickly, electricity moves much faster. Put another way, even though the time it takes for the drum to rotate one complete revolution seems very short, it is long compared with the speed of the computer processor. With a poorly optimized program the computer would spend most of its time waiting for the drum to rotate to the right spot.

45. An optimizing assembler is an assembler that tries to improve the program by analyzing the structure of the program and using the analysis to remove unneeded instructions, replace wasteful sequences with more efficient ones, and in the case of a drum computer, locate the instructions on the drum in an efficient way by modifying the location of the instructions in the program.

46. One thing an assembler does is take the symbolic assembly code and locate it somewhere specific in memory. Depending on where the assembler decides to place the code, all the addresses in the assembly program will have to be modified to take into account the exact location.

47. "Constants" are simply numbers that will come in handy to the rest of the program. These numbers are typically stored in known locations so the programmer can use them as the need requires. For example, if incrementing a value is a common operation, it might make sense to store a 1 at a known location so that you could always increment a value by adding the contents of that special location.

48. In an assembly instruction like ADD 100 104, the "ADD" is also called the "operation code" because it defines the operation that the instruction will perform.

49. Operation codes, like the "ADD" in the instruction ADD 100 104 are, themselves, coded as a series of 1s and 0s so that the computer can read them. Because these are just strings of numbers, they could also be considered numbers. For example, if the operation code for ADD was 0011, this could also be read as the binary number 3.

50. The operation code for ADD is 0011, which is also the number 3 in binary. So, if you wanted to multiply some value in the program by 3, you could conceivably multiply by the operation code for ADD since that operation code is, coincidentally, also 3.

51. You can imagine how difficult this would be to understand if you weren't looking for it.

52. "Hand-optimized" means that the improvements to the code were done by the programmer and not by any automatic means, like using an optimizing assembler.

53. "To massage" means to modify the code in some way. The connotation is that the structure of the program is changed by pushing, pulling, and molding the program code.

54. "Top down" design refers to a system design philosophy that starts by looking at the overall picture (the top of the design) and working your way down to the specifics. This is a "divide and conquer" method of designing large systems where large pieces of the design are split into smaller and smaller pieces until each of the individual pieces are small and simple enough to build. For software, this method of design would involve starting with the big picture of the whole program and then refining that idea into smaller and smaller units before even starting to write the code.

55. In contrast to the "top-down" approach is the "bottom-up" approach. In this method of designing large systems, you start with the smallest pieces: the ones that you already know how to do well. These pieces are then assembled into larger and larger units until you have the entire design. "Loops" repeat sections of the code some number of times. Suppose you were writing a

program to add a monthly bonus onto each employee's paycheck. You would write a program loop that would repeat the "add bonus" process on each employee's record. Now suppose that in each employee's record your program would have to loop again, perhaps to repeat the bonus process for each month of the year (this is a very generous company). The "repeat for each month of the year" loop would be an "inner loop" because it is a looping structure inside a larger looping structure. If this hypothetical inner loop repeated its function twelve times (one for each month), and there are one hundred employees in your company, this simple inner loop would execute twelve hundred times during one run of the program.

It is this property of inner loops—that they account for a large fraction of the total run time of a program—that makes them the first target for program optimization. A general rule of thumb in computer programming is that 90 percent of the execution time for a generic program is accounted for by only 10 percent of the written instructions. This is because a small number of inner loops execute over and over again. The other 90 percent of the code typically runs only a few times during the program's execution and so does not account for much of the total run time.

56. By placing the next instruction in exactly the right spot on the drum for the read head, the program would run much much faster.

57. Anthropomorphism is very common in the programming world. Computer programs are talked about in terms that make them sound like they are thinking, making mistakes, or otherwise behaving like people.

58. Even early computers were much faster at computing answers than the output devices (like printers) were at printing them. The modern solution to this problem is to send the information to be printed in one very quick burst to the printer, where the information is stored while the slow output device manages to deal with it. In the early days, however, it was common to write computer programs so that it slowed down enough to send one character at a time to a slow printer. The mechanism to slow down the program is called writing a "delay loop." A delay loop is simply a looping structure in the program that doesn't do any computation, but instead has as its sole purpose to waste time. After looping around doing nothing for a while, enough time will be wasted so that another character can be sent to the slow output device.

59. A Flexowriter was a very popular early computer printer and input device made by Friden. It was essentially a computer controlled typewriter that could also produce and read paper tape. Paper tape is an input/output medium that looks like an inch wide roll of paper with holes punched in it. A programmer might use the Flexowriter to type in a program and have that program put on a paper tape. The paper tape could then be fed into the computer to enter the program into the computer. Alternatively, the computer could produce the results of its computation to the Flexowriter and have those results stored on a roll of paper tape.

60. The interface to the Flexowriter was for the computer to send individual characters to the Flexowriter one after the other. The problem was that because the Flexowriter had to move physical objects in order to punch holes in the paper tape, it was very slow compared with the computer. If the computer sent characters to the printer too quickly, they were lost (or "dropped on the floor," as a programmer would say).

61. Locating the next instruction so that it was just past the read head when you

went looking for it means that it would take another entire rotation of the drum before the correct location appeared at the read head. This rotation is long as far as the computer is concerned.

62. Since 90 percent of the run time of a program is accounted for by 10 percent of the instructions, it doesn't make sense to worry about optimizing the other code since even if it were optimized to nothing at all, it could decrease the run time by only 10 percent. If you're a Real Programmer, however, you believe that all code deserves to be given attention and so even the initializer should be given the benefit of optimization.

63. A change request, sometimes called an ECO (Engineering Change Order), is a mechanism used by engineering companies to specify and track modifications to the systems they produce. These change requests follow a chain of command and allow large engineering groups to collaborate without losing track of what is going on. To an engineer, a change request from the sales department is not likely to be a meaningful engineering issue.

64. "Elegant" is a widely used term of praise and respect by programmers. If a solution to a problem is simple, efficient, or otherwise aesthetically pleasing to a programmer, it would be deemed elegant.

65. Generating random numbers is a generic problem that is used in all sorts of applications. Games, in particular, require random numbers so that the initial conditions are not the same each time you play the game. A computer program to play cards, for example, would use a random number generator to simulate shuffling the deck prior to dealing the cards.

In practice, generating truly random numbers is very difficult. Computer-generated "random" numbers are not actually random, but for purposes of shuffling a deck of cards, program-generated random numbers are completely adequate.

66. Older computers typically had a console on the body of the machine on which internal status information of the machine was displayed. Switches on the console could be used to modify the state of the machine. In addition to the switches dedicated to particular actions, some switches determined values during program execution. These switches, called sense switches, could be used for input to the program. At a certain point in the program the computer could sense the value of a switch on the console to determine what to do next.

67. Purposely making a program deceitful would definitely be considered by some as a violation of the Hacker Ethic.

68. It is well established in hacker lore that company higher-ups such as the Head Salesman and the Big Boss would know nothing about engineering, programming, and definitely nothing about the Hacker Ethic. The "Dilbert" cartoon series by Scott Adams has exploited this knowledge in a way that is both extremely humorous and possibly extremely close to the mark for most engineers. Scott Adams says that he gets many of his ideas for new comic strips from people working for big companies who send him ideas based on their actual workday experiences. The "Fellow Programmers" referred to in this passage are clearly not Real Programmers.

69. "The test" means testing the value of the sense switch to see if it is in the on or off position.

70. Although there are many stories about legendary programmers that circulate among programmers, it is thought by some that although they are admired

and idolized, it's probably a good thing that there aren't too many of them around. The tricks that make a programmer's code legendary typically make the code itself very hard to understand by anyone else.

71. Loops in a program are used to repeat a portion of the code a number of times. Each time the program executes the code in the loop a decision must be made about whether to loop again or continue on to different activities. The test is what indicates that the program should stop looping. If a loop had no test it would have to loop forever.

72. A program loop that has no test or has a test that is guaranteed to always evaluate to "true" is known as an "endless loop" or an "infinite loop."

73. That is, the program managed to check the loop's exit condition, find it changed, and exit the loop, even though no exit test was ever performed according to the code.

74. An index register is a feature of a computer processor that relates to the machine's addressing scheme. Using an index register in an addressing scheme involves adding the value in the index register to the value in the instruction for all memory references. If the index register is incremented automatically by the computer, the programmer could walk through sequential memory locations by simply setting the index register to the first location and then, with no further manipulation of the address by the program, look at sequential memory locations on each memory reference. This turns out to be a very helpful addition to a basic addressing scheme.

75. The singular of *data* is *datum*.

76. Data is commonly stored so that those related to each other are also closely spaced in memory. A list of names, for example, might be placed in consecutive memory locations. Walking through the list of names would involve operating on each datum in the list by looking at consecutive memory locations.

77. A machine register is a temporary storage location that is inside the computer processor itself. All the data that a program uses is held in the main memory of the computer (in the case of the LGP-30 and the RPC-400, this would be the drum, in the case of your PC this would be the RAM). To operate on this data the computer brings it into a machine's register in its CPU (central processing unit). The program typically operates on the data in the machine's registers until the operation is complete and then writes the updated values back to the main memory.

78. That is, write the updated value back to the drum to the location from which it came originally.

79. That is, instead of getting the instruction from the drum, which would be the normal case.

80. That is, he's walking through a list by executing a single instruction, but each time through the loop, the instruction itself is modified to point to a different location. There is no test that says when to finish this loop.

81. Single bits are often used as flags to indicate which features are enabled or being used in a particular program. Computers generally have a number of these bits, sometimes called a Processor Status Register, that is kept internally in the computer and accessible only to the operating system.

82. Although I don't have the exact instruction format for either the LGP-30 or

the RPC-4000, the bit that controls the use of the index register is in between the operation code bits on the left and the address of the data on the right. The layout is something like this:

operation code | index bit | address

83. Bits have only two states: on and off (also called 1 and 0).

84. Having the index register contain the value 0 means to add 0 to every address before it's executed. That is, use the index register, but since it's adding 0, it never has any effect on the actual address.

85. Memory in a computer is addressed by number. Each number corresponds to a different location in memory. These addresses typically start at 0 and go to whatever the highest number is for a memory of that size. For example, if a memory had 1024 locations, they would be numbered 0 to 1023. Locations with lower numbers are considered the bottom of the memory and those with higher numbers are considered the top of the memory.

86. Arithmetic overflow is caused when the result of an operation is larger than the maximum size allowed for the result. Consider if you wanted to use only numbers that could be expressed in two decimal digits. You would be restricting yourself to numbers between 0 and 99 because 100 must use three digits. Now, if you performed addition on two legal numbers, say 55 and 68, you would get overflow because the answer, 123, is too large to fit in the two-digit limit. Because computers have fixed-bit-width arithmetic units, overflow is an issue that must be considered carefully.

87. Another way of looking at overflow is to consider the extra digit of an overflow number as a carry to the next operation. Suppose you are adding 55 and 68. The computer adds the first digits: 5 + 8 = 13. Using overflow, the 3 is given as the first digit, and the 1 is carried to the next operation. Now add the second digits plus the carryover: 5 + 6 + 1 = 12. Again, the 2 is the digit and the 1 is carried to the next operation. If the operation is fixed at two digits long, the 1 is a carry out from the operation, which overflowed its size limit.

In the case mentioned in the tale, the carry out of the addition was added into the next part of the instruction word in the operation code. Because the operation code is just another stream of bits, this would be the same as adding 1 to the operation code, thus changing which operation code was being indicated.

88. A jump instruction is one that transfers program control to a different part of memory. When a program jumps it starts fetching instructions from a different location instead of from the next sequential one.

89. Consider that an arithmetic overflow in the right part of the instruction word has caused the carry bit that changed the ADD instruction into a jump. Because we were also told that the program was adding 1 to the contents of the ADD instruction to walk through data in a sequential series, it must be the case that adding 1 caused the overflow. If adding 1 caused the overflow, then the remaining bits in the right part of the word must be 0 because in binary, regardless of a number's total size, the next sequential number following 111 is 1000. So, the resulting instruction after overflow must have been a jump instruction with an address of 0, telling the program to start executing its next instruction from location 0.

CONCLUSION

The Future of Urban Legends

In 1984 Professor Thomas A. Sebeok of Indiana University (my alma mater) suggested (possibly tongue-in-cheek) that the U.S. government spread "curse of the Pharaoh" myths to warn future generations to keep away from high-level nuclear waste dumps. In a technical report—"Communications Measures to Bridge Ten Millennia"—submitted to the Office of Nuclear Waste Isolation (a branch of the Department of Energy), Sebeok reasoned that such a "false trail" could be created and sustained by an "atomic priesthood" appointed from among today's scientists and scholars. "The priesthood would be self-perpetuating. . . . When one member dies, the others would choose to initiate a replacement," as Sebeok was quoted in a *Wall Street Journal* report.[1]

When Sebeok noted that "conventional folkloristic devices, such as word of mouth" could be relied upon to spread these "myths," he seemed to put an amazing trust in the ability of oral traditions to survive in our technologically advanced age. However, he admitted that he "came up with the idea by watching old 'monster movies' about archeologists who meet tragedy when they violate the sacred tombs of Egyptian Pharaohs." Thus, popular culture as well as folk culture played a part in Sebeok's proposal. The parallels to urban legend tradition are obvious.

As I have shown in this book, a combination of oral tradition, electronic communication, and mass media exposure have sustained a wide range of modern urban legends over broad areas of space and long stretches of time. While no one can guarantee that all such stories will persist for centuries, let alone millennia, it is likely that similar legends will continue to be told as long as people communicate via the spoken and written word. Funny, ironic, scary, and bizarre stories that are alleged to be true and told by our friends, family members, and neighbors are simply too beguiling to fade away, even if the mass media alone already supply us with an ample number of juicy narratives. After all, there is also the added attraction in folk tradition of hearing something through the grapevine before it hits the media. The collection and analysis of urban legends afford a unique perspective to understand modern "folk" and their concerns.

A glance at the urban legends circulating during the spring and summer of 1998—the months when I was completing this book—demonstrates how vigorous the contemporary tradition is. In April, for example, when a new shopping mall opened in a suburb of Columbus, Ohio, a "new" horror story—recognizable as an old urban legend with a different twist—began to circulate by word-of-mouth and electronic mail. It was quickly denied by the mall management and thoroughly investigated and debunked by the local media, but the story continued to spread through the summer. Here is a version from an e-mail message headed "This is NOT a joke . . . Please share with everyone you know."

> This woman was shopping at Tuttle Mall in Columbus. She came out to her car and saw that she had a flat. So she got her jack and spare out of the trunk. A man in a business suit came up and started to help her. When the tire had been replaced, he asked for a ride to his car on the opposite side of the mall. Feeling uncomfortable about doing this, she stalled for awhile, but he kept pressing her. She finally asked why he was on this side of the mall if his car was on the other. He had been talking to friends, he claimed. Still uncomfortable, she told him that she had just remembered something she had forgotten to pick up at the mall and she left him and went back inside the mall.
>
> She reported the incident to the mall security, and they went out to her car. The man was nowhere in sight. Opening her trunk, she discovered a brief case the man had set inside her trunk while helping her with the tire. Inside was rope and a butcher knife! When she took the tire to be fixed, the mechanic informed her that there was nothing wrong with her tire, that it was flat because the air had been let out of it!
>
> The moral of this story is learn to change your own tire, call someone you know and trust to help you, or call mall security in the first place to assist you. Please be Safe and not Sorry.

The Tuttle Mall story—complete with its moral, expressed proverbially ("Better safe than sorry")—is a variation of the urban legend folklorists call "The Hairy-Armed Hitchhiker" or "The Hatchet in the Handbag." Despite its attachment here to a specific time and place, virtually the same story has been told for decades about shopping malls located literally from coast to coast. Also known in England, this legend can be traced there to pre-mall and pre-automobile legends of the midnineteenth century when the would-be assailant, often a man disguised as a woman, was recognized before he could harm riders in a horse-drawn carriage. In many modern American versions of the story the driver escapes on her own by asking the "helper" to stand behind the car and check her taillights; then she simply drives away, and she discovers the hidden weapons later in the day.[2]

The expensive recipe story—the Neiman-Marcus cookie version—kept rolling in unabated throughout the year;[3] then in late July someone sent me a parody in which a motorist visits an imaginary car service, "The Neiman-Marcus All Tune and Lube" in Dallas, and pays an outrageous price for the "recipe" for a special 20W50 motor oil. The parody concludes with the complex chemical formula for motor oil, which the victim is willing to share with one and all to gain revenge against the big bad company. To be successful, of course, a parody must refer to a story that most readers will be familiar with, and is there an Internet user anywhere in the world who has not had the expensive recipe story forwarded to his or her mailbox?

I had no sooner filed this parody when another attention-getting e-mail message arrived. It was headed "interesting, if true," and told the story of an engineer at the Pontiac Division of General Motors grappling with a customer's complaint that his new car stalled only when he drove out to buy *vanilla* ice cream, but never when he purchased other flavors. The solution:

> Vanilla, being the most popular flavor, was in a separate case at the front of the store for quick pickup. All the other flavors were kept in the back of the store at a different counter where it took considerably longer to find the flavor and get checked out.
>
> The engineer quickly came up with the answer: vapor lock. It was happening every night, but the extra time taken to get the other flavors allowed the engine to cool down sufficiently to start. When the man got vanilla, the engine was still too hot for the vapor lock to dissipate.

Ah, yes, "The Ice Cream Car" legend, once described to me as "a favorite at General Motors," not because it's true, but because it's so absurd, and yet it pops up again every few years, especially during heat spells.[4] The flavor of ice cream and the explanation of the car problem have varied somewhat since the 1940s and 1950s when it first appeared, but the essential plot remains the same. (By the way, how many stores do you know that arrange the flavors in relation to their front door in order of popularity, and who says vanilla is the most popular flavor bought for home consumption?)

Lest it appear that all the urban legends are circulating on the Internet nowadays, here's a list of the urban legends I can remember people buttonholing me to tell during summer and fall 1998: "The Obligatory Wait" and "The Bird Foot Exam" (two campus legends), "The Dead Cat in the Package," "The Kidney Heist," "The Lawnmower Accident," and "The Nude in the RV"; I've probably forgotten a few others. When I'm not receiving urban legends via the Internet or in person, I'm reading them in published articles. For example, the *San Jose Mercury News* on August 2, 1998, in an article on stress during airline travel told the story of "Passenger Judy" and her in-flight encounter with a candy bar thief:

> Not too long ago, Judy was rushing to catch a flight from San Francisco to Los Angeles. She hadn't eaten, and her blood sugar was in the tank. Dashing through the airport she zipped into a newsstand and bought a *People* magazine and a Kit Kat candy bar.
>
> Settling into a window seat, Judy dropped her magazine on the empty middle seat, nodded to the guy buckling himself into the aisle seat and prepared for takeoff.
>
> After the plane reached its comfortable cruising altitude, Judy unwrapped the Kit Kat, then put it back on the seat. But before she could dig in to it, the guy on the aisle reached down, broke off a piece and ate it. Judy was stunned.
>
> Before Judy could gather her wits, the guy grabbed the candy bar and polished it off. Now that was too much. Judy's incredulity turned to trembling, speechless rage. She gripped the armrests and boiled silently in her own bile all the way to L.A.
>
> They land, and the guy gets off the plane, followed by Judy—still in shock. Walking through the terminal, she sees the guy buying a muffin. Something snaps. She runs up to him, grabs his arm, takes a big bite out of his muffin and runs away.
>
> She felt great! Vindicated! Empowered!
>
> A few proud minutes later, Judy gets into her car and puts her magazine down on the seat. Out falls her Kit Kat.
>
> That candy bar on the flight had been the guy's.

Steve Farber, author of the *Mercury-News* article, declared that "in the airline business, this kind of thing happens every day." Well, maybe that *kind* of thing, but certainly not that exact thing, since "The Package of Cookies" (the usual form of the story) has been around for at least twenty-five years, was later claimed as an experience by author Douglas Adams, has been the subject of at least two short films, circulates widely in Europe as well as in New Zealand and Australia, pops up occasionally in newspaper advice columns, and on and on and on.[5] It's an urban legend that nicely demonstrates the possibility of misunderstanding a person's actions, but it never really happened. Certainly not, at any rate, to all the different people in all those various times and places described over and over again by storytellers. Farber's published version of the story has the stylistic flavor of an oral telling: "The guy gets off the plane" and "Out falls her Kit Kat," for example.

Doubtless there were other newspaper articles about urban legends published in the summer of 1998, but the second one that happened to catch my eye appeared just the day after the *Mercury-News* article, on August 3, in the *Akron Beacon Journal*. Sheryl Harris wrote about urban legends concerning business, beginning like this:

> Once upon a time, folktales had foxes and gnomes.
>
> Today they have . . .
>
> . . . fast-food chicken from Company X that can make you sterile just by eating it!
>
> . . . cactuses from Company Y that are so full of baby spiders they'll explode when you get them in the house!
>
> . . . the designer who doesn't want Asians wearing his clothes!
>
> Who needs the *Weekly World News* when you can rely on the friend of a friend for juicy tidbits like this?
>
> Urban legends, the folk tales of the 20th century, can sway consumers and affect companies' bottom lines.
>
> Are the tales absolute fiction? Definitely.
>
> But who cares?[6]

While some urban legends, as Harris documents, may harm companies, in another instance in 1998 a company was actually using such stories in its advertising. A news item released to the press in late July explained:

> Kmart breaks new advertising for Route 66 jeans
>
> TROY, Mich. (Reuters)—Kmart Corp. hopes customers will get their kicks from its first TV advertising for house denim brand Route 66.
>
> The spots, filmed on location at Route 66 outposts in California, use ironic, sometimes creepy tales in the urban legend genre to hook teens and young adults in the crowded jeans category. . . .
>
> One spot, "Last Dance," which broke Sunday [July 26], shows a young man picking up a young woman on the way to a dance. He lets her borrow a pair of jeans, but when he goes to her home later to reclaim them, he finds she has been dead for 20 years.

"The Cookie Caper" by Mike Parobeck © 1994 Paradox Press. All rights reserved. Used with permission of DC Comics.

A less ghoulish spot, which broke July 19, shows a jealous cement truck driver who mistakes the young man in his kitchen for his wife's paramour. Angered, he dumps cement into what he supposes is the man's convertible, only to find the man is a car salesman and he has just ruined his birthday present.[7]

Urban legends continued to be mentioned in the press through the winter of 1998–99. It's impossible for a book to stay up-to-date, but here are a few examples. The September 1998 issue of *The Rotarian* featured "The Truth about Urban Legends" by Gary Turbak, a freelancer from Missoula, Montana. Turbak reviewed the international circulation of such stories as "The Scuba Diver in the Tree," "The Rattle in the Cadillac," and "The Kidney Heist." The Fall 1998 issue of *U. Magazine,* distributed on college campuses, had a piece by Julie Keller, with splashy illustrations by Paul Adam of the University of Missouri; the article began, "Unless you live under a rock, you can't get through college, or life for that matter, without hearing at least one or two urban legends." In her December 11 column, Abigail Van Buren ("Dear Abby") included a story sent by a reader in Atlanta "told to me by a lady in the waiting room of a hospital here." It purported to be the chilling experience of a woman in a shopping mall in December 1966, but not only was it old news, it was also merely a version of the urban legend that I call "Sticking Up for One's Rights." (Armed woman orders intruders out of her car in a parking lot, except it's the wrong car.) Dozens of my readers sent me copies of the column along with their own versions of the story as it "really happened" in cities from coast to coast; as far as I've noticed, "Dear Abby" has never mentioned it again.

While the popular press and advertising were discussing (or exploiting?) urban legends in 1998, the more academic media were also keeping an eye on the genre. Examples: the fall 1997 issue of *Mid-America Folklore,* which hit my mailbox a few months after its cover date, contained an article analyzing the kidney theft legends.[8] The August issue of *American Libraries* had a nice piece on legends about libraries.[9] The September–October 1998 issue of *Skeptical Inquirer* (published by the Committee for the Scientific Investigation of Claims of the Paranormal) included a story about a state legislature supposedly trying to set the value of pi to the "Biblical value of 3.0" as "a new urban legend."[10] The Fall 1998 issue of *Arizona Law Review* had a lengthy article about legends concerning the civil justice system,[11] and the November 1998 issue of *Scientific American* contained a short essay on cyberlegends.[12]

But the primary media event of 1998 relating to urban legends would appear to be the release of a "horror-thriller" film "laced with humor" entitled *Urban Legend* (what else?) and produced by Columbia Pictures. Posters advertising the October premiere define the urban legend with fair accuracy as "modern day folktales that seem to arise spontaneously and spread by word-of-mouth. . . . [They] range from the silly (metal tooth fillings receiving radio signals) to the sinister (alligators in the sewers of Manhattan)." I feel obliged to point out that folktales and legends comprise two quite different categories of oral narrative, and that the poster's

"silly" example is really more rumor than legend. On the other hand, I was gratified to learn that *Urban Legend* not only uses one of my books as a prop in a campus scene but also shows someone consulting a book called *Encyclopedia of Urban Legends,* which just happens to be the title of my next project. While *Urban Legend* did not win any Academy Awards (it wasn't even nominated), it will certainly call even more public attention to this genre of modern folklore that fascinates so many scholars and lay persons alike.

The Last Word: Needless Needle Alarm

These two stories in various versions were zipping around the Internet and flying from mouth to ear in early 1999, just as I finished my final revision of the manuscript for this book. I quote these examples verbatim from e-mail:

> READ THE FOLLOWING PLEASE
> BE CAREFUL AT MOVIE THEATRE!!
> This has occurred in Hawaii and California and may be catching on. A young lady went to the movies—when she sat down she felt something poking her—she stood and found a needle with a note attached reading "Welcome to the real world, you're HIV positive." The needle was tested and contained the HIV virus. The needle was wedged into the seat fold. Please check where you sit—not just at the movies but all other public places—and watch where you put your hands. This is becoming a sick world—be careful.

> Not a Joke!!! IMPORTANT ISSUE
> PLEASE READ IMPORTANT MESSAGE BELOW AND SEND TO ANYONE I MIGHT HAVE MISSED!
> A very good friend of mine is in an EMT certification course. there is something new happening that everyone should be ware of.
> Drug users are now taking their used needles and putting them into the coin return slots in public telephones. People are putting their fingers in to recover coins or just to check if anyone left change, are getting stuck by those needles and infected with hepatitis, HIV, and other diseases. This message is posted to make everyone aware of this danger.
> Be aware! The change isn't worth it!
> P.S.—This information came straight from phone company workers, through the EMT instructor. This did NOT come from a hearsay urban legend source.

I trust that readers of this book will recognize the sure signs of urban legend tradition in these two stories. The clues include the vague FOAF attributions, the mocking note left behind (as in "The Roommate's Death," "AIDS Mary," and other stories), the supposed random attack on innocent parties, and especially the failure of these warnings to come through official government or media information channels. The fear of needles and infection, evident in both stories, goes back a long way; warnings against "white slavery" abductors in the 1920s and 1930s also mentioned needles stuck through theater seats.

Am I being too flippant and casual about such warnings? Could it be that drug users (also characterized in some of the warnings as "gang members") are really threatening the citizenry in this diabolical way? Certainly it *could* be true, but it wasn't. In late April 1999 the Federal Centers for Disease Control and Prevention, after receiving hundreds of telephone calls from concerned Americans, issued a denial of both needle stories that was widely publicized. My local paper, the *Salt Lake Tribune,* headlined its April 27 story "CDC Debunks Web Stories of HIV-Tainted Booby Trap." And, fighting fire with fire, the CDC also posted a denial on its Web site.

Maybe this is the true future of urban legends: rapid Internet circulation of doubtful stories, followed by rapid Internet denials. But, by whatever means they are circulated, you can be sure that the truth never stands in the way of a good story.

Notes

1. Con Psarras, "U. S. May Concoct Tales of Horror to Deter Trespass at Nuclear Site," *Wall Street Journal,* June 25, 1984. I quote the entire article in *The Mexican Pet: More "New" Urban Legends and Some Old Favorites* (New York: W. W. Norton, 1986), 205–7.

2. See my discussions of this story in *The Choking Doberman and Other "New" Urban Legends* (New York: W. W. Norton, 1984), 52–55; *The Mexican Pet,* 157–59; and *Too Good to Be True* (New York: W. W. Norton, 1999), 100–103.

3. In a version of the Neiman-Marcus story being e-mailed around the country in April 1999, "flour" was spelled correctly, but the recipe was directed to "cookie officianardo's"; then someone had added the comment, "I hate these big department stores that think they are God! This serves them right!!!"

4. See my discussion of "The Ice Cream Car" in *Curses! Broiled Again!: The Hottest Urban Legends Going* (New York: W. W. Norton, 1989), 121–22; and *Too Good to Be True,* 296–98.

5. For "The Package of Cookies" (called "The Packet of Biscuits" in England) see *The Choking Doberman,* 191–93; *The Mexican Pet,* 137–40; and *Too Good to Be True,* 30–31.

6. Sheryl Harris, "Legends and Lies," *Akron Beacon Journal*, Aug. 3, 1998.

7. For "The Vanishing Hitchhiker" see Jan Harold Brunvand, *The Vanishing Hitchhiker: American Urban Legends and Their Meanings* (New York: W. W. Norton, 1981), 24–40; *The Choking Doberman*, 210–12; *The Mexican Pet*, 49–55; and *Too Good to Be True*, 231–34. For "The Solid Cement Cadillac" see *The Vanishing Hitchhiker*, 125–32; and *Too Good to Be True*, 29–30.

8. Jeremy Freeman, "Are You Kidneying? An Analysis of Kidney Theft in Contemporary Folklore," *Mid-America Folklore* 25 (Fall 1997): 75–83.

9. Stacey Hathaway-Bell, "Satan's Shelving: Urban Library Legends," *American Libraries* 29 (Aug. 1998): 44–49.

10. David E. Thomas, "'Pi' April Fool's Joke Gets out of Hand—and Goes Round the World," *Skeptical Inquirer*, Sept.–Oct. 1998, 7–8.

11. Marc Galanter, "An Oil Strike in Hell: Contemporary Legends about the Civil Justice," *Arizona Law Review* 40 (Fall 1998): 717–52.

12. Paul Wallich, "Cyber View: This Is Not a Hoax!" *Scientific American*, Nov. 1998, 54.

INDEX

Edgerton, William B., 126, 127
"Elevator Incident, The" (urban legend), 26
Encyclopedia of Urban Legends (Brunvand), 207
Entities (Nickell), 123–24
Evening Star, 139, 146–47
Evening World, 139, 142, 146–47
Evidence for Phantom Hitch-Hikers, The (Goss), 13
"Evil Mother, The" (*madre mala;* urban legend), 50–51
"Expensive Recipe, The" (urban legend), 4–5, 201. *See also* "Red Velvet Cake"
"Exploding Toilet, The" (urban legend): first reported from Jerusalem, 108–9; circulated by news agencies, 109; national press coverage of, 109–10; reporters and readers doubt story, 110–11; story retractions, 111; in oral tradition, 112; incites examination of journalistic practices, 112–13; appears in tabloids, 113–14; variations of, 113–14; older outhouse version of, 114–17; two "true" versions of, 117–18; motorcycle version of, 118–19; summary of history of, 119–20; further journalistic reports of, 120–21; mentioned, 160

"Fatal Initiation, The" (urban legend), 6–7
Fields, Debbi, 73–74
Fine, Gary Alan, 71, 102
Fish, Lydia, 41
Flag Research Center, 157
Flexner, Stuart Berg, 89
FOAF. *See* Friend of a friend
FOAFtale News, 8
Folklore and Psychoanalysis (Carvalho-Neto), 50
Folklore Fellows Communications, 10
"Folklore of the Motor-Car, The" (Sanderson), 13, 17
Folktales of England (Briggs and Tongue), 13, 15
Franz, Marie-Louise von, 56
Freudian interpretations of urban legends: declined for "The Brain Drain," 27; for "The Baby Roast," 50–52; device of "projection," 56; parodied, 71

Friend of a friend (FOAF), 6, 13, 43, 44, 84, 155, 165, 208

"Ghost in Search of Help, The" (urban legend): "angel" version published by Billy Graham, 123–24; motifs in, 124; American "folk" versions of, 124–26; compared to "The Vanishing Hitchhiker," 125–26; oldest version of, 126; London version, 126–27; two subtypes of, 127; relationship of Dr. S. W. Mitchell to, 127–34; writers' variations of, 132; two recent versions of, 132–34; summary of conclusions concerning, 134
"Goliath Effect, the," 71
Goss, Michael, 13
Goulden, Joseph C., 39
"Grace under Fire" (TV show), 28
Graham, Billy, 123–25, 132, 134
Grapes of Wrath, The (Steinbeck), 3
Grizzard, Lewis, 29

Hackers (computer programming experts): negative image of, 170; urban legends about, 170, 180–82; admired by computer experts, 170–71; defined, 171; as programmers' heroes, 171; heroic, 171–78; "virtual home" of, 171–72; first wave of, 172–73; second wave of, 174; third wave of, 174–75; programming languages used by, 176–77; hacker ethic, 178–79, 181; concept of "magic" of, 179–80; distinguished from "crackers," 181. *See also* "Story of Mel, a Real Programmer, The"
Hacker's Dictionary, The, 171
"Hairy-Armed Hitchhiker, The" (urban legend), 200
"Hammered Child, The" (urban legend), 162–63
Hankey, Rosalie, 6, 125
"Hansel and Gretel," 51–52, 55
Harmon, Larry, 86
Harmony of Science and Scripture, The (Rimmer), 141, 143–44
Harvard Lampoon, 162
Harvard University, 162
"Hatchet in the Handbag, The" (urban legend), 200
"Haunted Street, The" (urban legend), 14

Jan Harold Brunvand, professor emeritus at the University of Utah, is the author of numerous books on urban legends, including *Curses! Broiled Again!: The Hottest Urban Legends Going,* *The Baby Train and Other Lusty Urban Legends,* and *Too Good to Be True.* He was general editor of *American Folklore: An Encyclopedia* and published *The Study of American Folklore* in 1968, which became a standard text in the field.

Erik Brunvand earned his Ph.D. at Carnegie Mellon University in 1990. He is currently an associate professor of computer science at the University of Utah. His main research interests are in asynchronous computer system design and integrated circuit design. He has published numerous technical articles related to these interests, but this is his first folklore study.

Typeset in 10/13 Sabon
with Green display
Designed by Paula Newcomb
Composed by Jim Proefrock
at the University of Illinois Press
Manufactured by Thomson-Shore, Inc.

University of Illinois Press
1325 South Oak Street
Champaign, IL 61820-6903
www.press.uillinois.edu